SHANGHAI SAGA

The Story of A City

JOHN PAL

Shanghai Saga

By John Pal

ISBN-13: 978-988-8552-83-2

© 2022 Earnshaw Books Ltd.

HISTORY / Asia / China

EB154

All spellings are as originally published.

Shanghai Saga was originally published under the name of John Pal with a copyright notice of ©1963 John Pal. John Pal was a pseudonym making the work a work of unknown authorship at the time of publication. Under the Hong Kong Copyright Ordinance, the term of protection of work of unknown authorship is 50 years from publication. Any enquires regarding copyright issues should be addressed to the publisher.

All rights reserved. No part of this book may be reproduced in material form, by any means, whether graphic, electronic, mechanical or other, including photocopying or information storage, in whole or in part. May not be used to prepare other publications without written permission from the publisher except in the case of brief quotations embodied in critical articles or reviews. For information contact info@earnshawbooks.com

Published by Earnshaw Books Ltd. (Hong Kong)

Contents

Foreword	1
Introduction	7
1 Sticky Start	27
2 Smugglers' Paradise	58
3 The Russian Invasion	92
4 Day of Fate	114
5 Theatre and Dogs	137
6 Japs, Dollars and Rickshaw Coolies	167
7 Reds, Racketeers and Pickpockets	196
8 Pirates and Secret Societies	220
9 'Squeeze' and Chits	240
10 End in Sight	252

Illustrations

Illustrations

View of down-town section of Shanghai in 1927   facing page 35
Shanghai's first Customs House   36
Tu Yueh-sen, head of Green Dragon Society   51
Shanghai Defence Force   52
The author meets Generalissimo Chiang Kai-shek   105
Terror meets terror   105
Grim warning to evil-doers   106
Man carries home heads of his two brothers   106
Captured criminals and terrorists under death-sentence   125
China's Lenin — Dr. Sun Yat-sen   126
The author's curfew pass issued at time of 1927 crisis   126
Monkey jockeys at Shanghai dog-track   179
Burning British ship abandoned by pirates in Bias Bay   180
China coaster burnt out by pirates   180
Hulls of Chinese nineteenth-century war-junks   199
Group of captured Chinese pirates handcuffed together   199
Gathering of international lawyers   201

FOREWORD
By Graham Earnshaw

JOHN PAL, the author of *Shanghai Saga*, was the pseudonym of Alan Palamountain, born in 1903 in Australia, probably in Launceston, Tasmania, and the son of a prominent local politician, John Richard Palamountain. It was published in 1963 and then almost disappeared. Of the little that we know about of the author, he appears to have been, amongst other things, an expert on opium smuggling, an active participant in the seamier side of Shanghai's nightlife and a player on occasion on the wrong side of the law.

He was the third of four children, and one of his siblings was named Paul. But he talks little about his early life in this book, which is probably fair enough in that what the reader wants is to be thrown straight into the stew of old Shanghai. But he does say that he signed up for a job in the city at the age of only seventeen.

Palamountain arrived in Shanghai in 1920 to be employed by the Imperial Chinese Customs service, an organization run by foreigners and charged with collecting customs duties on behalf of the Chinese government. The story of how he got there is told in brief in *Shanghai Saga*, starting with a chance encounter at a port in Australia, presumably Sydney. "World War I was just over," he recounts. "I met an old man peeling potatoes on board a ship down at the wharves. I was always hanging around ships, which fascinate me. The old, weather-beaten potato-peeler took a shine to me, perhaps because he liked to talk and I was a good listener."

SHANGHAI SAGA

The old man asked Alan what he planned to do when he left school, and the boy replied that he couldn't make up his mind. The man then painted for him a picture of the exotic Orient — "I saw myself wearing a smart tropical uniform, dashing around the harbor of a great port, boarding ships and giving orders right and left, saluting and receiving salutes, of natives kow-towing and of weird Oriental music playing at mealtimes, of pretty almond-eyed maids fanning me in hot weather and slipping Oriental sweets meats into my unresisting mouth."

He bought the dream, but to make it a reality, the old man told him he had to leave Australia and first travel to London. So he did.

He worked his way to England in the laundry of an ocean liner, but when he fronted up for the interview, the London representative of the Chinese Maritime Customs shook his head and said: 'A bit young, aren't you? No one under nineteen is taken on, you know.' But he added that if Alan went straight to Shanghai, he might be able to get hired anyway. The representative gave him a letter of introduction to the Shanghai Commissioner, and he found a berth of a ship heading for the Far East. When he got there, he presented the letter and was accepted. "The only stipulation attached to my appointment to the Customs was that I must serve twice the usual probationary period of six months. I was in."

For the rest of the story, I will leave most of it for Alan to tell in the book. But some of the important takeaways include a wealth of detail on how smuggling in and out of the port of Shanghai worked in those days — of opium and a vast range of other goods. The brunt of the customs inspection work was done by foreigners, presumably because Chinese people were considered more likely to succumb to the temptation of payoffs. But the foreigners were not immone from that temptation either.

FOREWORD

There is a mention of Alan in an article in the *North-China Herald* on December 30, 1922 about a court case involving the seizure of a cache of opium on board a ship. Palamountain went on board with another customs officer, named Doyle, to search a boat. Palamountain was in uniform, Doyle was not, and they did not report that they would conduct the search. Doyle was charged with corruption, and according to his own evidence, Palamountain was dismissed. He was not prosecuted, but his time as a Customs man was up, after two and a half years in the service. In the book, he says he quit, adding that the Customs Service had decided to send him for a two-year stint manning a customs house on the Burmese border, and he wouldn't do it. Another reference online says that he was in fact "dismissed."

The following year, 1923, Alan and his brother Paul were working for a Chinese man named Hip Han-ching, and were arrested on a charge of embezzling $30,000 from their employer. They were released on bail and there the case fades into obscurity with a comment in the *North-China Herald* that the matter was "being adjusted with the prosecutor." So it must have been settled out of court.

He became a journalist, joining the *Shanghai Times*, a newspaper which over the years developed a reputation for being pro-Japanese, and it appears he used the name John Pal in that capacity. In 1928, a salacious novel was published called *Shanghai Nights*, authored by Tasman Ile, who was almost certainly Alan. It was a love story set in the cess-pools of the city's nightlife, and featured a cast of newspapermen and a Eurasian girl looking for an American or British husband. It appears the book was a minor sensation judging by the reviews in the English-language newspaper of the day.

I haven't yet been able to locate a copy of the novel, but the review in *The China Press* published on December 9, 1929 described it as being "one of the most startling journeys ever made by anyone into the mad whirl of a city's night-life, where men forget their husbands, and wives their husbands."

In a preview of *Shanghai Saga* more than thirty years later, the book also revealed "the disgusting conditions prevailing nightly in so-called society beneath a curtain of hypocrisy, sham and deception." It was written, the review said, "by an author who had unparalleled opportunities for delving into the midst of things, for getting at the truth and for gathering facts from personal experience." The *North-China Daily News* described it as a "shocker", and the *Shanghai Mercury* said some readers would "delight in the realism of the book, while others will clamour for its suppression."

In August 1937, The Japanese military attacked east China and occupied all of Shanghai except for the foreign settlements. But life for foreigners there continued to some considerable extent as before, and Alan was married in January 1938 to Margaret Cecilia Talbot at the Church St. Pierre on Avenue Dubail in the French Concession, with his brother Paul acting as best man. The *North-China Herald* on January 11, 1939 announced the birth of their daughter, Peggy Ann. But by 1939, it was clear the Japanese intended to occupy not only the Chinese parts of Shanghai, but the foreign-controlled parts as well. So Alan and his family left. An item in the *North-China Herald* on May 24, 1939 said that he had resigned from his position as Racing Manager at Le Champ de Courses Francais, that is, the Canidrome. The family left Shanghai aboard the *Empress of Canada* liner on May 31, the *North-China Herald* recorded.

The couple subsequently had four children and Alan died in Australia in 1991. This information comes from a Palamountain family web page, for which we owe them much thanks. We have

FOREWORD

no information to hand about what he did after he left Shanghai in 1939, and the anonymity after his sparkling Shanghai sojourn is representative of the situation of many other foreigners who lived the high life in Old Shanghai and then faded into the fabric of life elsewhere. It may be that for most of them, and probably including Alan, the intensity and the glitter of that experience of living in Shanghai in the early 20th Century made life afterwards seem grey and slow.

Alan was not the only person to write a memoir of the life and times of old Shanghai in that dazzling era, but for most of his time in the city, he worked as journalist and he brought a journalist's eye to the marshalling of information and anecdote that makes *Shanghai Saga* easily one of the most readable of the Shanghai memoirs ever published. It is puzzling why it disappeared so completely after its publication in 1963, but such is the roulette game that is publishing. Some of the most prominent China books of recent decades have, in my opinion, been less than stellar.

But the word memoir does not really do justice to this book. It is also a history of the city, and a sociological analysis. It is all done in a non-academic way, but he covers all of the ground effectively, and with the confidence of having been there. This is not history written at a distance, it has the smell and the touch of reality about it. Journalism at its best is instant history, and Alan takes a journalist's approach to the story.

The core value of this sort of book is the cavalcade of vivid pictures that a writer can only paint if they were there, bringing to life just what it was like to be there at that moment. Such writers didn't necessarily witness or participate in the big events, and Palamountain was far from being a prominent member of the foreign community in Shanghai. But the kind of dynamic descriptions of the periphery such as given by Alan Palamountain in *Shanghai Saga* provide a wonderful counterpoint to the big facts of history. Palamountain did us all a great service by writing this book. It is a eulogy, but it is also celebration of a city living on borrowed time, a situation that was unique in so many ways.

Graham Earnshaw
June, 2022

Introduction

SCATTERED far and wide throughout the world today are the remnants of what was once a community entitled by every known definition to be called 'unique'.

It will never reassemble. There will never be another like it. It took a hundred years to come into being; less than five to break up. At the time of its collapse it was one of the world's great cities, a seaport ranking fifth to New York, London, Rotterdam and Hamburg.

Its name—Shanghai—gave legitimate birth to some of the foulest deeds ever done on the world's waterfronts—the forceful impressment of men into brutal service before the mast, known as 'shanghaiing'. As time went by and the nineteenth became the twentieth century, tourists called the place the 'Paris of the Orient'. Others knew it only as a sink of iniquity.

It was both.

British gunboats blasted the China Coast open to foreign trade and after a century of glittering, vibrant, sinful existence Chinese guns blasted the whites out again, some richer, many poorer, but all wiser.

For 100 years this great Oriental metropolis drew the adventurous from the four corners of the earth—including me.

Soldiers of fortune found outlet for many dark and dubious deeds; some found a page in history, like Frederick Townsend Ward, who rode across America on horseback, took ship to Shanghai and saved the city from sacking by the Taiping rebels.

SHANGHAI SAGA

Ward lies buried in a Chinese shrine some forty miles south of Shanghai, and before the Reds took over in 1949 an annual pilgrimage was made to his tomb by Chinese and foreign residents alike. And when Ward was killed while pursuing the rebels a hundred miles south of Shanghai, 'Chinese' Gordon, later of Khartoum fame, took over Ward's motley 'army' and completed the job set by this American adventurer.

The Taiping Rebellion of 1861 marked the first serious attempt by the Chinese to throw the 'foreign devils' back into the sea. The second was the Boxer Rebellion of 1900. It also failed, and cost China plenty besides. But the third attempt succeeded, forty-nine years later. Only this time, the Chinese government of the day went out with the 'foreign devils' and the Reds took over.

Shanghai began to grow from the moment the Taiping rebels threatened it, as native refugees from the bloodthirsty, head-lopping, pseudo-religious fanatics went berserk on a nation-wide rampage which ultimately cost 20,000,000 lives.

Starting with a scant 138 acres of 'trading territory' in 1846, Shanghai stretched to 470 acres two years later and by 1899 had been granted 5,583 acres. The French pioneers who set up shop alongside the early British and American, noting the trend, secured added acreage also from time to time, ending with 2,525 acres in 1914, at which figure it remained permanently.

To get Shanghai of the twentieth century into proper perspective you have to regard it as four cities, grouped so closely together that you merely crossed a street, sometimes only an alleyway, to pass from one to another. Perhaps in reality there were five separate cities, for 30,000 Japanese living in the Hongkew area of the International Settlement obeyed the Japanese consul-general first, the Settlement authorities second. And each passing year the Japs ran Hongkew more and more in the Japanese manner, of which more anon.

INTRODUCTION

Containing most of the business and industrial life of the city, the International Settlement dominated the port. Frenchtown, with its spacious parks, social clubs and wide avenues, offered more elegant existence than the twin Chinese cities of Nantao (south) and Chapei (north), which clung to the clean and well-governed foreign cities like cancerous growths, hideous examples of how cities should not be run: mute testimony to China's almost total ignorance of civil administration.

But then, of course, so long as Chinese officials handle revenue on the basis of 'One dollar for you — ten for me', very little civic improvement is likely to be accomplished.

It is important to note that most of the harbour waterfront, some five miles of it, abutted the International Settlement and French Concession. Only to the south Nantao, Shanghai's ancient walled city, had a slice of this 'inner' berthing space.

Surrounding all this — Chinese territory — was the so-called Greater Shanghai Municipality. Many Westerners built homes out in these more spacious areas, among them important residents able finally to squeeze further territorial concessions from the co-operative Chinese. These took the form of 'feeder' roads, Berlin corridors. Water, sewerage, light and telephones followed as a matter of course. So did permission for the foreign police to patrol such roads for the protection of non-Chinese residents; though they did not draw the line at helping the Chinese when necessary — which was often.

The Japs built a giant military garrison out at the end of one of these 'feeder' roads which passed through their Hongkew district, or 'Little Tokyo'. They also built and patrolled beyond the defined limits of foreign land concessions and lost no opportunity of provoking the Chinese into any sort of retaliatory action which might justify further expansion under the guise of protection for their nationals. It is well to remember this. It led to bloodshed later, such violent Chinese reaction, indeed, that the Japs came within a few yards of being massacred and thrown into the river.

Thus squatted the Queen City of the Pacific on the mudbank of the Whangpoo River, nearly ninety miles from the open sea. Fourteen miles upstream, where the Whangpoo joined the mighty Yangtze Kiang, there was a Chinese fortress with antiquated cannon which no one ever remembers being fired. When Japan invaded China in 1937 the Chinese had their first good chance to test their gunnery and, as everyone expected, the Japs put all the guns out of action in about twenty-four hours.

Born under gunfire, Shanghai may be said also to have died under gunfire, for the guns continued to explode from 1937 until that day, in 1949, when Generalissimo Chiang Kai-shek and members of the Central China Government quit the mainland of China to set up a shoestring anti-Communist Government in Formosa.

But what of the intervening years, which witnessed the growth of this mighty metropolis from a cluster of bamboo huts on the river-bank?

Even as late as 1920 the majority of male Chinese continued to wear the queue (pigtail), denoting loyalty to the Manchu Dragon Throne of Peking.

The foreign traders of Shanghai had been doing business for nearly fourscore years with their Chinese counterparts, yet they seldom met socially. The Chinese had a reputation abroad as 'mysterious, inscrutable', but the way they kicked their heels into the air when jazz swept the nation ten years later suggests, perhaps, that under the old Imperial rule they hadn't much to laugh about. As for the white man, he was held in great respect, if not fear, by the ordinary Chinese in the street — until the coming

INTRODUCTION

of the first White Russian refugees at the end of World War I.

The Chinese had watched the whites develop trade in Shanghai worth more than two billion (Chinese) dollars—60 per cent of all China's—out of a few shiploads of opium. They marvelled as a city with thirty-story concrete skyscrapers grew out of a small compound containing half a dozen bamboo huts. Perhaps these mad 'foreign devils' might have gone higher into the sky if the shifting, muddy subsoil of the Yangtze River delta had allowed them. Those were the days when a man called 'Boy!' and half a dozen soft-slippered Orientals came slithering across the floor to do the bidding of these free-spending, boisterously happy men from across the sea, the white men who enjoyed much 'face'.

Though the West declared opium trading in the East illegal, like the United States after the Volstead Act went into the statute books, a brisk business was done with the contraband at considerably higher prices, and Shanghai always remained the centre of this illegal drug traffic.

Civil wars ebbed and flowed around its boundaries year after year, seeking control of the city which controlled the opium traffic that, in the period of which I write, yielded between six and seven million dollars monthly. And within the city's boundaries hoodlums waged war of another sort; rubbing out rivals, hi-jacking dope cargoes, informing Customs officers of hide-outs on incoming ships, or Shanghai police of storage depots of dope already through the Customs' loosely drawn net.

Police, Customs, local government officers, pseudo-reform citizens, even diplomats, could not resist getting their fingers covered with the sticky brown poppy juice in get-rich-quick grabs, and some ended in disgrace, in jail, or in the Whangpoo River. Crusading newspapermen who dared expose the trade's machinations were smartly disposed of by professional removers attached to the merciless underworld organizations then fighting an underground war for supreme control over this vast, illicit business with customers counted by the scores of millions. Shanghai's streets at night literally reeked of opium fumes mingled with the pungent perfumes of pretty sing-song girls and a new class of Shanghai professionals making their appearance soon after the Russians arrived — the street-walkers.

This was the city whose every police officer carried a gun under official orders to remove the safety-catch going on duty. The city in which a few specialists in crime-busting even took their guns into the bathroom or the toilet!

Paradoxically, this same city was the centre of all Christian missionary effort throughout China, one of the largest missionary fields on earth. And side by side with those seeking to save the souls of the yellow race were many quiet, earnest 'missionaries' of another sort, who voluntarily watched incoming and outgoing ships and trains, trying to put a few spokes in the greasy wheels of the extremely active white slave traffic.

In Shanghai most of China's big piracies originated. It was the starting-point for operations which netted millions of dollars annually for this branch of crime on the China Coast.

Hovering over all the unlawful goings-on, like a black spectre with outstretched talons, reigned the underworld tsar to whom even China's president paid homage, the most powerful secret-society boss in many generations of outlawry. His authority reached into every city throughout the Far East which sheltered a Chinese community. Nor did it stop there, but followed Chinese around the world wherever they settled, like an Oriental Mafia, exacting tribute.

Generalissimo Chiang Kai-shek, head of the Nationalist Government in Nanking, was in this gangster's permanent personal debt and even had that not been the case he would still

INTRODUCTION

have been under his thumb, for Chiang and gang boss Tu Yueh-sen were blood brothers since long before the Nationalist leader attained prominence. To the outside world, Chiang was China's boss; but in Shanghai we knew who was Chiang's boss.

Here was a city—a country—which about this time never asked for passports. Everyone was free to come and go. And although there was a Customs service the 'foreign devils' had the country in the bag to such extent that Customs tariff was deliberately kept ridiculously low to the resounding benefit of foreign trade.

Any Tom, Dick or Harry could afford to drink the finest wines and puff the choicest of imported cigars. French ships landed elegant Paris perfumes at silly prices for the Russian dancing-girls who had started busting up the homes of established foreign residents. Liquor was so cheap, indeed, that rum runners from the United States called to load up during the prohibition era for a fast run back to Rum Row.

At one stage this crazy country used Mexican silver dollars for currency and permitted private banks to put their own banknotes into circulation, and in the 1920's the situation was so chaotic that even banknotes and dollars from distant interior provinces became mixed up with the stuff passing around Shanghai as legal tender. Inevitably, Chinese counterfeiters got busy gouging out the insides of the silver dollars—and even the copper coins—forcing every money-changer to tinkle each dollar passing through his hands. Thus was born the great Shanghai sonata, the sound of some 30,000-odd moneychangers ceaselessly flipping dollars against each other and listening for the 'dead' note which signified a 'refill'.

The upshot of all this was unavoidable debasement of the currency—inflation. When the Nationalist Government came to power money-changers were giving in exchange for silver dollars six twenty-cent pieces, one ten-cent piece and variably fifteen to thirty copper cents! Not bad for a supposedly 100-cent coin.

Little wonder that adventurers from all over the world headed for Shanghai. Here was a place where one could, literally, get away with murder.

For one hectic period a certain South American consul was selling citizenship rights to Chinese for 2,000 local dollars and building up a big string of 'protégés' among the drug and gun pedlars. Any of his protégés caught by Customs or police claimed protection and appeared for trial before the same consul who had previously sold him citizenship rights, by virtue of the system of extra-territorial privilege then in vogue for most Western nations. Thus the South American consul got it both ways, fees from registrations, fines from all subsequent convictions — Bonanza! When it became too obvious that almost every worthwhile Chinese crook was a South American 'citizen', Peking's Diplomatic Corps decided that this 'protégé' business had gone far enough and declared all such registrations null and void.

There was a big difference between living in the International Settlement and the French Concession. Control of the former rested in the hands of a body of diplomatic 'deputies' (of the Peking Diplomatic Corps) known in Shanghai as the Consular Body. This group of foreign consuls left the administration of the Settlement very much in the hands of the annually elected representatives of the ratepayers; but where matters of high, or international, policy were concerned, they had power to overrule Shanghai's Municipal Council.

As witness the occasion, in 1930, when the Chinese Government demanded the closing down of two greyhound race-tracks operating in the Settlement, accusing them of

INTRODUCTION

encouraging gambling among the oldest known race of gamblers in the world! The real reason was, of course, both tracks refused to contribute the very high sum of money demanded by the Chinese. Unfortunately, it happened to be a time when the Western powers were under heavy fire from the new Nationalist Government of China for — among other things — abrogation of the so-called unequal treaties between China and the Western power bloc; restoration to China of the areas set apart for foreigners nearly ninety years earlier, etcetera, etcetera. So the two tracks were forcibly closed down, notwithstanding a written franchise.

Not so the dog-track in Frenchtown. The French told the Chinese to go fly a kite, and their track was still operating even after President Chiang Kai-shek fled from the Japanese, to far-off Chungking eleven years later.

For a city of its size and importance, Shanghai had the most alluring small-town atmosphere, friendly and intimate, which made us love it.

Its atmosphere was not that of the ever-present stench of the Orient, nor the opium smoke nor the passing night-soil barges. It was an intangible something which every true adventurer 'felt' on impact. I saw travelling stage companies break up because a couple of key performers fell for Shanghai and refused to leave. I saw round-the-world tourists quit luxury liners after twenty-four hours ashore, send for their trunks and refuse to go any further. It was this something in the air which evidently made Will Rogers, the late lamented and celebrated American humorist, stand up in his rickshaw and 'Whoopee!' loud and often to the passing throng the night we rode the waterfront together in 1935.

Shanghai was big and brash in business, a collection of the world's shrewdies assembled in the Far East for one purpose only — to make a pile of money. To make it and spend it. Few of us ever intended to leave, although there was a time when residence in China was considered a form of exile. Business contracts, indeed, provided for 'home leave' every five years on full pay, passage paid, to compensate for having to 'endure' life in China.

The constitution on which Shanghai was founded was a model of brevity and tolerance. It consisted of a set of Land Regulations or municipal bye-laws, drafted to meet the needs of a group of pioneer international traders. There was no thought or intention in the minds of those framing these regulations to shackle either themselves, or future traders, with a lot of 'Thou Shalt Nots', or puritanical restraints of any sort whatsoever. The city's charter was drafted by traders, for trading purposes, by men who liked a noggin of ale and were not above casting a covetous eye upon any pretty wench happening along. The charter was drawn up in an atmosphere of sailing ships and rum, of hard barter and bar-room brawls. And none of us was ever allowed to forget that we lived in a city of the world neither English, American, nor South American, but a truly international melting-pot whose motto was 'Tolerance'.

From the very start Shanghai had to learn to defend itself if it were to live.

The Taiping Rebellion, and Admiral-General Frederick Ward, taught the early settlers the advantage of a civilian defence force, and for the entire hundred years of its existence Shanghai kept its powder dry and its army in training. Over 2,000 strong, the Shanghai Volunteer Corps boasted American, British, French, Portuguese, Chinese, German, Japanese and even Russian units as well as cavalry, artillery and tanks. Again and again it had to man the barricades and save the city from being overrun by battling Chinese mercenary soldiers and bandits. Through

INTRODUCTION

civil wars, riots and rebellions, through curfews and states of emergency, the world's most cosmopolitan 'army' alerted itself; soft-bellied tycoons mounted guard with junior clerks simply to keep the port open and the ships moving. 'Business as usual' became a proud tradition for every Shanghailander. The cargo was always kept moving, even though shells might be sailing overhead or occasionally dropping short into the city itself. Now and then a defeated Chinese force knocked at the boundary door and sought asylum. Shanghai never turned anyone away. Not only did it give shelter and food to the defeated ones, it also transported them back to their native province, sometimes a thousand miles away.

In this same city Chinese Nationalists plotted the overthrow of the Manchu Dragon Throne and Communists later plotted the overthrow of the Nationalists. Korean revolutionaries carried out acts of sabotage against the hated Japanese conquerors of their country and White Russians several times tried to burn down the Soviet Embassy.

So tolerant was Shanghai of other people's problems that the French authorities allowed one or two Chinese big-shots to mount protective machine guns on their garden walls. Every Chinese millionaire had a kidnap complex and kept his bodyguards on round-the-clock watch, but the man who carried the most protection wherever he went was the underworld boss, Tu Yueh-sen, himself.

'Uneasy lies the head . . . ?' Not in Tu's case. Tu had a private army of trigger-happy gunmen at beck and call. Some said he had 1,000; others 50,000. Ask the Japanese occupation forces between 1937 and 1945. Although the big chief was safely out of reach in Chungking, riding out World War II with members of the Nanking Government, Tu's followers made the Japs pay heavily for their occupation of Shanghai and their interruption of

SHANGHAI SAGA

Tu's criminal activities.

Crime? Here's a couple for the record. In the French Concession Green Dragon boss Tu Yueh-sen, king-pin of the crooks, was an honorary member of the French police force, sort of *ex officio*, and bore a title which, translated, meant 'chief of detectives'! Of course everyone knew the set-up in French-town. But over in the International Settlement the position was only a little better, for the chief Chinese detective of the Settlement police — fat, jovial, beer-drinking Loh Li-kwei was an old gangster himself, and almost every Chinese detective on the force had a criminal record! You see, the authorities there, like the French, figured that crime was there to stay. So they decided to let the pot merely simmer, leaving it to Loh Li-kwei to see that it never boiled over. Any other policy would have left most crimes unsolved; but for many years dozens of the worst criminals — armed robbers, kidnappers, murderers — convicted and sentenced to death, managed to beat the gallows at the eleventh hour by one of the most ingenious yet diabolical schemes ever conceived, details of which will be given in a later chapter.

Yes, Shanghai had its problems, but being Shanghai did not worry unduly about them. No reformer ever stayed to try out the standard hellfire and damnation treatment. The closest anyone ever got to it was a three-night stand by California's Four-Square Gospeller, Aimée Semple McPherson, in the thirties. Aimée arrived to try conclusions with the devil on sin in general and gambling in particular, and to show there were no hard feelings Shanghai loaned the visiting evangelist its largest gambling-hall for three nights at a nominal rental to see what she could do. Aimee's main difficulty, and the reason for her failure, was that most of Shanghai's gambling was done by the Chinese and Japanese; and none of these turned out to hear her message.

That great German chancellor Bismarck once said that 'the

INTRODUCTION

West would do well to let the sleeping Chinese giant go on sleeping, for if ever he bestirred himself . . .'. For nearly eighty years after the West forced open China's ports to trade, things went well. Trade boomed. Chinese and Western traders met by day, did business together and went their separate ways come five o'clock. There was very little fraternizing save, perhaps, in the highest circles of business and diplomacy.

The Chinese giant awoke from his slumbers in the 1911 bloodless revolution and got rid of the last Manchu emperor with a stroke of the pen. Nearly ten years of political chicanery and Machiavellian intrigue followed in Peking before the country plunged into four years of civil war, when Shanghai became the principal objective. The reason for this was the need for money to hire 'soldiers', and there was Shanghai with its monthly opium revenue of more than 6,000,000 dollars waiting for whichever battling warlord could capture it.

Meanwhile, Russians by the thousand were pouring in from Siberia as the Bolshevik Revolution of 1917 finally spread to the Far East and White Russians took to their heels. Looking back, they should have been called 'white ants'. From the day they first set foot in China the rot set in and Chinese began to see 'foreign devils', hitherto enjoying much 'face', in a far different role.

The Chinese giant, awakened by the 1911 revolution, now began to flex his muscles. And the more those early White Russian women threw themselves into the arms of white and yellow alike, the smaller grew the 'face' of the white man in China. Don't take my word for it. Matters on the morals front sank so low that the League of Nations (the United Nations of that period) appointed a special international committee to investigate the situation.

The relevant portion of their report reads:

'That the appearance of white women in such disgraceful

capacity as that of prostitutes among the natives of the lowest class, *affects very deeply the prestige of the Western nations in the Orient.'*

I'm not taking sides: I'm merely reporting. I happened to be there when they began to arrive from the north, and as I was in the Customs service at the time I saw first-hand what they possessed — or didn't possess. And they had to eat!

The years 1919 to 1939 in Shanghai brought terrific social changes. The ancient Chinese order of things was turned almost completely inside out. The next ten years, from 1939 until 1949 when the Reds took over the country, don't really matter from my point of view. World War II was fought, Chiang Kai-shek resumed his fight with the Communists, lost and fled from the mainland; but there was very little social change to report.

And now, Shanghai under the Reds. You can have it!

The irony of it is that this great city, which helped so much to modernize and encourage the Chinese colossus and get him on his feet, was the first to be devoured by him.

What we regret is not the billions of dollars' worth of assets abandoned by the whites in China, nor the magnificent city which they built and left behind; it is the sad thought of that vanished, happy-go-lucky community which showed the world how people of sixty-three nations, of diverse colour and creed, could live and do business together. Now they are dispersed to the four corners of the earth once more. Some, we learn, have started another Little Shanghai in far-off São Paulo, fastest-growing city in South America. Showing rare prescience, a Chinese mill-owner of Shanghai looked into the future in 1948, packed up his mill machinery and flew to São Paulo with his family, servants, and the entire mill staff, several hundred in number, at a cost of U.S. $1,300 each for the flight. His example was followed by others, until today in São Paulo there is a small

INTRODUCTION

replica of the old Shanghai and, I trust, a continuation of the old community spirit.

Not all were so wise as that industrialist, however. Nor so lucky. Steeped in a tradition of gunfire, most Shanghailanders elected to stay put when Chiang Kai-shek was being driven out. Other Chinese leaders in the past had been driven out of Shanghai. Perhaps this was just another changeover. Career men in the foreign areas, particularly, chose to remain: members of the police, health, public works departments, many on the eve of retirement, clung to their posts hoping for the best. Instead, they witnessed the rapid disintegration of a once proud and mighty city. Its throbbing business life all but dried up; its gay social life gave way to the Red culture—lectures, propaganda, brainwashing and the firing squad.

Soon the choice of remaining or departing was no longer in the hands of the 'exiles'. Exit permits came into being and the price was high. The Reds put the squeeze on Western business men, making no secret of their intention to bleed them of the profits of the past hundred years.

Today the Reds, have an empty shell of a metropolis. The population has risen to 6,000,000 but the port has silted up and no longer attracts the great ocean liners of yesterday—just river and coastal ships, an occasional Red liner and, of course, the junks. Such a clean sweep of the old order was made that even Tu Yueh-sen and his hierarchy had to pack their opium pipes, gather up their many concubines and hit the trail for Hong Kong where the police were not so easily corrupted. Tu and all his Green Dragons shrank in size and importance, and he himself died in 1950, just a year after abandoning his Shanghai throne.

This account of that period in China between the fall of the monarchy and the rise of the Reds also happens to encompass the entire chapter known as the Soong Dynasty, shortest but possibly most dynamic of China's many dynasties. It lasted but twenty-two years and is scarcely more than an exclamation mark on the pages of Chinese history.

Those who say 'Shanghai's end is no loss' may be right or wrong; but the fact is, Shanghai *did exist* and in its heyday was one of this world's great port-cities. It played a leading part in creating, unwittingly perhaps, the present-day Communist Government of that country. It tried desperately to avoid political involvement but its very neutrality opened the door to plotters and revolutionaries.

'The Shanghai people [who] inhabited a mudflat and turned it into one of the world's great cities were without background, but even so, were a pronounced type — smart, aggressive and unashamedly ostentatious', wrote Christopher Rand in his book, *Hong Kong, the Island Between.*

'The women dressed lavishly and the men were big spenders and loud talkers. They were easy to spot in the [Hong Kong] streets, to where they shifted when Shanghai fell to the Reds.

'Suddenly there were more millionaires in Hong Kong than in New York, representing a huge concentration of brains and energy.'

According to Rhoads Murphy (*Shanghai: Key to Modern China*):

'In Shanghai, China for the first time learned and absorbed the lessons of extra-territoriality, gunboat diplomacy, foreign "concessions" and the aggressive spirit of the nineteenth-century Europe... while it lasted, foreign Shanghai was an exciting place, justly famous as one of the wickedest cities of the world, a place where two civilizations met and where neither prevailed; where morality was irrelevant, or meaningless, each man a law unto himself... an atmosphere which was apparent, even to the casual visitor.'

INTRODUCTION

Yet another passing writer (Hauser) had this to say in *Shanghai: City for Sale*:
'Shanghai was the most realistic republic ever to have existed in this world.'
Of its charter, the Land Regulations, Hauser wrote:
'These made Shanghai the most unconventional municipality in the world and created the proper atmosphere for the exuberant growth of a money-making, unsentimental, optimistic, wide-open city.'

Of more than passing interest is this fact; that once (in 1862) a group of go-getting traders tried to have Shanghai declared a 'free and independent city', entirely self-governing, and they proposed to tie up the municipal franchise system in a manner that would give permanent control of the city to property owners only, whether they be Chinese or foreign, the latter, of course, to represent (and control) the former by proxies, a voting system that, by the way, was adopted and endured to the end. But the British consul of the day blocked the scheme, declaring Shanghai territory to be 'on loan' only from the Emperor of China, under treaty.

These treaties clearly stated that whereas the emperor allowed the 'foreign devils' to live on Chinese soil according to the laws of their own countries (i.e. extra-territoriality) he retained sovereignty over his own people living in all the 'concessions' set apart throughout China for Sino-foreign trade.

In actual practice, however, the emperor's subjects living in Shanghai and any of the other foreign 'concessions' in China became subject to the legal jurisdictions of those areas, and were arraigned before special courts consistent with Shanghai's whole strange and original set-up. These were a mixture of foreign and Chinese administration, and the 'foreign' judges invariably dominated the scene, though the laws which they applied were

Chinese! They were even *called* 'Mixed Courts' and the name was used both in the International Settlements (Shanghai, Hankow, Tientsin and other large treaty ports) as well as in all French Concessions throughout China.

On one point only did the emperor stand firm and it was this: should any Chinese be sentenced to death in these Mixed Courts, the sovereignty of China over all her subjects was to be expressed by having the condemned prisoner executed by Chinese authorities, on Chinese soil. The emperor who made that stipulation should have known better. He should have known that even in his own capital city of Peking the post of executioner was one eagerly sought after by court officials anxious to get rich. Indeed, under the lap big bribes were paid to the court chamberlain for the job, reasons for which will be clarified in due course.

One of the more recent descriptions of Shanghai is contained in *In Two Chinas*, by K. M. Pannikar, Indian ambassador to China (1948 to 1952), who describes the city of Shanghai as an 'unreal, fantastic creation... proud Queen of the Pacific'.

In this book I shall try to describe in greater detail some of the facets of life in Shanghai which contributed to impressions like those formed by the Indian ambassador, while at the same time trying to convey the truth that Shanghai was also a kindly, friendly and charitable city.

Like most happy-go-lucky fortunate people, Shanghailanders were generous to a fault. And the strangest feature of all is that although sixty-three different nationalities made up its population, they were as one in the pride they felt in their city.

Could they be asked today, the vast majority of Chinese residents of Shanghai who lived under foreign control would vote for a return of the old conditions. And they would talk it over in the 'Shanghai dialect', a specially created Chinese

INTRODUCTION

language born in Shanghai for the use of Chinese from all parts of the country who could not speak to each other in any other way — save in English.

And that is no opium dream!

1

Sticky Start

WHAT COULD be more fitting than to begin this story at the same point where Shanghai itself started — the opium trade? Especially as the oldest and largest trading firm in the city — nay, in all China — grew out of the profits made from opium dealing before it was outlawed. Everyone in the Far East has heard of Jardine, Matheson (Jardine was a canny Scot). This firm dominated Shanghai throughout its existence and its financial foundation was millions of pounds sterling representing opium profits. When the Reds arrived (1949) to take over the city, the Jardine, Matheson commercial empire included a large coastal and river shipping fleet, extensive cotton mills, dockyards, wharves, breweries, engineering works, insurance companies, real estate and, last but by no means least, a large voice in how Shanghai was to be run.

Another one-time big-shot of influential proportions whose bank balance was also built up on opium was Edward Ezra, owner of whole down-town city blocks, who is best remembered for launching an American-style newspaper in Shanghai called the *China Press*.

So far as is known, neither Jardine nor Ezra ever dabbled in opium again after the 1917 international convention placed a voluntary ban on the drug in an effort to save the Chinese from becoming a race of drug-fiends. But others did. Thousands of opium-smugglers went to work to feed the opium appetite which these two pioneers had helped to create.

For some strange reason, opium grown in China is inferior to opium grown in India, Turkey or Persia and these three places furnished — and no doubt still furnish — the high-quality smoking of those able to afford it. There was, indeed, an outrageous difference between the market prices of the imported and the locally grown opium. In the period 1919 to 1939, of which I write (mostly), imported opium fetched around Ch.$500 per pound while the China-grown stuff was struggling to get Ch. $50.

Before Shanghai's uncrowned ruler, Tu Yueh-sen, gained virtual control of the narcotics trade, hundreds of petty operators sought to supply the lucrative Shanghai market in large or small shipments according to their cash resources. There are many roads, rivers, creeks and canals leading into Shanghai. The trick was to select one of these unbeknown to the gangs of hijackers and hoodlums who waited to pounce.

Estimates were that 90 per cent got through.

On the white powder market — morphine, heroin, cocaine — Dr. Wu Lien-teh, Chinese port health administrator under Generalissimo Chiang Kai-shek, estimated that twenty-seven *tons* entered annually into Shanghai, basing his guess on the 10 per cent seizures made by Customs and police. How much of this was used in Shanghai itself, how much went out to the 200,000,000 Chinese living in the Yangtze River valley which looked to Shanghai for most of its supplies of luxuries, no one can say with certainty.

Four times a year the Customs authorities destroyed all seized narcotics in a gigantic bonfire which for twenty-four hours put a black cloud over the city, representing several millions of dollars' worth of opium dreams — or sniffs, or injections. It was quite a

STICKY START

ceremony. Seized drugs stored for months in the Customs House strong-room were taken out under strong guard, ferried across the river to a special enclosure containing two large brick kilns and there, watched by high Chinese and foreign Customs and diplomatic officials, burned to the last ash.

Not everyone knew it, but that little bit of Bund at Shanghai between the Customs House situated on the Bund foreshore and the Whangpoo River always remained Chinese territory even though it was within the International Settlement ceded by treaty to the 'foreign devils' for trading purposes. All seizures of contraband made by the Chinese Customs men had to be transported by water to the Customs House strong-room. They were put ashore at the Customs Jetty which faced the Customs House. Necessarily, therefore, they had to remain under Chinese Customs jurisdiction until locked away in the Customs House. Hence the invisible Chinese passage across the Bund.

That is why armed Chinese troops were permitted to form a corridor across this busiest of all Shanghai thoroughfares on those occasions described above, and why traffic was halted to give way to the column of coolies bearing their burdens of valuable contraband to the waiting launches and, eventually, the kilns.

I have already said that in 'fees' (protection and otherwise) Shanghai was worth upwards of $6,000,000 monthly to Chinese in authority. By that I mean the heads of the Chinese territory police and military garrison. These, whoever they were, remained in office only as long as they 'held the fort'. Any ambitious bandit able to muster enough followers to take over Shanghai did so, and a new set of collectors set up shop. It can be better appreciated, therefore, how Shanghai found itself in the centre of the civil war years (1921-7), when the spoils of victory usually went to the warlord able to hire the most mercenaries — a very different type of Chinese soldier from what the world knows today.

Similarly, it can be understood why the volume of narcotics flowing into Shanghai grew so rapidly in the same period, and why Chinese local government officials of whatever allegiance gave every assistance and encouragement to the drug-smugglers. Let me give an illustration of the ramifications of this drug traffic and its relationship with the civil warfare of the period.

The whole of China was in a state of chaos. The authority of the Peking Government, following ten years of plot and counterplot, had completely broken down. There was no longer an emperor: the country had turned republic, there was much jealousy and jockeying among those eligible or ambitious for power. Inevitably some turned to force, and sides were quickly drawn so that banditry broke loose all over the country and it was no longer safe to travel in the interior.

New and powerful names began appearing in the Press, names like Wu Pei-fu, Chang Tso-lin, Feng Yu-hsiang, Yen Hsi-shan, while over in distant Szechwan Province, a thousand miles as the crow flies from Shanghai, Governor Yang Sen's name crept more and more into the stories relating to internal pillage and banditry.

Yang Sen's ambition was to dominate the north-west region, containing some of the most fertile areas in all China. He was not much interested in politics or what went on in Peking. He knew that money won wars and that his soldier-bandits would remain loyal to him—and keep him in power—only so long as he paid them. So Yang cast his eyes upon the distant opium market of Shanghai. He ordered the farmers of Szechwan to plant poppies instead of their usual crops and brought virtual famine to his territory as a result. Since his greed had no bounds he ignored this fact and concentrated on the problem of how to get his opium to market.

STICKY START

In those days the only—repeat *only*—way to Shanghai was the long, long trail down the Yangtze Kiang River, 1,200 miles of it. So Yang Sen sent emissaries down to feel out the Shanghai military garrison commander. Safe conduct was arranged over the final stage of Yang Sen's trek to market, from a small river-port known as Lu Shing on the south bank of the Yangtze. From here a military escort from the Shanghai native garrison accompanied Yang Sen's opium as far as the border of the French Concession, where hired guns from the Shanghai underworld took over. Occasionally, when the tip-off arrived in time, opposition hoodlums, locally known as *pi-sehs* (loafers), hi-jacked the dope and left Yang Sen lamenting—but this was a rare occurrence.

It was the journey downriver from distant Szechwan to Lu Shing which earned newspaper headlines for General Yang Sen; or should I say the many journeyings? Yang's usual practice was to put his opium aboard any river boat heading for Shanghai out of Ichang, Szechwan port of call for all vessels plying the Upper Yangtze River. A large squad of Yang's soldier-bandits accompanied the cargo. They never asked permission and never paid for their passage. And none dared deny them passage.

Such was the state of affairs at this time that even Customs officers were unofficially warned against tangling with Yang or any other soldier-bandits transporting themselves from one part of the river to another. One small shipping company tried to get fares from a party of bandits changing scenery. An argument developed and when the next foreign gunboat appeared the merchantman had the 'deadheads' forcibly put ashore. From then on all foreign merchant ships plying the Yangtze River were used for target practice by bandits encamped along the river-banks, and walls of armour plate six feet high had to be erected around the decks of all ships to protect those on board from trigger-happy bandits.

SHANGHAI SAGA

All foreign ships painted their national flags on bow and midships in a futile warning which, if anything, only drew more fire. Twelve hundred or more miles of river needs a lot of patrolling, and the international fleet of gunboats which half a century earlier had sent the natives a-running, now worked overtime trying to give protection to the commerce which gunboat policy had built up.

The mighty Yangtze Kiang River begins in the Himalaya Mountains back of India, dominated by Mount Everest. Between winter and summer there is a rise and fall in the water level of more than 200 feet! When the thaw sets in among the mountains a raging torrent pours into the Yangtze through precipitous gorges, and only flat-bottomed vessels with powerful engines can get upstream to China's World War II capital of Chungking, which is the terminus of river schedules. Shooting the rapids of this upriver region can be dangerous, and every summer sees at least one steamer impale itself upon hidden rocks while dozens of native junks go ker-plunk to pieces. Indeed, there is one spot not far from Ichang, No. 2 port of the Gorges, whose inhabitants derive their livelihood from the wreckage and washed-up cargo of the failures.

In September 1927, after several years of cat-and-mousing with the foreign gunboats, Yang Sen finally came to grips with them in a big and final way. He seized two British upriver merchant ships, *Wanhsien* and *Wantung*, at the minor riverport of Wanhsien, slightly downstream from Ichang, where he had temporary headquarters. Both ships were officered and engineered by foreigners, and incoming reports said Yang held them all prisoner. For years after the incident it was debated why Yang Sen seized these ships and of the various reasons put forward those held most likely were: (I) They had refused to carry Yang's opium downriver, (2) their captains had double-

STICKY START

crossed Yang in some manner, or (3) Yang wished to find out how far he could really push the Customs and naval authorities who were supposed to control the river.

Whatever the reason, the British Admiralty took a very poor view of Yang's bold deed and Admiral Cameron, commanding the British Yangtze River patrol, went into immediate action to recover the seized ships. Using Hankow as a base, the admiral worked out what he believed to be a good scheme. He knew that Yang Sen had over 400 soldiers aboard the *Wanhsien* and *Wantung*, while he could only muster about sixty officers and men in a hurry — and he was in a hurry. The British Navy's 'face' was at stake. Naval headquarters reported only two Yangtze gunboats in the Gorges, *Cockchafer* and *Widgeon*, and Cameron wirelessed instructions to both of them to head for Wanhsien and await further orders 'out of sight' of the two captive, anchored merchantmen. At Hankow, called the 'Chicago of China', 600 miles upriver and capable of berthing 10,000-ton ocean liners at high-water periods, Admiral Cameron commandeered the Jardine, Matheson river boat *Kiawo*, big enough to carry the rescue party and all necessary supplies.

Although supposedly secret, even to the extent of repainting the *Kiawo* during darkness, the well-known 'bamboo wireless' of China somehow managed to get word to Wanhsien of the impending naval expedition. Cameron expected to have to fight to recover the two merchant ships. The days when Chinese slunk away at the first show of force by foreigners were over, at least for men like Yang Sen and his followers.

The ultimate expedition setting out from Hankow consisted of sixty-three naval ratings and five junior officers headed by Lieut.-Commander Darley, an Australian in the British Navy, the main armament being a pair of Lewis guns. The *Kiawo* approached the port of Wanhsien towards dusk, and through binoculars Darley could see but a handful of bandits scattered about the decks of the two impounded river ships. He at once suspected a trap and selected the *Wanhsien*, closer of the two, for boarding purposes. Apart from an occasional glance in their direction the bandits went on with their evening meal on deck.

Darley's orders were to recover the ships and release the imprisoned foreigners, so the *Kiawo*'s engines were cut and the vessel allowed to drift with the current towards the *Wanhsien*. 'Prepare to board!' ordered Darley, and his men did just that. Some stood by with grappling hooks to make fast to the *Wanhsien*, both Lewis gun crews took up crossfire positions to cover the boarders and Darley, naval cutlass in right hand and revolver in left, stood near the rail to lead his men into attack.

When the gap between the two vessels was less than ten yards the *Wanhsien* suddenly came to life. The few bandit-soldiers who had been putting on the peaceful-evening-meal scene disappeared ominously, and up from the bowels of the ship and out of suddenly opened doors and other shelters came pouring a yelling, cursing, shooting horde of Chinese bandits.

The two ships now bumped gently; grappling hooks thrown by tensed British bluejackets clutched and hung on to the *Wanhsien's* rails. The Lewis guns opened up into the oncoming swarm of Chinese, but for the majority it was rifle and pistol-fire. The Chinese appeared to have no rapid-fire weapons of any sort, and unquestionably it was just as well. As it was, the Lewis gunners had a field day, pouring hot lead in two steady streams into the thickening swarm of Yan Sen's 'five dollars a month and loot' mercenaries. As fast as they fell, replacements poured up from 'tween decks and other hiding-places. Bodies piled up so high in front that newcomers on deck had to push the dead and wounded out of the way to get a shot at the British sailors, who were not by any means escaping their share of casualties.

STICKY START

View of down-town section of Shanghai in 1927

Shanghai's first Customs House

STICKY START

However, the Lewis gunners had charge of the situation and the terrific din of this battle pushed echoes up and down those cliff bound Gorges, the like of which had never before been heard thereabouts.

At the height of battle the two gunboats *Cockchafer* and *Widgeon* hove into view around a nearby bend of the river, crews at action stations. Both gunboats mounted small-calibre cannon forward as their main armament, backed up by machine guns, but to both commanders it was soon obvious that this fight was one exclusively between the *Kiawo* and the *Wanhsien* desperadoes, for the two ships were literally locked together in a death struggle.

I happened to have just been made cable correspondent for an Australian group of newspapers at this time and sent a lurid description of this epic Yangtze Gorges battle some twenty-four hours after it occurred — just as soon as the facts came to hand. Unfortunately, I had not had time to build up a reputation as a sane and trusted correspondent and the gory details received by the Australian editors were viewed somewhat sceptically, no doubt in the belief that I was trying to get off to a good start. Thus my accurate description of the *Wanhsien's* scuppers literally running with blood and guts was toned down unrecognizably, to my great discontent.

When it appeared to Commander Darley that the spirit of the Chinese had been broken, he made the mistake of his life and leaped from the *Kiawo* to the deck of the *Wanhsien*, brandishing his cutlass and firing his revolver as he yelled to the boarding party to follow. One of the Chinese bandits shot him down immediately and rammed a bayonet through his throat. Several of his bluejackets fell with him and the other would-be boarders halted in their tracks. Less than ten minutes had passed since the point-blank battle had commenced. Most of the 400 Chinese aboard the *Wanhsien* were either dead or so badly wounded as to be useless to Yang Sen and his treacherous scheme.

Not only were the Lewis guns running dangerously hot: they were also running critically short of ammunition. Meanwhile *Cockchafer* and *Widgeon*, spoiling for a fight and helpless to do anything for Darley and his men, slipped over towards the village of Wanhsien nearby and bombarded Yang Sen's bamboo headquarters with H.E. shell. Almost instantly the village became a raging inferno.

During the battle all but one of the imprisoned foreign officers and engineers of the two captive vessels managed to escape from their ships and swim to the off side of the *Kiawo*. The bandits sighted only one of them and shot him dead as he swam, the swirling waters of the Gorges carrying him swiftly downstream beyond recovery.

Darley's next in command, aware of the ammunition shortage but not quite realizing how close was victory, ordered immediate withdrawal, but first, recovery of the bodies of the fallen which still lay amid the carnage on the *Wanhsien's* deck. While the Lewis gunners beat back the last of the bandits a boarding party made a desperate but successful recovery of their fallen comrades, whereupon the *Kiawo* broke off action and cut adrift almost as the last available bullet sped towards the cowed enemy aboard the still captive British merchant ships.

But everybody had had more than enough for one day. Escorted by the British gunboats, the *Kiawo* returned somewhat dejectedly to Hankow under orders from Admiral Cameron. The eventual recapture of the *Wanhsien* and *Wantung* was an anticlimax. Although prepared to continue the chastisement of Yang Sen, a second naval expedition bore down upon the anchored ships at Wanhsien only to find them completely abandoned. The dead had been thrown overboard and the wounded removed

STICKY START

for treatment. Both ships were taken to Hankow and Admiral Cameron's mission was accomplished.

For a classic example of hi-jacking an opium cargo one must go back to February 26, 1924. Almost all of China was involved in civil war and one had to look to the areas under foreign control for any sort of law and order. In Shanghai a group of opium dealers had pooled their cash and bought heavily in the Turkish opium market.

Vladivostok, Russian warm-water port of Siberia on the Pacific, and recently come under Bolshevik control, was now an active receiving centre for contraband of every description, and it became general practice for European contraband to be consigned to the Russian port whence it ricocheted to Shanghai by well-tested rail and ship routes. A million dollar cargo of high-grade Turkish opium left Constantinople (Istanbul) per Nippon Yusen Kaisha's European liner *Kamagata Maru* in January of that year — destination, Vladivostok. Or should we say Shanghai?

The Japanese captain of the *Kamagata Maru* yielded to temptation. A rival gang of opium-smugglers who knew of the Turkish cargo successfully propositioned the skipper, and he hove to off the China coast near Shanghai at midnight on February 26. A Chinese junk slipped alongside and some fifty chests of opium were sold by the double-crossing Jap to the junk for an undisclosed number of American dollars. I first heard of this when a telephone call reached me at the Mixed Court of the International Settlement, where I had a daily assignment for the Shanghai newspaper on which I worked as reporter at this time. The call came from Assistant Commissioner of Police M. O. Springfield, in charge of narcotics suppression for the International Settlement.

'Come down to Number 51 Canton Road,' Springfield told

me over the 'phone. 'We're searching the place and it looks like a good story.'

I stumbled upon an incredible set-up. But in passing I must draw attention to that little act of the assistant police commissioner to illustrate the sort of friendship Shanghai just naturally handed out to those living there. There was only one level of society, and even the beachcombers were offered jobs, food and shelter, or passage back to their home country if they so desired.

It seemed to Police Commissioner Springfield at the time that he had merely uncovered an elaborate storage depot for imported opium. He summoned me, he said, to show me an ingenious arrangement of false walls, secret doors, tunnels and other amazing forms of camouflage in Fu Manchu style, the like of which even he had never seen before. Actually, he said, his 'information' had given a number on another street, half a block away. But after three or four hours of probing with crowbars and axes, Springfield's police searchers discovered what they had come for, ten feet underground and a hundred yards from where they started!

This case later became famous, with international repercussions. Among the stuff Springfield seized was a large batch of documents in different languages, which needed a month to translate and get ready for presentation as evidence in court. The 'tip' given to Springfield came from — believe it or not — a man named Ezra claiming Spanish nationality!

'I represent a syndicate which had a cargo of Turkish opium stolen,' Ezra told police. 'Some of the stolen opium is believed to be hidden at 51 Canton Road. We ask for a search to be made.'

Pressed for more information, Ezra told Commissioner Springfield that the opium had been consigned to Vladivostok, where its importation was legal. How it got back to Shanghai, he

STICKY START

declared he did not know.

'How did you get into this, Mr. Ezra?' asked Springfield. 'I always thought you were an active member of the Opium Suppression Society.'

'So I am,' replied Ezra. 'But this is purely business. I shall receive a commission on whatever opium is recovered.'

'How could you prove any opium we found belonged to your syndicate?' asked Springfield.

'By its markings,' replied Ezra. 'The syndicate can identify any of the opium found by marks on the wrapping.' (It ought to be explained that opium experts can tell the origin of any raw opium by the method of its preparation for shipment, shape, size and weight as well as style of wrapping and trade-marks.)

In Shanghai the market was so well organized, so sensitive to supply and demand (with consequent effect upon price) that the impact of a newly arrived Turkish cargo was unavoidably felt. Word got around quickly and, inevitably, the unfortunate syndicate learned the fate of its cargo as soon as it hit the market.

But only the syndicate and those who had hi-jacked the *Kamagata Maru*'s midnight cargo had the full story. A hurried conference and some legal opinion came up with the bright idea which ultimately led to the meeting of opium-suppressionist Ezra and policeman Springfield. Though Commissioner Springfield told me he disbelieved Ezra's story from the start, his main interest was to get hold of the opium, irrespective of its owner. A search warrant was immediately issued and we are now back in the Mixed Court of the International Settlement where eight occupants of 51 Canton Road faced charges of both possessing and stealing opium.

The case opened sensationally when the British judge questioned the nationality of the prosecution's leading witness, Ezra.

'I always considered you as a British subject, Mr. Ezra,' the judge said.

'I am a Spanish protégé,' replied the fat little Jew, wiping his brow. 'I renounced British nationality years ago.'

'I am not questioning your right to renounce British nationality,' the judge came back, 'but there may be some doubt as to the right of the Spanish consul to confer Spanish nationality on you.'

The case was adjourned to refer the matter to the Peking Diplomatic Body. The latter, to Ezra's consternation, ruled that the Spanish consul 'lacked power' to confer on Ezra Spanish privileges. Having renounced British nationality, therefore, Ezra reverted to the nationality of his parents, who were Turkish.

As the Mixed Court judge unfurled one argument after another at the little Jew, and finally nailed him as a Turk, without any extra-territorial privileges and subject to Chinese law, Ezra squirmed and sweated and hastily went into a huddle with his attorney, Italian Chevalier G. D. Russo, once (1923) kidnapped by bandits travelling from Shanghai to Peking by train.

Ezra's position had now become parlous indeed. Turkey, like Germany, Austria and other Central European powers against whom China fought in World War I, forfeited all treaty privileges the day China joined the Allies and one of the main losses to Shanghai from this was that the fine German brass band no longer gave concerts to the foreign population from the balcony of the German Club on the Bund foreshore on summer evenings. All Germans, with their allies of that time, henceforth fell under Chinese law, and the fine German Club became the Bank of China.

Attorney Russo's solution to Ezra's dilemma was to drop the Case and he asked leave of the court for Ezra's withdrawal as one of the complainants. By now, of course, the court had sized

STICKY START

up the situation, and Ezra's true role was suspect. He was placed under a bond to appear whenever called upon, thus short-circuiting any idea he may have had of taking the first ship out. Furthermore, 'in the interests of justice', the court insisted on continuing with the hearing, naming the police as complainants.

By now, however, it was not the 400 lb. of stolen *Kamagata Maru* opium discovered at the Canton Road underground hideout which interested the court, or police, but the translations of those documents found on the searched premises. These revealed the existence of a world-wide organization, a brotherhood of opium dealers spread over many countries. Certain brochures proved to be trade circulars extolling the virtues of Persian opium, quoting prices f.o.b. and many details relating to duration and methods of delivery.

The narcotics division of the old League of Nations showed great interest in the Canton Road documents, particularly when a high British official then stationed in Persia confirmed their information and further reported that the industry was heavily backed by, Persia's leading bankers, merchants and even a smattering of Church dignitaries who were deriving income from the poppy-fields.

Seeking ways and means to counteract the opium traffic, one special committee of the League recommended setting up a search barrier for Far Eastern ships passing through the Suez Canal. Without Japanese support, however, the scheme was doomed to failure and was never adopted.

The tremendous plant which General Douglas MacArthur found manufacturing narcotics in Jap-controlled territory at the end of World War II may explain Japanese reluctance to collaborate in any opium-suppression scheme propounded by well-meaning Western powers. Japanese drug factories had been churning out opium by-products such as morphine, cocaine and heroin in such vast quantities that Chinese coolies were able to afford daily injections on coolie wages! This was Japan's method of levelling down the enormous manpower disparity between the two nations, an ever-present fear haunting ambitious architects of Japanese supremacy in Asia, for a nation in the grip of debilitating drugs is a pushover for any smaller, but physically fit, power.

I have already mentioned in my 'Introduction' how Shanghai was drawn into the civil warfare in China in the 1920's because the fighting warlords needed the opium revenue to pay their armies. The smoke of opium and the smoke of gunpowder were never far apart in those wild, uncertain days. At one period in the civil war three separate 'armies' surrounded Shanghai, doing a little fighting with real bullets, but spending most of their time negotiating with rich bankers and merchants inside Shanghai for loans — in silver dollars which, in time, were cynically dubbed 'silver bullets'. And they won wars, too. Of course they had to make promises to the moneylenders and the big problem for the latter was to know who to put the money on. And in such deals what collateral do you think they offered? Opium revenue!

'It is safe to say that whoever holds Shanghai has $6,500,000 a month from opium revenue as surely in his hand as if it were deposited with the Bank of England.'

So wrote Bertrand Lennox Simpson, who as 'Putnam Weale' edited an English-language newspaper known as *The Peking & Tientsin Times* which from time to time crusaded against graft, corruption and kindred evils. Simpson was also one of that small army of 'advisers' with which the Peking Government of those days surrounded itself in order to get a cheap line on the foreign viewpoint of things.

'The Shanghai Opium Trust,' wrote crusader Simpson, 'has its headquarters in the French Concession, where its stocks are

STICKY START

safely stored under police immunity. More than 20,000 chests of Persian, Turkish and Indian opium are stored there annually. In addition, 1,500 chests of Chinese opium are stored there monthly, bringing the total revenue of six and a half million dollars to those controlling the opium traffic.'

Mr. Simpson then wrote his own death warrant by declaring: 'I can name the street in the French Concession where the head depot of this trust is situated. There are 200 foreigners working in and around Shanghai for the Opium Trust and about forty miles outside the Shanghai harbour there is a port for transhipment of overseas shipments of opium.'

Next night a quiet-looking, bespectacled young Chinese, dressed in Western-style clothes, knocked on the front door of Mr. Simpson's home in Peking. This was not unusual, for Mr. Simpson had many friends among the Chinese, especially students. He himself opened the front door to the visitor, who handed him a card which the Englishman took, half turning towards the inner light to read it more easily. The young Chinese suddenly drew an automatic pistol from inside his long native gown and shot Simpson stone dead, so that he never had another chance to name the place where the Shanghai Opium Trust kept hidden its huge store of millions of dollars' worth of opium. A Chinese servant witnessed the murder. The card handed to the ex-political adviser to the Peking Government was of the type used to invite sing-song girls to come and join the party!

Perhaps the chief result of Simpson's murder was the sudden change of command in the Frenchtown police force. Le Commandant Bulgari terminated his services somewhat prematurely, the French Government replacing him with a promising, supposedly 'untouchable' junior commandant named Fabre from France's Tientsin concession. It was widely whispered of the outgoing incumbent that a thick wad of what the underworld called 'greenery' lay embedded in his breakfast napkin every morning. The change of command proved to be just a bit of official window-dressing, however, for the opium trust remained in business and, like all monopolies, waxed fatter with the years.

One of the principal improvements after 1927, the year in which civil war ended and the Nationalist Government of Chiang Kai-shek came to power, was that it was no longer necessary for the Trust to use that port of transhipment mentioned by the late Lennox Simpson. Henceforth, it was commonly held, all big shipments sailed gaily into Shanghai in a Chinese man-o'-war, thumbing its bowsprit at the Customs House on the way up to the officially protected unloading centre. Every time a Chinese cruiser passed upstream during the brief Soong Dynasty, Shanghai residents exchanged winks, commenting, 'Another load of European opium has arrived safely.'

One man had created this amazing situation. He was king of the underworld. He was also blood brother of the President of China, and his name was Tu Yueh-sen. I called him 'Old Snake-eyes' and if you look at his photograph facing page 48 you will understand why. Those are the eyes of an opium smoker as well as of the Al Capone of the Orient.

Tu wasn't always a big-shot. I recall, as a very young officer in the Chinese Maritime Customs, that he was just one of hundreds of petty dope-smugglers trying to get their stuff past the Customs. Tu and I met many times and both as a Customs officer and later as a newspaperman I attended many Chinese dinners given by this super-crook, who was once a fruit-pedlar on the streets of Shanghai! His rise to criminal eminence culminated a career of violence which left rival gangsters either corpses or working for Tu. In the end he got himself elected head of the Green Dragon Society, one of China's oldest secret clans. China is and always

STICKY START

has been riddled with secret societies, though not all exist for criminal purposes. By far the majority are mutual aid societies, better known as 'guilds'.

The twentieth century, however, witnessed the emergence of two major underworld organizations, the Green Dragons and the Red Dragons, whose overseas agents fought many bloody tong wars in the Chinatowns of San Francisco, New York, London, Chicago and elsewhere. But, like the leaders of North American underworld gangland, the Chinese saw the futility of rivalry and so the two societies merged and Tu Yueh-sen, as head of the Green Dragons and blood-brother of Chiang Kai-shek, was a natural to become supreme head of this vast criminal empire.

'There is no doubt of the immense hold that Tu came to have on Chiang all the time the former was alive.'

Those words were written by the Indian ambassador to China (1948-52), K. M. Pannikar, in his book *In Two Chinas*.

Ironically, all of Shanghai was in debt to Tu Yueh-sen. He saved the city from a blood bath in 1927 in a breath-taking demonstration of underworld power and the facts are these: Generalissimo Chiang's 1926-7 military campaign was going well. His Nationalist forces had foot-slogged it from Canton up through central China, cleaning up the battling warlords of the civil strife as they went. Chiang reached the very gates of Shanghai, greatest of all prizes. But the city was bristling with foreign troops and warships ready to defend itself against this Nationalist army which had been assembled, trained and marched northwards with the avowed purposes of recovering the foreign concessions from the foreigners, cancelling the so-called 'unequal treaties' and establishing a Chinese Government which could look the Western powers square in the eye and say: 'You've had your day. From now on we do business as equals.'

Friendly Chinese in Hong Kong had warned the British

Government in the middle of 1926 of the purpose for which this Cantonese force was being assembled and the British had passed the news to other interested powers, with the result that by the time Chiang Kai-shek and his victorious army reached the outskirts of Shanghai that city was an armed camp, with some 25,000 international troops entrenched around its boundaries and upwards of fifty assorted warships, including aircraft carriers, tied up in the harbour.

The United States of America in those days usually sent the U.S. Marines to trouble-spots. For this crisis Washington despatched the famous Fourth Marines with Major-General Smedley ('Gimlet Eye') Butler in command, plus regular army units from the Philippines. Britain sent General Sir John Duncan with General Lord Gort, v.c. (of Dunkirk fame in World War II), as second in command and, among other troops, a battalion of the famous Coldstream Guards, complete with bearskin 'busbies' and the regimental band.

Sepoys from India, Ghurkas, Punjabis, Annamites from French Indo-China, Japanese, Italians, Swedes, Norwegians, Portuguese; almost every nation with a 'stake' in China despatched reinforcements to 'save' Shanghai, even though several were but token forces for legal purposes. It was decided to name this international army the 'Shanghai Defence Force' — 'Shaforce' for short. It commandeered rooftops of high buildings on the city's outskirts and placed lookouts and light artillery thereon. It sent armoured cars on regular patrol up and down outlying roads wherever foreigners had their homes, reassuring the occupants (most of whom had evacuated such areas anyway) and warning the ambitious Nationalists. Still the big question remained — 'Will Chiang try to take Shanghai by force?'

But the Nationalist leader was having troubles of his own. Within the Nationalist movement was a powerful group of

STICKY START

violent left-wingers, rabidly pro-Communist. These had already launched riots and seized the British Concession at Hankow, in central China! At Nanking, just ahead of the Nationalists, they had joined with the rabble in a wild orgy of burning, looting, rape and murder, killing several foreigners and necessitating British and American naval intervention. In the general confusion the blame for all this was put upon Chiang Kai-shek's army which, of necessity, had to go in and restore order out of the chaos created. This was just what the Reds wanted, and they went ahead with a diabolical scheme for repeating these tactics at Shanghai, but on a grander scale, hoping to embroil Chiang Kai-shek with the Western powers. Consequently, when Chiang and his forces reached the outskirts of Shanghai, the left-wingers led a revolt in Chapei and Nantao, the Chinese sections of the city. Allegedly led by present-day Red China's Premier Chou En-lai, this rabble burned, looted and killed, setting fire to several native police stations and seizing their armouries. In terror, most of the gendarmes deserted, and those who did not were butchered.

Inside the barricades of the calm and peaceful foreign areas of Shanghai we watched from the tops of high buildings and saw incendiarism rampant, with the unmistakable signs of petrol and oil smoke everywhere. By night the native sections had a hundred large fires burning simultaneously, and shooting could be heard in many directions.

Flushed with the success of similar tactics at Hankow a month or two earlier, when the British Concession had been stormed and overrun at the height of confusion, the Reds intended to storm Shanghai's barricades as soon as Chiang's forces moved into Nantao and Chapei to restore order. But Chiang Kai-shek saw the trap, and instead of giving his men the order to go in he got in touch with Elder Dragon, Tu Yueh-sen.

Like most correspondents for overseas newspapers about

49

this time, I was attached to a local paper. And like most local newspapermen I shifted around from one Shanghai paper to another from time to time as various moods, needs, or rows-with-the-boss dictated. I was on the *China Press*, brain-child of the late opium magnate Edward Ezra, at the period under review. This newspaper saw many interesting personalities come and go during its existence. To name a few who come to mind — Thomas Millard (*Millard's Far Eastern Review*); J. B. Powell (*My Twenty-five Years in China*), *Chicago Tribune* correspondent and proprietor of the *China Weekly Review*; Elsie McCormack, witty columnist in more recent years of the *New York Times*; Larry Lehrbas, press relations officer with General MacArthur in World War II; and Charlie Sloan!

Charlie would easily qualify for 'the most interesting personality I have ever met'. He was, of course, from the U.S.A. Those big, horn-rimmed glasses, the fast talk, the 'bull', to say nothing of those ever-present golf trousers — just look at Charlie in that photograph with General Chiang Kai-shek and myself (opposite p. 96). Sloan, like hundreds of other newspapermen and women who passed through Shanghai, never intended to remain. All of them worked their way around the world, picking up enough material for a series of articles, or a book, maybe.

Well, Charlie blew into the *China Press* one day like a fresh breeze and, as the pink sports page was in rather inept hands at the time, by noon Charlie was installed as sports editor and he certainly looked the part! From that day forward, until he left Shanghai and a mighty bundle of cabaret chits behind, Charlie had the *China Press* in the palm of his hand.

When Edward Ezra died he left two young sons and a widow as heirs to his well-lined estate. Now Mrs. Ezra had two brothers. Arthur and Theodore Sopher, known to all fun-loving Shanghailanders as 'The Bing Boys'. As minors, Ezra's sons had to

STICKY START

Tu Yueh-sen, head of Green Dragon Society

SHANGHAI SAGA

Shanghai Defence Force

STICKY START

come of age before acquiring papa's opium fortune. Meanwhile, Arthur and Theodore persuaded their widowed sister to leave the management of the Ezra estate in their hands and, to keep an eye on each other, the Bing Boys became inseparable. Hence, no doubt, the title.

Arthur and Theodore adored Charlie Sloan from the first meeting. Charlie responded by pumping out a long editorial two weeks after joining the *China Press* in which he eulogized these two worthy 'newspaper magnates' and threw the dictionary at them. Charlie then moved into a sumptuous apartment, above and behind the *China Press* offices, five floors up. By coincidence it faced my flat. We both had balconies, with big french doors.

I mention this merely to tell how Charlie used to wake me up about ten o'clock every morning with some of the most brilliant piano-playing ever heard from an amateur in the Far East. I could see him from my bed, naked to the waist, sitting in his pyjama pants, minus the horn-rims, which gave him a terrible squint: indeed his eyes could scarcely bear sunlight without them. I often glanced down into the street below when Charlie was playing. There was always a fair crowd of music-lovers gazing up in the direction of the fifth floor. It was a grand piano, by the way, and the Bing Boys put it there for Charlie as part of the 'furnished apartment'.

One day I saw Charlie putting a lot of wiring and electrical stuff on the wall of his office and I learned that he was quite a radio mechanic. He had suggested to the Sopher brothers that Reuters, Associated Press, United Press, International News and other news services were holding back on important news items, therefore he intended bringing in the news himself!

Every afternoon about four o'clock Charlie put on the headphones, and when I asked 'What for?' he said that the warships in port always received news bulletins by Morse code and he was 'tapping' everything not in secret code.

I thought he was nuts until one day I saw him typing furiously on his silent typewriter and I sneaked up behind him to watch. An amazing thing was happening. Sloan was decoding Morse out of the air, 'padding' and typing his story as he went along. ('Padding' means that he was typing in all the extra words customarily left out of telegrams.) When finished he pulled the sheet out of his machine, called for the copy-boy and, after slapping a headline on his story, sent it straight to the linotypes. I still wasn't sure. The story was about a Frenchwoman who had just been decorated at Buckingham Palace for heroic behaviour towards some British soldiers shot down in France in World War I. But when Reuters came through with the same story forty-eight hours later my respect for Charlie Sloan consolidated.

I happened to mention to Charlie one day that the widow Ezra lived in a fine mansion in Frenchtown, with ballroom, swimming-pool and a magnificent white-and-gold grand piano. Two weeks later the widow Ezra extended an invitation (through her brothers) to the entire *China Press* staff to a Sunday lunch in the ballroom, with an orchestra in attendance, and the affair ended in a tea-dance with Charlie Sloan and the widow on astonishingly familiar terms.

Charlie's next milestone was to write a song entitled the *China Press*, in waltz time, with lyrics — an undoubted dedication to the widow Ezra. And one Sunday night (a big movie night in Shanghai) Sloan talked the leading (Majestic Hotel) ballroom orchestra into introducing the song to Shanghai from the stage of the theatre at the interval!

From a position of such strength it was, therefore, a simple matter for Charlie to persuade the Sopher brothers to put a couple of their limousines at the disposal of *China Press* staff on twenty-four-hour service with day and night chauffeurs to boot. Thus,

STICKY START

when Generalissimo Chiang Kai-shek reached Shanghai and halted on the outskirts, and nobody seemed to know what his next move would be, Sloan's mercurial mind decided there was but one thing to do and that was go and ask the Generalissimo!

We had working with us on the *China Press* a handsome young Chinese, pale-skinned, delicate and obviously an aristocrat. His beautiful sister had delighted Shanghai theatregoers with her amateur stage performances, notably in the star role of *Lady Precious Stream*. The father of these two delightful young people was a noted elder statesman named Tong Shao-yi. One of the negotiators of the Manchu emperor's abdication in 1911, Mr. Tong had acted as intermediary between the Imperial household and Dr. Sun Yat-sen's revolutionaries and had supervised the signing of the instrument of abdication in the old Shanghai Town Hall.

'You're going to fix up an appointment with General Chiang for the *China Press*,' Sloan told Tong Yu-li, son of Tong Shao-yi who, somehow, did that very thing and had the time set within twenty-four hours. I told Charlie I would be tagging along, too, for my readers in Australia. I wanted to be there when Charlie put the sixty-four dollar question to the Generalissimo — 'Are you going to try to take Shanghai by force, or negotiate?' Many world capitals were waiting on the answer to that question. Sloan knew it, but he did not represent any overseas newspapers and the idea of letting a scoop go begging disturbed his mercenary mind. For scoop we knew this was going to be. 'Charlie,' I said to Sloan, 'a lot of people may not believe our story. Let's take along a photographer and get some pictures.'

Chiang Kai-shek told us he had no intention of starting hostilities to get possession of Shanghai, but we could see that he was a very worried man none the less. He willingly posed for several pictures after we'd all had tea and cakes together at the Chinese Bureau of Foreign Affairs just outside Frenchtown, where he had established temporary headquarters. (Incidentally, that young Chinese in the picture with us was not Tong Yu-li, but a young Cantonese interpreter.) Sloan's first act upon returning to his office with story and pictures was to contact all leading news agencies and offer his scoop to the highest bidder. He did very well out of it, too.

Next day reports came filtering in from the Chinese areas which were somewhat difficult to believe, but subsequently proved to be true. Chiang's appeal to his Elder Brother was bearing fruit. Tu Yueh-sen had ordered his private army of gunmen into Chapei and Nantao with orders to kill the revolt within twenty-four hours. They did just that, putting Chou En-lai's Red adherents to death or to flight in one of the grimmest, bloodiest, ask-and-give-no-quarter fights ever associated with a revolt. One by one the fires died down and one by one the police-stations were recovered and handed back to the gendarmes. And as word got around of what was happening, tension all round the perimeter began to ease, for Charlie Sloan's story had now been substantiated most convincingly.

That is why I said earlier that Generalissimo Chiang Kai-shek owed the notorious gangster Tu Yueh-sen a debt which could never be fully repaid, for it is quite certain that had the Nationalist army been caught up in a real fight with the international force then assembled at Shanghai, the young military commander from Canton would have sustained the first defeat of his campaign. And it is equally certain that the Reds could have mustered sufficient strength to finish him off!

It is significant that less than a year later Tu Yueh-sen honoured his dead parents by erecting an expensive shrine at their village birthplace in Chekiang Province, not too far from Shanghai. Celebrations lasting a week were held in the village and the

STICKY START

native Press, in particular, carried long and detailed reports of the daily events at the shrine. Diplomatic representatives from several important Western powers followed Eastern custom by sending appropriate gifts accompanied by illuminated scrolls eulogizing the gangster and his deceased forebears. According to reports, gifts sent by the head of the Nationalist Government were worth an aggregate of $600,000!

The Frenchtown slum product and fruit-pedlar had come a long way. He had, in fact, acquired the opium monopoly — among many other things — of the Shanghai valley, catering to about 200,000,000 customers!

2

SMUGGLERS' PARADISE

THEY CALLED Shanghai 'an adventurer's paradise', and that was true: but it was even more a smuggler's paradise.

Smuggling is second nature to a Chinese, like 'squeeze', the percentage which has to accompany every deal to make it worth while. Even your houseboy must get his 'squeeze' or he starts looking for another job. The anti-'squeeze' wife of a prominent Hong Kong official was hacked to death with a meat-chopper while taking her regular afternoon nap in the 1930's. The reason? She held her native cook to a strict accounting of all food purchases. He stood it as long as he could. One day 'mississee' went too far. She openly charged the cook with theft. Strangely, most people were in sympathy with the ancient cook when he was arrested and confessed in a welter of tears.

After the Chinese, Japanese were the next best smugglers. A few foreigners beat the Customs for paltry amounts. Chinese and Japanese defalcations totalled millions of dollars annually: about 30 per cent of China's trade! This was considered good return. Had the Chinese Customs service been administered by the Chinese themselves, there might have been a leakage of 70 per cent with 30 per cent collections!

If you find it difficult to believe that, I quote from the history book, as follows:

SMUGGLERS' PARADISE

'Owing to the difficulty of finding Chinese with the necessary qualifications as to *probity*, vigilance and knowledge of foreign languages required for the enforcement of a close observance of Treaty and Customs House regulations...'
(italics mine).
Therefore the consuls of the pioneer foreign trading nations were invited to undertake the collection of dues on cargo.

Out of this typically topsy-turvy Chinese arrangement grew a fine Customs organization which, besides collecting import and export duty on behalf of the Chinese Government, also assumed control of inland transit trade, coastwise traffic, pilotage, lighthouses, coastal surveying with responsibility for navigation aids, emigration, weights and measures, harbour control and the compilation of China's trade statistics.

To mention the Chinese Customs service without paying tribute to Sir Robert Hart, the Irish genius behind this fascinatingly cosmopolitan outfit, would be on a par with describing the history of aviation without mentioning the Wright brothers. 'No foreigner ever wielded such power in the Celestial Empire,' wrote several Western diplomats after a study of Hart's career. 'He was the acknowledged intermediary between the Western nations and China.' Queen Victoria created him Sir Robert Hart, Bart., G.C.M.G., 'for developing a strong, loyal, well-organized and cosmopolitan service'.

He had such an amazing life that he cannot be dealt with summarily, and here is a rather broad thumbnail sketch of his career.

Hart was born at Milltown, County Armagh, Ireland, in 1835. He attained his B.A. degree at the age of eighteen, his M.A. at thirty-six, and the honorary degree of LL.D. from the University of Michigan in 1882.

In 1864, at the age of twenty-nine, he received from the

Emperor of China the brevet title of An Ch'a Ssu (Provincial Judge), with civil rank, 3rd class; brevet title of Pu Cheng Ssu (Provincial Treasurer), with civil rank, 2nd class in 1869; Order of the Red Button 1st class in 1881; Order of the Double Dragon, Second Division, 1st class and the distinction of the Peacock's Feather in 1885; Ancestral Rank, 1st class of the First Order and made retrospective for three generations, with Letters Patent in 1889; brevet title of Junior Guardian of the Heir Apparent in 1901.

He was received in audience by the Empress and Empress Dowager in 1902 and in the following year, upon applying for leave, was created President of the Board, brevet rank, in appreciation of his services.

At one stage of his career Hart accepted an appointment with the British Government as Envoy Extraordinary and Minister Plenipotentiary to the Empress of China and the King of Korea but, at the urgent request of the emperor, rejoined the Customs service.

Not to be outdone by the many picturesque titles conferred upon this modest Irishman by China, the nations of the world honoured Hart with the following decorations:

Chevalier of the Order of Wasa (Sweden-Norway), 1870;
Knight Grand Cross, Order of Francis Joseph (Austria), 1885;
Order of Pope Pius IX (Rome), 1885;
Knight Grand Cross, Order of Christ (Portugal), 1888;
Knight Grand Cross, Order of Polar Star (Sweden), 1894;
Knight Grand Cross, Order of Orange Nassau (Holland),1897;
Order of the Crown, 1st Class (Prussia),1900;
Knight Grand Cross, Order of the Crown (Italy), 1907;
Knight Grand Cross, Order of St. Olav (Norway), 1908.

He was also created Knight Commander of the Order of St.

SMUGGLERS' PARADISE

Michael and St. George (Great Britain), 1892; Knight Grand Cross of the same Order in 1889 and a Baronet in 1893. To mark their appreciation of his services in connection with the successful issue of negotiations between France and China in 1885 the French Government created Hart a Grand Officer of the Legion of Honour.

In short, Hart 'was the permanent trustee of foreign interests in China'.

One might also say that, under his wise guidance and honesty, he was likewise the permanent trustee of Chinese interests, for the Customs service of China when Sir Robert Hart passed on was a very efficient organization and he thoroughly deserved the statue they made of him and erected on the Bund facing the Customs House.

As soon as he was made boss of the Customs Hart went straight to London and bought a fleet of gunboats 'for the suppression of smuggling, rebellion and piracy'. He then appointed 'inspectors' for each trading port, naming himself Inspector-General, with headquarters in Peking, capital of the nation until Chiang Kai-shek came along in 1927, when Nanking became the seat of government. Hart empowered his inspectors 'to appoint any assistants of whatever nationality to aid in the collection of dues, prevention of smuggling, etc.'. By 1907 Hart's force of collectors included twenty different nationalities in a total of 1,387 foreigners employed in the Imperial Maritime Customs, as it was called before the 1911 revolution. Of this total 738 were British, 170 Germans, the balance being distributed among Frenchmen, Italians, Scandinavians and Japanese, with but one or two Americans.

I travelled a distance equal to the length of the equator to get into this Customs service. But I made it in 1920, and at the age of seventeen-and-a-half was the youngest recruit ever allowed to

61

SHANGHAI SAGA

join. For that privilege I had to thank Commissioner of Customs L. A. Lyall, in charge of Shanghai at the time.

World War I was just over. I met an old man peeling potatoes on board a ship down at the wharves. I was always hanging around ships, which fascinate me. The old, weather-beaten potato-peeler took a shine to me, perhaps because he liked to talk and I was a good listener. He had sailed around the world not once but many times. He asked me what I intended to do with myself when I left school. I said I couldn't make up my mind. So the man said that if *he* were my age, he'd know what to do. I was still listening so he went on to paint a fascinating picture in which I saw myself wearing a smart tropical uniform, dashing around the harbour of a great port, boarding ships and giving orders right and left, saluting and receiving salutes, of natives kow-towing and of weird Oriental music playing at mealtimes, of pretty almond-eyed maids fanning me in hot weather and slipping Oriental sweets meats into my unresisting mouth.

If I ever meet up with that potato-pellet in the hereafter I shall thank him for urging me into the Far East.

'London,' he said to me. 'You'll have to go to London to join up.'

So it was London, pushing an Orient liner's laundry through hot, steaming presses all the way — a swim in the yellow waters of Colombo harbour; through the Suez Canal by
 moonlight; red hot lava pouring down the side of Stromboli island in the darkness; the
 majesty of Gibraltar and finally — London.

'I'm awfully sorry,' said the London representative of the Chinese Maritime Customs. 'A bit young, aren't you? No one under nineteen is taken on, you know.' (Observe the change of name. Since the 1911 revolution it was no longer the 'Imperial Chinese Customs'.)

SMUGGLERS' PARADISE

'I'll wait,' I told him.

But when he got the rest of my story he suggested that I might get a local appointment if I made application on the spot. He offered me a letter of introduction to the Shanghai Commissioner. All I had to do was to get to Shanghai!

That proved easy. A co-operative Board of Trade official gave me a list of names and I struck pay-dirt at the second call. A Far Eastern shipping company was despatching an ex-German reparations ship to the Far East within two weeks and I was offered a working passage, without pay. This vessel, the *Vogtland*, 8,000 tons, carried but five passengers and all were Shanghai-bound to supervise the construction of most of the present magnificent buildings on Shanghai's Bund which came out of wartime profits. The only stipulation attached to my appointment to the Customs was that I must serve twice the usual probationary period of six months. I was in.

The examining officer handed me several official pamphlets to teach me something of the service I had just joined. I learned, for instance, that China charged export, as well as import, duty. This was fixed by the Western powers under treaty at 5 per cent *ad valorem*; that is, of the value of the goods. The Customs, for the most part, accepted the valuation of goods declared but, where disputes arose, Customs expert appraisers had the final say. An additional 'Famine and Flood Relief' surtax of 2½ per cent sought to boost national revenue to take care of these recurring disasters. In addition, China had a unique system of collecting a provincial boundary duty on goods passing from port of entry into the interior, known as *likin*. Vessels in port stopped work at 5 p.m. but night-working permits could be applied for at a fee.

I learned that in spite of such low tariff China managed to collect Stg.£5,000,000 in 1907, which subsequently rose to Stg.£10,987,500 by 1922 and Stg.£19,095,000 by 1929. And it is worth mentioning that, whereas by 1914 the number of foreign firms doing business *in* — as distinct from *with* — China was 3,421, by 1925 the number had risen to 6,995, all having offices or branch offices actually in China.

I learned that there were two distinct branches of the Customs service — the indoor staff, representing the 'snooty', socially eligible members, and the outdoor staff. The indoor boys held down the desk jobs handling such matters as statistics, China's repayments of foreign loans, Boxer Indemnity remittances and the like. They wore civilian clothes. We outdoor members did all the dirty work, took all the risks, wore uniforms, occasionally got tossed in the harbour or 'bumped off' when we looked like hitting a gang of smugglers too hard in the pocket.

'*Tiffin!*' announced the examining officer, as the overhead Customs clock boomed out the noon hour.

'Lunch — back at two o'clock,' he explained, when I didn't seem to catch on. (China borrowed the word 'tiffin' from India.) Then he remembered. I needed quarters, uniforms, chits to this person and that before I could properly be considered 'in' the service.

Living quarters, provided free for unmarried members of the outdoor staff, were in Quinsan Gardens, situated in what had once been the American section of the International Settlement — hence the name 'Broadway' given to its main thoroughfare. Quinsan Gardens was an eminently satisfactory assemblage of red-brick, two- and three-storied terraces surrounding a delightful public park mainly used as a gathering-place for native amahs airing the children of their foreign employers.

Altogether about a hundred bachelor Customs men were given free quarters in and around this square, but they came together in a common mess in the main building. Adjoining this were clubrooms for the staff — large bar, card-rooms, billiard-rooms and one of the best dance-halls among clubs of that period. There was a weekly tea-dance every Wednesday.

Though barely furnished, each bed-sitting room allocated to outdoor staffers possessed a private bath with toilet, and quarters were serviced on every floor by native boy, coolie and 'learn-pidgin' boy, a youngster between twelve and fifteen picking up pointers from Number One boy as to the manner of caring for 'foreign devils'. The Number One boy was, in short, the ideal manservant, able to produce anything from a meal at midnight to a bed partner.

The central mess-hall was in charge of a petty opium-smuggler who provided an excellent table at the flat monthly rate of Ch.$25 (U.S.$12) at that time. No limits were set. Besides three hot meals, early morning tea, afternoon tea and supper were thrown in. The menus would have done justice to the best city hotel and, as already stated, no growls came up from the kitchen if one demanded a hot meal even in the small hours of the morning.

The fat, Buddha-like steward received recompense for all this generosity from the many 'assists' given to him when necessary by certain of his boarders among the outdoor staff. An unwritten law fixed payment to the servants. Seven local dollars monthly from each of us covered the lot—boy, coolie, 'learn-pidgin'—for the finest room service outside the Waldorf-Astoria.

In due course along came my eagerly awaited uniform with brass buttons. 'It is generally reckoned in the service that each brass button has the value of a machine gun in the eyes of Chinese,' my Customs House mentor advised me. 'Your authority on the waterfront is supreme, and don't ever forget it.'

I had occasion to remember that remark many times.

By common practice, Customs officers attached to ships operating the cargo hatches dined on board, in the First Saloon.

SHANGHAI SAGA

Now and then a ship's steward new on the China Coast attempted to relegate me to a lower meal rating and it became necessary, under Standing Orders, to insist on first-class privileges. Occasionally, this insistence had to be demonstrated by going out on deck and giving orders to the Chinese stevedoring foreman to cease work until such time as the offending ship's steward saw the light. The practice never failed.

The duties of an outdoor Customs officer were both trying and dangerous, but never dull. We were continually up against some of the world's trickiest smugglers, though, in fairness, it must be said that the vast majority were good losers. Japanese and European smugglers were the ones to watch for reprisals.

The Japs generally employed a few *ronin* (hoodlums) for protection and these relished any opportunity to practise the more dangerous feats of judo, while on French ocean-going liners it was always good to bear in mind that the unsavoury waterfront of Marseilles supplied most of the crew members engaged in pushing the contraband.

Like the city itself Shanghai waterfront was never quiet. The tempo merely slowed down a little from midnight until dawn, and we of the outdoor staff knew that somewhere someone was smuggling something all the time. The trick was to find out who, where and what.

We had the greatest incentive payment system in any Customs in this world. Pay was little more than 'peanuts'. Perhaps it was kept at its low level to drive us harder on the job. If we caught a merchant shipping ten cases of silk instead of the six declared on his Customs papers we took the lot, and if the seizure 'stuck' we received 10 per cent of what the contraband fetched at the next public auction.

Shippers worked in cahoots with *compradores*, a Portuguese word describing the Chinese chief clerk carried by coastwise

SMUGGLERS' PARADISE

and river ships whose nearest counterpart on foreign ships is the purser. The original *compradore* was the middleman between the foreign trader and Chinese merchant, but as time passed the term acquired wider application. No worthwhile business of any description could get along without its *compradore* as Sino-foreign trade developed. As a class they were mostly wealthy, those attached to the big hongs and banks being invariably millionaires, raking it in from both sides, as middlemen usually do. More than one *compradore* was known to have rescued a sinking firm with his own money.

When pirates captured a ship the first person they looked for was the *compradore*. Not only did he carry the keys to the ship's safe, containing the passage money of all the deck passengers as well as passengers' cash and valuables for safe-keeping; he also kept the ship's cargo manifest and knew just where to lay hands on the most valuable packages. Ship's *compradores*, therefore, took extraordinary steps at the first sign of a pirate attack to disguise themselves and many provided themselves with secret hide-outs, leaving it to trusted assistants to keep them in food and drink until the pirates left the ship.

Unlike most major world ports Shanghai possessed no 'lock-up' wharves, and everything was wide open. Ships entered the harbour, tied up at wharf or at buoy in midstream and it was up to the Customs to find a way of keeping ship and cargo under observation.

A selective system was employed. Ships from certain countries, or ports of call, were always suspected of bringing narcotics — and in this connection every ship from the Russian port of Vladivostok was kept under constant surveillance. If, as often happened, we received advance information of contraband on board, we sent a launch downriver to board the ship coming upstream. There were special launches with a suitable turn

SHANGHAI SAGA

of speed for this type of work. We never asked a ship to slow down. We ran alongside, took hold with long bamboo poles, and our men simply went up the same bamboo poles which held ship and launch together. Haiphong, in Indo-China, provided another 'must' for the searching parties for, like Vladivostok, the French port was a well-known transhipment centre for high-grade narcotics from Europe; and like the French Concession of Shanghai, all activities in Haiphong connected with dope were by permission of someone with the necessary authority.

The total absence in China's ports of sealed docks, where overseas ships could discharge their cargoes for Customs inspection, created a very unusual Customs set-up. Each wharf had its resident Customs examiner! He lived in a solid, two-storey red-brick house adjoining the godowns (warehouses) where all cargo passing through his wharf had to come for inspection. Ships tying up at buoys in midstream directed their cargo through one of these wharves, according to the company or agency handling the ship.

The same system prevailed at all coastal or river ports in all parts of China, and even on the faraway Burmese border athwart Marco Polo's route there lived a trusted Customs examiner with a native staff assigned to the difficult task of spotting smugglers when not engaged in collecting revenue. It is said that most of the early Eurasians in China originated from the lonely outposts of the Customs outdoor staffers and other types of bachelor employees who settled down in real exile with some local woman.

It was the task of juniors in the service at the big ports to supplement the work of the examiners by keeping an eye upon the ships themselves. The day shift was spread over the harbour on ships at the discretion of the officer in charge of the watch. The harbour was divided into Upper and Lower Ashore; Upper and

SMUGGLERS' PARADISE

Lower Afloat. This took care of the 'inner harbour', containing the great majority of wharves and tie-up buoys.

The 'suburbs' of the harbour were under separate command. These were designated 'Upper Station' and 'Lower Station' and each had a floating hulk for headquarters, whereon its foreign and Chinese staff lived together, though in separate compartments. Each hulk had its 'fleet', consisting of motor-launch and several sampans. Moored about fifty yards offshore, the hulks were equipped with telephones and electricity.

There were two other residential hulks attached to the Shanghai Customs administration. One was a mere native houseboat permanently tied up in a major creek some ten miles from the Customs House. Its role was to tally and check the passes of the thousands of barges and sampans which annually brought down millions of sacks of cocoons for the silk mills at Shanghai. They were one of the most important cogs in the machinery producing the bulk of China's vast silk output.

The second was a floating hulk down at Woosung, where the Whangpoo River joins the great Yangtze Kiang. At one time this hulk handled all ships over 10,000 tons which could not get up the over-silted Whangpoo River. But as dredging cleared the way and ships up to 25,000 tons ultimately reached Shanghai, the role of the Woosung hulk became one of merely reporting names of incoming and outgoing ships to the Shanghai Customs Jetty on the Bund.

In those days, when most ocean-going liners dropped anchor fourteen miles downriver from Shanghai at Woosung to discharge both cargo and passengers, the latter with their baggage were always transported to the Shanghai Customs Jetty by special tender. Likewise, all outgoing overseas passengers left Shanghai from the same Customs Jetty and thus, as the official point of arrival and departure for most of Shanghai's passengers, it can well be imagined that it had developed into quite a busy spot in the daily social life of the port-city, where a minimum of ten ocean-going passenger liners berthed daily. Do not, however, be misled by the term 'jetty'. It was vernacular for a group of huge floating platforms, suitably protected against bad weather, capable of accommodating several thousand people and of berthing several large tenders simultaneously.

The night-shift for Customs 'ships watchers' began at five o'clock, and I shall, for the moment, concentrate upon the duties of the inner harbour staff. We signed-on at the Customs Jetty, then reported to the officer in charge of the watch who called out names and assignments. I will take you with me on 'Wharf Patrol—Upper Section' for a glimpse into the unusual work of a beginner in the service of the Chinese Maritime Customs—in the year 1920.

'Upper Section—Wharves' is a stretch about a mile and a half long, the dirtiest, smelliest and most dangerous of any on the entire waterfront. It embraces the Bund of the French Concession and the shorter but even more sinister Chinese Bund of the old walled city on the south side known as Nantao. I am unarmed, carrying only a torch. I visit each ship in turn, and note in my book whether it is 'Quiet' or 'Working Cargo'. If the latter, I call for the 'night-working permit' and observe whether this allows for work until midnight or right through the night. If a ship is working without a permit I am empowered to stop work and there are no 'ifs' or 'buts'. The Chinese coolies know my word is law. Any ship working after 5 p.m. without a permit may be heavily fined.

On this, my first round, I do not stop to check any of the cargo. I am, however, supposed to take a quick look over the river-side of the ship to see if any suspicious-looking sampans or unregistered lighters are nearby with cargo aboard. These

SMUGGLERS' PARADISE

are always worth a second look, because in them may lie some worthwhile prize-money. In my notebook I write my time or boarding and leaving each ship, adding comments as to what condition I find it in, e.g. 'Loading general cargo for Hong Kong and way ports'. At the end of my beat, or patrol, which may last an hour and a half; I turn around and retrace my footsteps, revisiting every ship on the return journey, again entering in my notebook time of boarding and leaving ship, as well as what each ship is doing. If a ship is not working, my entry simply reads: 'Quiet.'

Between 5 p.m. and midnight I must go up and down my beat twice, visiting each ship four times. If my wharves are well filled I naturally have little time for detailed checking of any cargo. I have authority, however, to halt any package entering or leaving a ship on my beat and to demand that it be opened for examination. In course of time I get cunning. I watch for stacks of cargo just off the wharves, in the shadows behind godowns, or otherwise suspiciously placed for quick loading as soon as my back is turned.

It is well to explain that, whether ships be native or foreign-owned on the China Coast, all cargo carried must be okayed by the chief *compradore*. Therefore any smuggler wishing to add several cases of goods to the number declared and passed by the Customs examiner must, perforce, first seek approval from the *compradore*. The foreign captain, officers or engineers couldn't care less! The *compradore* alone knows the ship's capacity for this 'extra cargo', and after he has received all shipping papers for honestly declared goods he is able to calculate the amount of available space for the undeclared stuff; and it is in the hope of getting some of this surplus space that shippers hold goods ready in the shadows, just around the corner, with strong coolies waiting for the signal to grab and make a run for it. This is done, of course, as soon as I have gone my way. If I have been lucky enough to get a good look at those goods waiting in the shadows, and on my next visit find that they have vanished, I know that this is my cue to go aboard and make a quick search of all likely hiding-places. If I can locate the stuff and prove — by the absence of the well-known Customs examination chop (stamp) — that it is contraband, I then summon the ship's foreign officer on watch, and hold him responsible for the non-removal of the cargo while I telephone my officer-in-charge at the Customs Jetty.

If nothing unusual happens during my spell of duty, my relief appears shortly before 1 a.m., whereupon I return speedily by rickshaw to the Customs Jetty, transfer my report from notebook to official ledger, sign off and go home. There are, however, traps for the unwary. Smallish native river steamers, identical in appearance, often slip in or out, exchanging berths and offering no evidence of having done so which anything except a close inspection of the name on bow or stern will verify. Hardly a man in the service escaped that pitfall.

That, in short, is the official picture. It takes no account of the wholesale bedlam assailing eyes and ears along the entire waterfront. Hollywood conceptions of New Orleans catering to a fleet of Mississippi steamboats about to cast off, offer but fractional evidence of the last hour on the Shanghai waterfront. The greasy, cobbled Frenchtown-cum-Nantao Bund is alive with cargo, coolies, taxis, pony-carriages, hawkers, portable kitchens, touts, pimps, white-slavers, thieves, pickpockets, passengers and family friends. The melodious chant of cargo-carrying coolies rises above every other noise. Into the bowels of the ships, through side doors, they jog-trot, collecting their tiny bamboo tokens when passing the tally-clerk. Every once in a while one stacks his stout bamboo pole, wipes the sweat from his noble brow, heads for the nearest steaming, portable kitchen, digging

SMUGGLERS' PARADISE

into his dirty cloth money-belt as he goes towards the ever welcome bowl of noodles, the fried pork with native cabbage, the small bowl of green tea and the whole or half cigarette which every such kitchen is able to provide.

On board, though sailing time may not be until dawn, there are deck passengers already abed by 9 p.m., spread across the decks and surrounded by their baggage. One steps gingerly between their sprawled, quilted forms on going the rounds of the ship. For some it may be just an overnight jaunt to nearby Ningpo, where Admiral-General Townsend Ward met a premature death chasing Taiping rebels in 1863; for others one of the longer, more permanent trips to Hong Kong, Hankow or Tientsin. There is always an element of risk travelling by a Chinese coastal ship. Ninety per cent of all piracies occur on them, especially those under a foreign flag, and it is by such vessels that banks transfer bullion — silver dollars — worth millions, annually. Piracy is not dead. It is still the scourge of the China Coast and every passenger looks askance at his neighbour, wondering if he is one of a gang which will take over at gunpoint as soon as the ship reaches the open sea. Nearly every piracy is an 'inside' job, but we will deal more fully with that later.

To the patrolling Customs officer it is the vessel about to leave which is worth attention. Time is usually well spent watching — from behind some dark corner — for the last-minute rush of undeclared cargo from out the many hiding-places. The experienced eye selects what the nature of the packing suggests will be the most valuable, should there be more than one smuggler at work. One waits until the last package goes aboard, then follows it like a good 'tail', hoping to be led direct to the whole cache.

My first few attempts at this were failures. One of the lookouts spotted me before I even reached the side of the ship.

SHANGHAI SAGA

At a shouted warning the coolies dropped their bundle on the pontoon and calmly lit cigarettes, leaving it to me to go aboard and try — if I could — to locate the earlier packages. I seldom did. The *compradores* usually co-operated to the limit with any shipper overcarrying any cargo, and short of delaying departure to give the whole ship a thorough going-over — a very risky procedure — my chances of discovery were negligible. But through experience I learned how to leave the ship ostentatiously behind, then double back on the riverside by sampan, climb aboard and watch from the inside. At other times I took steps to hide my brass buttons and my service cap, and do a Sherlock Holmes act which invariably paid a handsome dividend.

As I have said, most Chinese were good losers. Faced with inevitable seizure, most of them sent a middleman along with a proposition and it was then up to the individual Customs officer to decide whether to go along with the unhappy shipper, or seize the stuff and await the customary 10 per cent at auction. With Japanese or Frenchmen things were never so easy. I once intercepted a dimunitive Japanese coming ashore from a European liner with a brace of Mauser pistols for sale to the underworld tucked inside his tunic. As I stepped out of the shadows, around 8.30 p.m., he dropped the guns and took to his heels. The wharf was busy and there were plenty of people about, including armed Indian wharf policemen, but he got clean away in the crowd.

At the same wharf six months later, around 2 a.m. when all was quiet, I stopped two Japanese stewards carrying a couple of bundles between them. They became truculent and backed away when I tried to seize the bundles. Then, as I grabbed one of the Japs by his coat, the other stepped behind me and I woke up in bed several hours later with a very sore neck. All that my senior officer said was, 'You've got to learn discretion in this service,

SMUGGLERS' PARADISE

young man.'

It seemed that I was determined to learn the hard way, in spite of such warnings. One night, near knock-off time at midnight, for example, I observed two large sampans heading into the anchorage between pontoons on the French Bund, loaded to the waterline with reed bags of native salt, perhaps two tons in all. Now native salt was a Chinese Government monopoly, and its transport from one province to another required tax payment; so I made known to the boatmen my intention of seizing the salt when they failed to produce any permit for its shipment by the outgoing river boat, which they admitted to be their intention. The men simply shrugged their shoulders when I pointed downriver to the Customs Jetty, sat myself on the bow of the foremost sampan with the second tied in tow and took off on the ebb tide with my booty — as I thought. With the salt duly lodged under lock and key, I completed my report and went home to bed.

Called by telephone several hours later, I rushed down to the Customs Jetty to find a near-riot outside the bonded go-down where my seized salt had been stored, and knew by the look on my senior officer's face that I had guffed it again. It appeared that the salt was legitimate cargo and had, through my blunder, missed the boat. Its owner had come up with his permit only an hour before the ship sailed, to find out I'd seized his salt! But what worried my senior officer even more was my stupidity in riding with the salt back to the Customs Jetty, perched like Columbus near the bowsprit with the boatmen all behind me. 'If these men really had been salt-smugglers,' he told me, 'they only needed to tap you on the bean with a paddle, push you overside and who'd have been the wiser?'

Right from the start I was wary of the French smugglers. No product of the Marseilles waterfront is going to see his investment grabbed by any interfering Customs official, not while he can stalk him around the deck and on to the wharf if necessary with a wicked-looking knife in his belt. And they proved once or twice that they were not afraid to use these knives. While I was in the service—a mere two and a half years—the score stood at one Customs officer dead and two half-drowned after being thrown overboard from a French liner into the Whangpoo River. Even the captains of such ships, we learned, did not monkey around with their crews.

There were, of course, always those Chinese able and willing to betray their countrymen, and found it profitable to prowl around the environs of the wharves tabulating the stacks of 'excess cargo' waiting in readiness for the final dash past the Customs. From length of practice these professional informers were able to assess with astonishing accuracy the potential return from such cargo. But their end of any bargain depended solely upon the generosity of the giver—the Customs officer to whom they gave the tip-off. In course of time this very numerous brigade came to know the comparative handful of patrolling officers fairly well and had them pretty accurately sized up. Of necessity, however, they sometimes had practically to give away a valuable tip, because a 'meanie' was the only officer on duty when the vital moment arrived.

There was always a gamble about payment on the spot for tip-offs on contraband; but a newcomer to the service had to build up confidence. The veterans, I discovered, had their regular informers who worked in relays on suspected ships. A well-known opium ship from Vladivostok, for instance, might be in port thirty-six hours before any word reached shore concerning the stuff on board. Then the Customs quarters in Quinsan Gardens might have a 2 or 3 a.m. visitor and someone was pulled from bed with the admonition to 'Come velly

SMUGGLERS' PARADISE

quick' — in the unlikely event that he could not speak Chinese. The native night watchman who admitted such a visitor knew from experience to admit him in a hurry, and the visitor in turn knew from experience to oil the key which opened the door to him. This is known as 'old custom' and is a brand of 'squeeze'. It is often practised by servants upon tradesmen who fail to obey the courtesies of the tradesmen's entrance. It can almost certainly lead to friction between tradesman and the master, which is not something the former profits by, therefore 'olo custom' is usually observed — pronto.

The thirty-six hours' delay, more or less, represents time spent by the professional informer hovering in the vicinity of the suspected ship and often actually aboard, shrewdly piecing together by eavesdropping, observation and skilful deduction the telltale evidence which will eventually pinpoint zero hour for the smugglers. When conclusions have been drawn a confederate is despatched swiftly to the known whereabouts of their favourite official. With him they always keep in touch. They know his roster of duty, the day it is changed and where to reach him at any given moment. Without several such characters on your unofficial payroll your Customs 'seizure money' could not amount to much. But given a few good contacts one could run up several thousand dollars in a month with very little effort — all legitimately.

My first such contact was a Chinese dentist who worked the wharves. He specialized in fixing the teeth of ship crews who had very little time en voyage for such things. Chen Paw-yen nailed me the day I arrived in Shanghai on the *Vogtland* when he saw a couple of decayed front teeth. He handed me his business card and promised me fast and cheap repairs. He looked clean enough, but I preferred to delay an appointment until I knew my fate with the Customs, to whom I had yet to apply. At mention of the Customs Chen laid his skill at my feet and pressured me into an immediate appointment.

Like the native tailors in many parts of the world who can measure you and deliver a dozen suits in twenty-four hours if necessary, Chen and his team of mechanics operated what was probably the fastest dental dock in the Far East. Most ship crews in port got shore leave, and Chen's consulting-rooms behind the 'Lower Section—Wharves' had a constant stream in and out from 5 p.m. onwards. Chen drummed up business aboard by day and did the fixin' by night. Deliveries, when necessary, were next morning.

I eventually agreed to enter this assembly line on the clear understanding that if I failed to make the Customs service I owed Chen nothing. I was always grateful to Chen for the sheer confidence this arrangement engendered in me from that moment. We remained firm friends for many years, and the beautiful bridge with which he replaced my decayed front teeth required no attention until thirty-six years later!

But, busy though he was as a dentist, Chen managed in the course of his wanderings about ships to ferret out a bit of information now and then in the manner of the professionals. Nor did he think it unethical to relay such information to quarters best equipped to make use of it. His speciality was opium brought in by British India and P. & O. ships from Bombay, Calcutta and Indian ports other than Ceylon, whence opium seldom emanated. Over many years of attending to Indian teeth Chen acquired a useful smattering of their languages which, however, he was very careful to conceal, and his reticence in this respect handsomely supplemented his income from dentistry.

It must be conceded that every dollar picked up by those prone to pimping on the smugglers was well earned inasmuch as they ran great risks. And though the ordinary run-of-the-mill

SMUGGLERS' PARADISE

Customs defaulter regarded his efforts as a battle of wits and any loss a gambling loss, the narcotics-smuggler was a coyote of another colour. He struck back, savagely, whenever he located the louse who turned him in. Several years out of the Customs, as a newspaper reporter, I once helped police to put together the pieces of a man collected from the gutters of the wharf district. Someone had dismembered him, wrapped the severed legs and arms in newspaper and tossed them into different alleyways, leaving the head in a rubbish-bin and the torso in four parts in unmentionable places. As we laid out the bits and pieces on the slab in the morgue like a jigsaw, and the head was finally brought in by an attendant after washing the features clean of refuse, I was a bit taken aback to recognize one of my regular informers of other years. He had finally blundered. He would inform no more.

Conditions had changed in the interval, of course, and this may have been his undoing. Narcotics-smugglers, playing for higher and higher stakes all the time and frequently with huge sums invested, took out insurance by hiring professional muscle-men able and willing, if necessary, to spill blood in defence of their loot. In China, however, dismemberment in the manner described was usually reserved for informers, whether professional or inspired by civic responsibility. Also, it had to be remembered that after Tu Yueh-sen's elevation to underworld boss of China, narcotic-smuggling was so well organized and protected that no informer dared to operate in what became a closed shop, with official status.

After a course of wharf patrol, the *griffin* (new chum) Customs officer was next given a three-month spell of 'steamer duty', being assigned to any ship selected by the duty officer, where he stayed put for the full eight hours of his watch. As there were always more ships in harbour than Customs officers to watch them, duty officers had to use their discretion plus any information which might be in their hands. Ships loading for export overseas headed the list and it was my job when placed on board such a ship to acquaint myself as speedily as possible with the ship's cargo manifest. I was supposed to know at any given moment what cargo was entering which hold, and to check the shipping marks on such cargo against those on the manifest and now and then to count a batch of cargo. There was never the same sort of collusion between shippers and *compradores* on overseas vessels as on the coasters, simply because there were no *compradores* on foreign overseas ships. Occasionally a Chinese exporter would try slipping through substituted goods of superior quality in the same cases bearing the Customs chop and then it became a simple matter between the shipper and the Customs officer on the loading ship.

It can readily be seen that the Customs examiners, distributed around the Shanghai wharves, bore great responsibility. Through their hands passed all inward and outward cargo for the ships tied to their wharves and others moored midstream to the buoys as well. They operated on the hit-or-miss system. Time did not allow every case of cargo to be opened, so they picked a few at random! It was this very Customs practice which stirred the gambling instincts in every Chinese merchant. It was similar to fan-tan, or the West's thimble-and-pea of the sideshows, that most of them were willing to take a chance on the examiner missing the packages containing the higher-duty, or excess, goods. If they were detected—*Maskee*! (As common a word as a French shrug, and having virtually the same meaning. The Russian says—'*Nichevo*'.)

On steamer duty one had always to remember when certain overseas ships were loading and, on the eve of departure, that this might have been the time selected from the beginning to put

SMUGGLERS' PARADISE

the contraband ashore, when the hot breath of the searchers no longer blew down their necks.

A ship working through the night was always a spell of interesting duty. There was life, activity, hot coffee, a chance of conversation with interesting people. On ships sailing at dawn there were gay parties, music. But a 'quiet' ship was filled with boredom and in the freezing temperature of January, out in the middle of the harbour, a period of true penance. Placing an officer on a 'quiet' ship—that is, one which had already completed loading but did not sail until several hours later—was done solely to ensure that no further loading was done. Under such conditions there was always the temptation to seek the warmth of the steam-heated saloon or smoke-room. Indeed, there were cases of men on such duty succumbing to the temptation of 'forty winks' in a snug (empty) cabin, and of waking up fifty miles out to sea. How could anyone explain that away?

Of other branches of duty, such as a spell of attachment to one of the floating hulks aforementioned, there is little worth saying here, save, perhaps, to reveal that such spells were considered vacations by men in the service, though modern radio and television would have enriched the experience considerably had they been in vogue at the time. Perhaps I should have mentioned that in my own case the Shanghai Customs commissioner of the period, L. A. Lyall, a kindly, partly crippled man, appeared to be right behind me, shoving me along with all the influence usually associated with nepotism. Consequently, as soon as my year's probation ended, having included wharf patrol (afoot), harbour patrol (launch), ship-watching and a spell of lower-harbour hulk, I found myself in charge of one of the baggage-inspection parties, of which there were two. For the next six months the ways of the world grew upon me and my waning teenage lapped them up.

It astonished me to discover the lengths people would go to

get their trunks through Customs unopened. It did not mean they wished to smuggle something in. On the contrary, most of their China smuggling was done on the *outward* journey when, theoretically, there was also an *ad valorem* tax of 5 per cent on many goods. The Customs, in those days, never bothered with outgoing luggage, and the favour such people sought was, it seemed, merely to prevent strange hands rummaging through their private effects, or to ensure prompt baggage release — but in most cases I concluded that the real reason was to impress others with their importance.

So many travellers thrust business cards into my hand expecting this to forestall examination of their effects that I developed a collector's mania. To this day I have hundreds of such cards, from men of every colour and nationality, including the unfortunate Lennox Simpson, who threatened in his newspaper, *Peking & Tientsin Times*, to expose the hideouts of the big Shanghai opium combine and was murdered in consequence.

The year 1921 was one of bitterest gall for the young Republic of China. The Chinese delegates to the Washington Disarmament Conference had gone to the United States as representatives of the victorious allies of World War I. They had confidently expected removal of some of their long-time grievances, such as having Japan removed from China's back, the granting of tariff autonomy and other concessions from grateful allies. But Japan was a Western Ally too and, in those days, one more worthy of appeasement; and although the Western powers realized that tariff autonomy would have to be granted sometime, the postwar necessity to rebuild trade seemed good enough reason to postpone that unwelcome day.

Thus, from my front seat at the baggage-inspection counters, I witnessed the return in high dudgeon from Washington of many of the delegates who walked out of the conference and sailed for home—men who later became cabinet ministers in a more respected Chinese Government, all of them important names in one sphere or another.

All their trunks and suitcases bore labels proudly printed for the momentous conference, topped by the five-bar-colour flag of the shortlived Peking republican government which crumbled before Chiang Kai-shek, six years later. And it was into Chiang's lap that the Western powers dropped the plum of tariff autonomy.

All the world's great musicians, singers and other entertainers dropped in on Shanghai at one time or another in this era and I can still see Efrem Zimbalist, Mischa Elman and Fritz Kreisler coming ashore one by one clutching the violin-cases containing their precious Stradivari. The Tibetan Panchen Lama of the time paused in saffron robes just long enough to allow his astrologer to give my palm a brief reading. Chaliapin, great Russian basso of his day, delighted everyone who saw him in his multi-coloured little skull-cap, which so resembled the local style of Oriental male headgear.

Peter B. Kyne, author of the immortal *Cappy Ricks*, discovered quite early that a smile in China—in those days—brought a better one. Jascha Heifetz, another of the Strad violinists, is best remembered by his comment after a short stay: 'China needs jazz.' By 1936 he might have been compelled to admit that China had a surfeit of jazz. In Shanghai alone (8,000 acres in area) there were over 300 cabarets, whereas in Jascha's time there was not a single Chinese-style honky-tonk anywhere on the horizon.

Hotel ballrooms in the period under review were Shanghai's principal whoopee centres. The day of the night-club and cabaret was not yet. All of Shanghai met for good times either in hotel ballrooms or private clubs, of which there were scores in the great and growing city. Perhaps the most famous of these was the celebrated 'longest bar in the world' Shanghai Club, which lost the title to at least three other overseas clubs before the Reds breasted it. One's social standing received a distinct upward thrust by becoming a member of this exclusive club of the *taipans*.

Observe that word! Oriental equivalent of the West's 'tycoon'. Its explicit meaning was 'head of the firm' and one could be a tycoon without being a *taipan*. But in Shanghai to be a *taipan* was also automatically to be a tycoon. By an unwritten rule one end of the Shanghai Club's famous bar was reserved for *taipans* as members daily assembled around noon for the ritual of gin-and-bitters, or what-have-you. Lesser fry left a gap between themselves and the great city's most prominent citizens, though not, as might be believed, through any social distinction. This daily gathering of the industrialists and diplomats was an integral part of commercial life, an opportunity for interchange of commercial, political or banking information; for the pooling of cabled and other reports (including those from Chinese sources) likely to prove useful at the 2 p.m. resumption of business.

Perhaps in no other city in the world was so much gambling done in foreign exchange, where eighths and even sixteenths could turn profit into loss, or vice versa, for those dealing in millions, as many of these men were. I sometimes felt almost as one of them in consequence of the special attention I always received from Shanghai's hotels during my tenure of office as a Customs baggage inspector. This was inspired, of course, by the baggage clerks attached to the hotels, whose job was to meet ships and relieve incoming hotel guests of the worries of baggage.

Of all the baggage runners Tetsu Minami, manager of a Japanese professional baggage agency, gave me the most laughs. Thin and toothy, invariably wearing dark glasses with his well-tailored suit and grey Homburg, Minami and I hit it off well from

SMUGGLERS' PARADISE

the start. His small but active staff gathered in a fair share of the incoming Japanese passengers, many of whom had made no hotel bookings and were sitting ducks for Minami's boys to steer to their favourite Japanese hotels. Runners from the foreign hotels always had specific persons to meet and care for. Minami's boys—only sometimes. By extending to Minami the privilege of entering the baggage compound to tout for business, we baggage inspectors were helping ourselves as much as the diminutive Jap, for he had developed a brilliant technique in the handling of Japs unused to our Customs methods. In short, he and his men helped us to clear our compounds in less time than otherwise.

Minami taught me useful Japanese words for dealing with Jap passengers and as our friendship grew my vocabulary grew also. Not all the *geisha* houses were in Japan. Minami showed me where there were three Shanghai branches of Tokyo's most famous ones and I learned that, owing to the large number of wealthy tired Japanese business men in Shanghai, these houses despatched regular batches of their leading *geisha* to our city to keep the T.J.B. happy in their so-called exile.

Even after I ceased to be of use to him Minami continued to entertain me, and I spent many evenings in his home, dining (on the floor, of course) and listening to his buck-toothed wife playing her *samisen* (stringed instrument) and trying to sing. It was often a nerve-racking experience, but for the sake of good international relations it had to be done. Then, around Christmas time, I became entangled with some of Minami's neighbours in a Christmas pastime the name of which I forget.

All guests squatted on the tatami-covered floor, shoes off. The host turned off all lights and scattered a jarful of dried beans around the floor—hundreds of 'em—and at the word 'Go!' everyone scrambled around on hands and knees in the dark, feeling for the beans and collecting them, always remembering the proprieties.

The collector of the most beans won a prize, and the game had hilarious possibilities!

A curious sidelight on Shanghai's dry-cleaning business came to my notice about this time. Observing many baskets and trunks filled with beautiful Japanese silk kimonos arriving on every ship from Japan, my urge to levy duty on them was prevented when Minami explained. Had these gorgeous garments been immersed in any local liquid containing Shanghai water – highly chemicalized – fast deterioration would have resulted. Therefore the kimonos had to be returned to Japan whenever dry-cleaning became necessary, and the hundreds I saw returning on every ship, seemingly new, were merely on their way back to their owners in Shanghai.

In the outdoor branch of the Chinese Maritime Customs one had to make a choice of career sooner or later. We all began as 'Tidewaiters', a curious term, but one that almost explains itself, for in the early days before steam Customs men waited on the flood tide to bring up the ships to the harbour anchorage. From Tidewaiter – Probationary one advanced in the service to Tidewaiter (4th Class), Tidewaiter (3rd Class), Tidewaiter (2nd Class), Tidewaiter (1st Class), Assistant Boat Officer, Boat Officer, Assistant Tide Surveyor, Tide Surveyor, Chief Tide Surveyor. This was commonly referred to as the 'Boating Service'.

Or one could choose the Examination Service, progressing through various grades of Examiner and ultimately becoming an Appraiser, an expert who could tell from which province any type of hog-bristles originated, assess the market value of a sample of soya-bean sauce or put a price upon a piece of pink jade. There was no substitute for experience in the Appraising Service! And the best proof of this was the fact that when the

SMUGGLERS' PARADISE

Nationalist Government of Chiang Kai-shek came to power in 1927, it began sacking all foreign employees immediately on a progressive scale, only these Appraisers remaining to be bled white of their expert knowledge to serve the ends of what proved to be a rapacious regime.

The 'granting' of tariff autonomy to China by the Western powers proved a turning-point in history. At long last the finances of China had a chance to get out of the red. Hitherto saddled with indemnities and foreign loans, the awakening giant which Bismarck feared so much now had the means of becoming a free and independent nation. Finance Minister T. V. Soong, brother-in-law of Chiang Kai-shek, lost no time introducing new tariffs which sent the dream-life of foreigners in China up into the celestial sky and away for ever. No more cheap champagne or Paris perfume for the dancing-girls. No more imported Scotch under the old benevolent 5 per cent import duty. The Kuomintang clique at Nanking had vengeance in their hearts when framing their new schedule of tariffs, and all foreigners living in China had to tighten their bulging belts. Many firms even insisted on employees observing regular office hours! It became as bad as that!

But to Japan the idea of China having money in the bank kept the war office awake at night. A China in constant poverty suited Japan's plans well: a strong, armed China—not at all. One of the first things General Chiang Kai-shek did when Customs revenue began pouring in was to cast around for supplies of modern arms, and in this he was ably assisted and advised by an old friend of revolutionary leader Dr. Sun Yat-sen. The China Coast still rings with the hoarse belly-laughs of Morris 'Two-gun' Cohen—thick jowled, rotund, black-haired life pensioner of the Kuomintang reputed to have saved the life of the old Chinese revolutionary when Peking Imperialist agents were hunting him down in London. Cohen was likely to pop up in hotel lounges anywhere in the world, on buying missions for the Kuomintang. A colourful figure, always jolly, with an infectious laugh.

The Japanese eyed Cohen's missions apprehensively. Though they were prepared to admit that Chiang Kai-shek needed more and more equipment to beat down the Reds who were spreading over the land like a bush fire, they also knew that their own days of sly conquest of China were numbered; that is, unless they did something quickly to consolidate their many ill-gotten gains. Japan had a blueprint for the conquest of Asia. Korea had already been gobbled up. But the Koreans had never forgotten and the Korean Revolutionary Party always had members in Shanghai ready to take pot shots at any high Jap official. Blueprint for Asian conquest had been drawn up by the notorious Baron Tanaka and Koreans had the baron No. 1 on their list for liquidation.

By chance the baron came through the Customs during my spell of duty with the baggage team in 1922, and I had a front seat while some Korean revolutionaries tried to rub him out. They were waiting for their arch-enemy the moment he emerged from my compound and greeted him with pistol shots and a Mills bomb, but without effect. The shots missed the baron, and a passing British sailor picked up the bomb and tossed it into the nearby river. The baron's bandy little legs broke records and got him safely behind some bales of cargo, but unfortunately an American woman tourist following the Japs out of the compound stopped one of the bullets and died some hours afterwards. She was a Mrs. Snyder, of Indiana, on her second honeymoon. Police pursued the fleeing Koreans, and a running street-fight occurred in and out among the downtown banking section of the International Settlement. All were either killed or captured.

We sent a wreath, in sympathy, to Mrs. Snyder's funeral. It finished up on the victim's grave—beside one from the baron,

SMUGGLERS' PARADISE

whom most of us would have preferred as the victim! While on the subject of Korean revolutionaries, the Japanese Foreign Minister who signed Japan's unconditional surrender aboard the U.S.S. *Missouri*, Tokyo Bay, August 1945, was one Mamoru Shigemitsu. He had an artificial leg and walked awkwardly with a stick, Korean revolutionaries having wounded him in 1932 when he was reviewing a Japanese victory parade in Hongkew Park, on the Japanese side of Shanghai, after Japan and China had tangled viciously for four weeks in the Japanese quarter as a result of Japan's seizure of Manchuria several months earlier. Just another step in the Baron Tanaka's plan for conquest.

The Chinese had shifted an unusually large number of their best troops into Chapei, the Chinese city overlooking Little Tokyo, as Japan's section of Shanghai was known, and Japan became suspicious of these troops—why were they there? China wasn't telling, but it certainly looked as though she intended doing a bit of unannounced annexation on her own account so the Japs struck first (as usual) and for nearly four weeks the two lifelong enemies slugged it out, toe-to-toe. The crack Chinese troops gave the Japs—and the world—a taste of things to come. The Japs were driven back to the river and many of their nationals had already taken to the boats and were speeding down the Whangpoo River en route for Japan when the Western powers intervened and brought the belligerents to the peace table. Was this done to save Japan's face? Many of us thought so.

In spite of swelling Customs revenue, Chiang Kai-shek was not getting enough money to pay for the arms and ammunition which he claimed he needed. Two-gun Cohen was shopping around in Czechoslovakia, Germany, U.S.A., England—but although Chiang's forces received ample supplies of small arms the Red armies, which were the bane of the Generalissimo's existence, repeatedly surrounded his men and took the arms away from them! The Nanking Government was hitting at foreign traders in other ways, too, by going into business for itself and competing on terms which could end up in only one way. As a front, the government set up the giant Kian Gwan company, Chinese business octopus with headquarters in Indonesia and dealers in any type of commerce one can mention. Control of the Chinese Maritime Customs, too, began passing into Nanking's hands — as it had every right to do, so long as foreign loans were secured. Finance Minister Soong was showing the Western world that the days when foreign banks could arbitrarily fix the value of the Chinese dollar had ended.

Soong's life almost ended, too, at the hands of rabid left-wingers within the Kuomintang, or *agents provocateur* — who knows? Soong arrived at Shanghai's northern railway station by train from the new capital of Nanking. He strode along the platform accompanied by his personal assistant — none other than handsome young Tong Yu-li, our colleague on the *China Press*, whose resignation was now explained. As usual, the railway vestibule was crowded with Chinese coming and going, when suddenly a series of shots rang out and young Tong fell dead. Minister Soong, the real target, made a quick dive to the ground and found cover as the would-be assassins shot wildly in his direction. A home-made 'bomb' hurtled through the air also, but luckily failed to explode. Railway guards, never too eager or willing to get into an actual fight, unslung their rifles and shot into the air, unsure of a target in that crowded and panic-stricken place. The effect was good, however. The gunmen took to their heels and escaped in the crowd.

Two hours later I was looking down upon the lifeless but still handsome features of my erstwhile colleague as he lay in the embalming room of the Shanghai Funeral Parlours, expensive American burial firm and first to introduce the bronze casket to wealthy Chinese at $10,000 each. Tong, I observed, rated one of these.

But I had no easy task getting in. Minister Soong was inside ensuring first-class treatment for his short-lived private secretary and wherever Minister Soong went, there went twenty trigger-happy bodyguards also, from that moment on.

My Customs career ended when I found myself, two and a half years after joining up, on the transfer list (issued half-yearly) to what was reputedly the loneliest of many lonely Customs outposts, far away on the Burmese border. Since it usually required more than a month to reach Mengtze, changes of personnel occurred every two years instead of the usual six months. I did not relish the prospect of being virtually buried alive for two years and there was no Commissioner Lyall around to appeal to, as he was absent on leave. Furthermore, I was both homesick and desperately anxious to splash around some of the small fortune I had already amassed from seizure-money. By normal regulations I was not due for 'home leave' for another six and a half years, for in the Chinese Maritime Customs they made you wait nine long years for your first home furlough.

I quit.

3

THE RUSSIAN INVASION

RUSSIANS BEGAN reaching China in large numbers about two years after the October 1917 revolution, the Bolsheviks having needed that length of time to consolidate in Europe before moving eastwards into Siberia.

Then began what the *New York Herald* termed 'one of history's unparalleled curiosities', as some 60,000 White Russians commenced their mass migration from Siberia. On foot, ox-cart, train, ship or Mongolian pony they made their way into Manchuria and China, the one country within reach not requiring passports. A last-ditch stand was made by a handful of Tsarist troops under Commander Ataman Semenov, but it was only a rearguard action to gain the safety of a small fleet of ships waiting to evacuate them from Vladivostok.

Two of these Russian vessels found their way to Shanghai under the command of Admiral Stark and dropped anchor at Woosung, entrance to Shanghai's river, the Whangpoo. They were jammed to the rails with bearded Ivans and Borises, all jack-booted and heavily armed. Alarmed by the quantity of firearms carried by the two ships, the *Okhotsk* and *Mongugai*, Chinese authorities sent word to the Russian admiral in charge of the 'fleet' that no one was to land, and to back up the ultimatum a Chinese warship came downstream from Shanghai and dropped

THE RUSSIAN INVASION

anchor half a mile from the two refugee ships.

This was a period in Shanghai's history when arms and ammunition were at a premium; when provincial warlords were gathering men and guns together; the civil war period when the nation was without any central governing authority.

A Mauser pistol with fifty rounds of ammunition fetched as high as Ch.$500!

As baggage inspector in the Chinese Maritime Customs I had seen thousands of these White Russians arrive on ships from Vladivostok, Dalny and Dairen (Port Arthur). Russian was not one of Shanghai's common languages then, and it was generally left to the ubiquitous little Jewish carpet-baggers, who were earliest among the Russian refugees to arrive, to act as our interpreters. They were only too willing, for among them were the trail-blazers for the wave of Russian white slavery soon to sweep over our city and, indeed, all China! The contents of some of the luggage of the refugees — church ikons, silver candelabra and sackfuls of Russian coins — also suggested that more than a little looting had been done during the escape from the Bolsheviks.

These refugees made a sudden and unwelcome impact upon the social life of Shanghai. To them too must be given the dubious credit of introducing cabarets to the Paris of the Orient. Ways of earning a livelihood simply had to be found to supplement the meagre handouts from the Russian Relief Society hurriedly formed by well-meaning Shanghai citizens to succour the new arrivals. So Shanghai got its 'Trenches'; an unsavoury conglomeration of slum tenements in greasy, cobblestoned alleyways in Chapei, Chinese territory.

By knocking down walls to join ground-floor rooms, draping a few coloured streamers around and economizing on the candle-power, Chinese owners and Russian *entrepreneurs* went into the night-club business with the help of half a dozen scattered

Filipino dance bands. These dim dives hung so close together that if the bouncer knocked a man out of one, he fell into another; and though the flesh-hungry Oriental customers spoke no Russian, the language of the banknote overcame all difficulties. At first, the refugee girls danced for drinks — little red or green glasses at fifty cents apiece — and commission. They wore cheap, tinselled evening frocks lent to them by the carpet-baggers, who let them out at night to work like Japanese cormorant fishermen, who take the big ones and let the birds have what midgets they can swallow. For these sordid spectacles the local Chinese gendarmes took the licence fees behind their backs. What's more they stood around the doorways every night, rifles slung across their shoulders, grinning at the goings-on. Cavortings such as these they had never seen. Nor had the majority of erstwhile staid and fairly steady Shanghai.

Shrewdly the refugee Russian girls, many of them blonde, beautiful and bewitching in the eyes of young and exiled Englishmen and Americans, sensed their power, and it was because of the nightly brawls for their affections, the clash of tempers, fits of jealousy and never-ending hostilities, that the district became known as the Trenches. But bad as it became it never reached the low level depicted in the Broadway hit The Shanghai Gesture, in which an old harridan, reputedly born a Manchu princess, nightly auctioned off white girls to wealthy Oriental bidders. Sooner or later it had to come. A man was killed. But this happened to be a somewhat important young man, the tourist son of a wealthy American family. Someone knifed him in a fight over a Russian refugee girl. Presently the Trenches ceased to exist. Under pressure from the American authorities the local Chinese administration — weak and subservient in those days — barricaded the doors.

Meanwhile, down on the *Okhotsk* and *Mongugai* at Woosung,

THE RUSSIAN INVASION

nearly a thousand ex-Tsarist soldiers were getting tired of being cooped up aboard their overcrowded and unsanitary ships. Despite the Chinese cruiser playing sentinel half a mile away, they took turns to slip ashore in native sampans after dark to sell their guns for money to buy food and wine, especially wine. After a few months of this the two vessels were hell-ships filled with drunken derelicts who had neither country nor future.

For two years Admiral Stark and his two runaway ships rode anchor at Woosung, then finally negotiated a permit to proceed to Manila, in the Philippines, where the few remaining men of Ataman Semenov's army found a home and Admiral Stark sold the ships. 'There is no direction for this mass migration,' reported the *New York Herald*. 'These people are being washed up on shores anywhere from the South Seas to Broadway.'

The closing of the Trenches was but a minor interruption to the Russification of Shanghai. The refugees soon found their way into other avenues of trade, and by 1925 had so lowered the moral tone of our city that the then League of Nations became alarmed, and formed a special committee to investigate the effects upon Shanghai, and China generally, of female Russian penetration. It found:

'That, owing to the growth of the number of Russian girls and women engaged in prostitution, and competition between them and the numerous prostitutes of Oriental nationality, Russian women and girls of Shanghai are driven to offer themselves to Chinese irrespective of the latter's social position.

'That this extensive prostitution of Russian girls and women and the breach by them of the natural racial barrier which has, until recently, existed between white women and natives in China, cannot but have a demoralizing effect on women and girls of other Western nationalities in China who are very often in the same unfortunate position as the Russian women and girls.

SHANGHAI SAGA

'That the appearance of a white woman in such disgraceful capacity as that of a prostitute among natives of the lower classes, affects very deeply the prestige of the Western nations in the Orient.'

Elsewhere than in the brothels, too, they were causing heartburn. A dozen cabarets operated in Shanghai's foreign areas by now and well-groomed Russian girls in hundreds paraded nightly as 'respectable dance hostesses'. The Trenches had pointed the way for numerous well-heeled Chinese and foreign investors, and Shanghai's night-life shifted from the hotel ballrooms to the less inhibited atmosphere of Mumm's, Palais, Del Monte, Maxim's, Alhambra, Wintergarden, Carlton *et al.*

Instead of coloured drinks, customers bought dance tickets at fifty cents apiece with managements and girls splitting fifty fifty and drink commissions on a sliding scale. With dancing came floor shows — Cossack Whirlybirds, balalaikas, Salomes in spangles — all very upsetting to the hitherto placid domestic life of the community, especially when the Russian beauties discovered that as fast as they picked up the English language they picked up an Englishman (or an American) with it. And how they wanted to do just that!

By the middle twenties the Shanghai correspondent of the London *Daily Express* summed up the situation succinctly in the following despatch to his paper:

'The conduct of the pretty Russian women refugees in China has precipitated a crisis in the homes of British and American residents, particularly in the treaty ports [Shanghai, Hankow, Tientsin etc.]. British wives in Shanghai declare that these fascinating rivals from Russia and Siberia, some of them so-called aristocrats and virtually all of them possessing no fortune other than face and figure, have lured husbands away from them and broken up their homes.

THE RUSSIAN INVASION

'English girls with fiances in the Far East similarly assert that the fair Russians are causing their betrothed husbands to break off engagements.

'An English judge in the Shanghai British Court makes the unequivocal statement that most of the divorces he has tried recently have been almost entirely due to the fascinations of these Russian refugees who are characterized as "real vampires" of the kind made famous in films.

'The judge's statement has let loose a flood of letters from indignant British and American wives on the one hand, and from protesting Russian women on the other, which appear in the daily press.

'The British wives attack the morals of the Russians and demand their expulsion from China! The Russians retort by describing the British wives as "flat-chested, flat-footed, worn out by hunting, hockey and golf".

'The Russian women refugees, in fact, are presenting another Far Eastern problem which no one seems able to solve. They are unable to find employment as typists or schoolteachers [virtually the only avenues open to white women in China] owing to their ignorance of the English language.

'Many of them, owing to their good looks and attractive appearance, secure employment as singers, exhibition dancers and dancing partners in restaurants and cabarets.

'There is always a scarcity of white women in the Orient and the alluring Russians have quickly attracted young English and American bachelors who are in China on business contracts containing a clause forbidding them to marry during the term of their first contract.

'Older men, husbands and fathers, many of whom sent their families home owing to the local unrest, have also come under the spell, in many cases, of these fascinating Russian women in

SHANGHAI SAGA

the treaty ports.'

Soon Shanghai was eating *zakouska* and caviar washed down with vodka like mad. Russian-style restaurants and night-clubs branched out and every man looked around for a mistress. Boom times in the twenties were rip-roaringly reminiscent of San Francisco in the gold rush. White, yellow and bronze dangled the dollars before the eyes of the voluptuous vampires from Vladivostok and many a bankroll took a hiding before things settled down. What they settled down to was an entirely new social order, and Chinese were caught up in the swirl even more than foreigners. If you doubt this I refer you to an official memorandum issued to Chinese Government personnel soon after the Nationalists came to power reminding them that their offices were at Nanking, the capital, not in the cabarets of Shanghai!

Perhaps the fact that Generalissimo Chiang Kai-shek wed Soong Mei-ling (Madame Chiang) in the ballroom of the magnificent Majestic Hotel established a precedent for his people. It was a glittering spectacle Shanghai liked to remember. Chiang had two weddings, in fact; the first in deference to his ancestors, native style. The second, out of respect for his Wellesley-College-educated bride, a Christian ceremony attended by all the top hats and gold braid. There never was, before or since, so much gold braid in Shanghai, due to the presence then of Shaforce, the international defence force built up by some twenty Western nations for the bloody defence—if need be—of this Paris on the Whangpoo against Chiang's own army. (Quaint, that Chiang should turn round and invite them all to his wedding nine months after taking over the country.) Prominent among the wedding guests was Old Snake-eyes—Tu Yueh-sen and, of course, Charlie Sloan and myself; representing the *China Press*.

The Majestic Hotel ballroom was born on a boom and died

THE RUSSIAN INVASION

in a depression. A Shanghai millionaire merchant had three sons and built a mansion that they might all live together. He was not Chinese, though some said he was not pure white either. The merchant was so wealthy, influential and popular that he was elected mayor of the International Settlement for more than one term. But when the merchant died his dream of all sons always together under one happy roof died with him. They went their separate ways. One of those ways led to Europe and Paris, and a Follies girl who separated son No. 3 from his inheritance and left him—but for periodical handouts from his brothers—an unrepentent, unredeemable degenerate.

The mansion found its way into the real-estate market. The powerful Hong Kong & Shanghai Hotel chain snapped it up and remodelled it, regardless of expense, as a hotel for tourist millionaires. Named the Majestic Hotel, it boasted two magnificent ballrooms, undoubtedly the finest in all Asia; perhaps even beyond that boundary. It was the Taj Mahal of world hotels, and had a wonderful garden of several rich acres planned by Japan's best landscape gardeners for lovers of beauty and people in love. Mussolini's son-in-law, Count Ciano, when consul-general for Italy in Shanghai, was among the more prominent hosts favouring the Italian-style summer ballroom in the hot months.

In a far-off city where almost every nationality had its national day of celebration, the Majestic was a place where the host nation could really justify itself. It was said that, if a man cared to, he could live on the free handouts from Shanghai's annual celebrations—and live high. For the same reason that the Englishman is said to dress for dinner in the Brazilian jungle, the numerous nationals of our city magnified their celebrative days into grandiose fireworks and champagne binges. Hardly had citizens recovered from Chinese New Year wine before the annual round began to weave its unsteady way through Empire Day, St. George's, St. Andrew's, St. David's, Fourth of July, Bastille Day, Washington's Birthday, Garibaldi's Day, Hallowe'en, spring and autumn Racing Carnival (each ten days) — the correct order does not matter.

Take Bastille Day: I took it first time representing an afternoon paper. The flag-raising ceremony at 8 a.m. with Annamite troops of the French army firing a salute in the grounds of the French consulate-general, went off without incident. This was followed by an official reception within the same consulate at 11 a.m. when felicitations were customarily exchanged between diplomatic representatives of leading Western nations and — when there was no civil war on hand — representatives from the Chinese local authority. The temperature on these midsummer days might be around the century mark by 11 a.m., yet one had to *'Vive la France!'* again and again in pony-glasses of iced champagne and nibble at the trays of food circulating in the hands of white-gloved Chinese servants, come what may. At 3 p.m. the French community played host in the Frenchtown Gardens to any foreign children at all who cared to be present for the sports, the fun fair and, of course, the huge tables of food and drink free, gratis and for nothing. The *pièce de résistance* was the grand ball at night in *Le Cercle Sportif Francais* (French Club), a full-dress-and-medal affair which invariably slopped over from *Le Juillet Quatorze* into *Le Juillet Quinze*. I never made this the first time. The 11 a.m. reception, plus the humidity, got between me and my assignment.

In later years I learned how to paste up the previous year's report, altering only names of speakers and officials present. A newspaperman in Shanghai did not require to be a product of the Missouri School of Journalism, nor did he have to worry much about the laws of libel. It just wasn't done to say nasty

THE RUSSIAN INVASION

things about local residents: not the same buddies you played mah-jong and drank with in this or that club night after night.

One of my newspaper offices overlooked notorious 'Blood Alley', on the other side of Avenue Edward VII which divided Frenchtown from the International Settlement. In a feature article a *Collier's Magazine* writer once said that every time a riot started in the alley I put another notch on my typewriter, implying that I fused these fights to get a scoop for my paper. Did I get mad? I was tickled.

That was a very handily placed newspaper office, as a matter of record. Just across the avenue were at least a dozen cabarets, and a habit grew among the desk men of transferring to one of these on quiet nights. Copy-boys beat a path between office and cabaret, and we put our papers to bed 'mid blare of brass and swish of skirt.

On the floor above the office worked a real product of the Missouri School of Journalism, the China correspondent of the *Chicago Tribune*, likewise editor and publisher of the *China Weekly Review* — one John B. Powell (*My Twenty-five Years in China*). Powell disliked the British and loved the Chinese. Also, the Japs hated Powell because he continually championed the cause of China in an era of swashbuckling Japanese militarism. When the Nationalist Government of China first took over the country, most foreigners and especially Britons were edgy, possibly fearing the end of their pre-eminence in the lucrative China playground. Powell's unceasing support of Chiang Kai-shek's government aroused resentment even among fellow Americans until the point was reached when he was asked to resign from the American Club! In a place like Shanghai that was as bad as firing Ben Hogan from the Golfers' Union!

Powell came back, of course, and was all buddy-buddy once more. Mellowing co-existence between the new Nanking

Government and the Western powers had much to do with this. Besides, 'J.B.' continued his one-man war against the Japanese, who furnished him with plenty of ammunition for his *China Weekly Review* and daily despatches to Chicago. Japanese annexation of Manchuria, coinciding with the timely disposal of Marshal Chang Tso-lin, Manchurian ruler, was good for months and months of vigorous Powell journalism. Right through the interval between the Manchurian grab and the start of the Sino-Japanese war six years later, Powell kept on after the Japanese, exposing their expansionist aims under the euphonious catch-phrase of 'co-prosperity'.

No wonder the Japs gleefully seized Powell almost as soon as the bombs dropped on Pearl Harbour and threw him into the freezing cells of the notorious Bridge House Jail. They did not kill Powell: they wanted him to suffer. But suffering was not new to this battling journalist from Missouri, for he had been among those captured by Chinese bandits Peking-bound from Shanghai by the Blue Express in 1923 and held captive in a mountain hide-out for fifty-three days. When Powell was released at war's end in 1945 his feet had been amputated because of frostbite. He lived long enough back in the U.S.A. to write his memorable book *My Twenty-five Years in China* and tour the country lecturing.

When the world depression finally reached Shanghai about 1931 one of its first victims was the millionaires' Majestic Hotel. Hong Kong & Shanghai Hotels Ltd. discovered that it had a real white elephant on its books and quickly unloaded into the local real-estate maelstrom. Speculators tossed it around for some six months like a hot potato while the diehards of the city tried scheme after scheme to keep its prize high-kicking centre extant. The final plan submitted before the wreckers moved in was for an international club—but the city already had a surfeit of clubs, international and national. Thus, into a tumble of broken bricks

THE RUSSIAN INVASION

and other rubble fell a rich man's — and a city's — fondest dream. Within a couple of months Generalissimo Chiang Kai-shek's wedding roof had caved in and just to complete the humiliation felt by all Shanghai at this grievous loss, the Hagenbeck Circus arrived on a world tour from Germany some weeks later. It set up shop on the vacant lot and its elephants left their calling cards right, left and centre.

I have already mentioned how the granting of tariff autonomy to China, effective from 1929, caused many firms to tighten up on their employees, even to the point of keeping regular office hours. The days when certain foreigners were kept on the staff payroll simply because they were good jockeys, played bridge well or had a fund of good humour, were over; and the crowning insult came when some bars and cabarets began demanding cash instead of chits from unfamiliar customers.

Through all the city's vicissitudes Russians kept coming to Shanghai from North China and Siberian cities, lured by tales of opportunity in the great southern metropolis. And opportunities there were. Though those early White Russian refugees had paid a terrible price and even pulled the props from under white prestige, those who followed fitted well into the cosmopolitan community and in the end won for themselves a respected place in the city. Some began humbly as domestics and night-watchmen. Soon, when they learned enough of the English language, they became chauffeurs, mechanics, engineers, bakers, bootmakers, pastrycooks, shopkeepers, clerks, typists and nurses. Racing men gave them jobs in stables and at the race-tracks; hundreds became bodyguards for Chinese millionaires; several died in defence of their Chinese employers in a city where kidnapping occurred every other day.

This was, perhaps, the only city in the world having both White and Red Russian newspapers published daily a few

SHANGHAI SAGA

hundred yards from each other; not merely papers sympathizing with a cause but one backed by Moscow, the other by Russian royalists. Inevitably, Shanghai gained a Russian choir to go with its semi-professional symphony orchestra and, in the 1930's, to supplement the voluntary civilian defence force which had kept the peace since the Taiping Rebellion of 1861, Shanghai got its first full-time 'army', a battalion of White Russian troops who were first into the field at every disturbance.

When a count of heads showed upwards of 15,000 Russians living in Shanghai the police of Frenchtown and the International Settlement discovered the need to have Russians on the force. A Russian became assistant to the British registrar at the Mixed Court of the International Settlement; another a famous cartoonist on Shanghai's leading British newspaper. Most Russians favoured residence in Frenchtown and a 'Little Moscow' grew up along the Avenue Joffre, main stem of the French half of Shanghai. A Russian church was built, a reminder of Moscow and the motherland of nostalgic memory, with its onion-shaped turrets. We already had Russian bouncers in most cabarets. Soon we had Russian boxers to climb into the ring against British, American, Filipino or any other kind of pug. When World War II began, Russians far outnumbered all other foreigners in Shanghai, save Japanese!

One night in 1927 a whole thousand Russians boosted the census in a dramatic manner. We were in the last days of fighting between North and South, between a coalition of northern warlords and Chiang Kai-shek's new Nationalist army which had marched on foot all the way up from Canton. One of the warlords had a battalion of White Russian mercenaries on his payroll. He was General Chang Tsung-chang, 6ft. 4 in. giant from Shantung, chiefly noted for the international flavour of his harem. Chang had put the Russians aboard an armoured train

THE RUSSIAN INVASION

The author meets Generalissimo Chiang Kai-shek

Terror meets terror — punishment of captured gunmen as warning to others

Grim warning to evil-doers

Man carries home heads of his two brothers for proper burial

THE RUSSIAN INVASION

drawn up alongside a platform at Shanghai's northside railway station, where Finance Minister Soong was almost assassinated some months later. The Shantung warlord knew his jig was up. He left the Russians to cover his retreat. This they did right well, Chang and the rest of the Chinese forces getting clear away and over the Yangtze River into Shantung province. Then the abandoned Russian mercenaries came to a decision. Under a flag of truce they approached the barricades manned by Shaforce, requesting asylum. A hurried conference among the civic fathers of foreign Shanghai agreed to admit them, providing they left all arms and ammunition behind. Quietly and secretly they were let in through the barricades shortly after midnight. The darkness and silence of a 10 p.m. to 4 a.m. curfew swallowed them up. They became a part of Shanghai and the war between North and South was over.

It is quite true, however, that at one time White Russian refugees begged from Chinese in the streets, sold newspapers alongside Chinese paper-pedlars and even tried pulling rickshaws for a living! These performances, like those of the women and girl street solicitors after nightfall and the previously described activities revealed in the League of Nations' report, could not help but pull the foreigner down from his pedestal in Chinese' eyes, and one of the first big changes occurred at the top level of administration. Both French and International sections of Shanghai were run by annually elected foreign councillors. The Chinese attacked the weak spot first—the International Settlement—knowing the French to be more resistant to their ambitions. Though they paid the bulk of the taxes, Chinese had no voice in the administration of either area, and they demanded a voice in both.

The councils agreed to admit them. After 1929 the International Settlement was governed by five British, two American, two

Japanese and five Chinese councillors, the last-named being elected in a separate election by the Chinese themselves. Frenchtown reconstituted itself into a council of nine Frenchmen, two Britons and five Chinese. There was one important difference between the two administrations, however. The French consul-general was the supreme local authority, exercising the power of veto over the actions of the Frenchtown councillors. He was answerable only to the French Minister to China and the French Government. On the other hand, any elected group of foreign consuls (the Consular Body) could overrule the municipal council of the International Settlement and any appeal from its decisions had to go to the Diplomatic Corps which, naturally, backed up its consular representatives.

The Japanese always felt held down under British and American pressure in Shanghai, and repeatedly demanded greater Japanese representation on the Shanghai Municipal Council (International Settlement) on a population basis. Although only the Japanese consul-general knew the exact number, it was plainly evident that Japanese outnumbered all other non-Chinese nationals in Shanghai combined. Year after year, at the annual ratepayers' meeting of the International Settlement, Japanese speakers mounted the rostrum to voice their annual protest against the policy which limited the number of Japanese on the council to two. In the declining years of Shanghai's existence, when the Japanese Army was already bogged down in the Sino-Japanese war touched off in July of 1937, a tough delegate from the Japanese Street Unions, mouthpiece of Japanese ratepayers, pulled a gun and shot wildly into the half-circle of municipal councillors at their annual meeting. He grazed a couple of startled councillors but nothing more.

Two years after this incident, Pearl Harbour was attacked and, of course, the Japs took over Shanghai completely. As with

THE RUSSIAN INVASION

J. B. Powell the journalist, so with Stirling Fessenden, American lawyer and permanent secretary-general of the Shanghai Municipal Council. He was a short, thick-set man with beautiful white bushy hair, who wore thick-lensed glasses without which he was as blind as the proverbial bat. The Japs' idea of paying off old scores was to take away Fessenden's glasses and prevent any friends from helping him. When last seen he was in wretched poverty, half starved and very sick—a sorrowful fade-out for a man who once largely directed the destiny of Asia's greatest, happiest and friendliest city.

During the 1930's Japan's secret-police system reached right into Shanghai and every Japanese resident was listed at the consulate so that none dared move in or out of the city without police permission. The secret police had a dossier on every Nipponese citizen who, in turn, carried a kosekei, or police passport. Just as Russian police were enlisted to assist in the government of the growing Russian population, so Japanese police were taken into the International Settlement police to patrol Little Tokyo, or Hongkew. Extra to these, however, were the Japanese consular police, responsible only to the Japanese consul-general and assigned to special duties, mostly political. Their main job was espionage, and for this purpose they had many Japanese who looked and even spoke like Chinese. It goes without saying that they dressed like Chinese most of the time as well. These were the men the Korean revolutionaries in Shanghai feared most, yet they outwitted even these Japanese S.S. men again and again, to wit, when they bombed the official stand at that victory parade in 1932 and cost the then Consul-General Shigemitsu one of his legs. They paid dearly for such triumphs, however. Always smarting under such defeats, the Japanese S.S. men again and again caught a Korean revolutionary, and when they did all Shanghai felt a strong sympathy for the little men from the 'stolen kingdom'.

There was a strongly barred detention-house in the grounds of the Japanese consulate. Any man, or woman, wanted by the S.S. squad could be held there and slipped aboard an outward-bound Japanese ship under cover of darkness to vanish forever. Many did, and their arrest and disappearance would never have been known but for wives, relatives or friends who carried the news to the legitimate police of the city. No S.S. man had power to make an arrest until first receiving an okay from the Settlement (or French) authorities, but the Japs always forgot to get this.

Two major aims of the Chinese Nationalists had been successfully accomplished. They had tariff autonomy and revenue was pouring into the Bank of China and they were represented on the municipal councils of both foreign areas of the city. A third and comparatively minor demand was now put to the Western powers—their right to enter the foreign parks of Shanghai, including the grass lawns along the Bund foreshore. This was also agreed to, but in order to prevent these little oases of pleasure and fresh air from being swamped by the city's coolies, turnstiles were installed at the gates and a fee—calculated to be beyond the reach of any coolie—charged for admission.

Next to come under attack were the two Mixed Courts, wherein Chinese and those foreigners without extra-territorial protection were subject to the Chinese Criminal and Civil Code of Laws. Once more the Western powers gave in. The dominant voice in judicial affairs at these courts switched from the foreign to the Chinese judges and the courts were re-named 'Provisional Courts'. That is to say, they had to pass through a term of probation satisfactory to the Western powers before acquiring absolute power within the foreign areas of Shanghai. To any who may be thinking that all this was as it should be, let it be remembered that Shanghai grew into a big city largely because

THE RUSSIAN INVASION

Chinese wanted to live there under foreign protection and do business.

It wasn't long, however, before the newly constituted Provisional Courts under Chinese control began to be used as instruments of blackmail. Someone in the new Chinese government was trying to get rich in a hurry. Reports of abductions of wealthy Chinese kept coming into police headquarters and many rich Chinese doubled their bodyguards as a precaution. One millionaire mill-owner must have been hard to get at. So the unseen power in the Nanking Government tried a new dodge and it was my misfortune one day at the Provisional Court to see this well-known Chinese grovelling on the floor of the court, tears streaming down his face as he begged the court to believe his story. An application had been made for this man's extradition from the International Settlement to the native-controlled courts outside. A number of charges had been made which the terror-stricken accused insisted were frame-ups just to get him outside foreign jurisdiction. 'If you hand me over to them they'll kill me for sure!' he wailed, a pitiful object and far from the 'immutable, inscrutable emotionless Oriental' of fiction.

Before the change-over from 'Mixed' to 'Provisional Court' and the accompanying switch from foreign to Chinese dominance the situation could easily have been handled by refusal of the extradition application. Things were different now. The Chinese judge had the big voice and foreign judges did not even hold the power of veto. At best they could enter written protest against any court decision or judgment in which they disagreed. Pity the poor Chinese judge in this case. He might want to do right and refuse extradition; then at once he fell foul of the unseen power seeking that extradition. He could even lose his job, or his life. There might be a couple of million dollars involved in this! On the other hand, he knew the spotlight was upon his court and it was in bad enough public odour already, within a year of the change-over! His dilemma was resolved by the quick-thinking American judge, who held a short, whispered discussion with his bench colleague. There was prima facie evidence sufficient to grant the extradition application. So be it. Hand the prisoner over, the court decreed, 'but have him where we may come and inspect him at any time we so desire'. Enough to make any extortionist sick in the stomach. No torture, no cutting off of ears or fingers to speed up payment of ransom money. Worst of all, the court's decision short-circuited what was to have been a neat, regular and easy method of getting hold of the bodies of many other victims whose names were on a long list to be systematically separated from their wealth.

One of the first changes made by the new group of Chinese judges installed in the new Provisional Courts was to abolish the Mixed Court's practice of banishing convicted criminals from the foreign areas. It had been customary for many years to add a rider to every sentence in these words: 'Expelled from the International Settlement' or, in the case of the French Concession, 'Expelled from the French Concession'. This meant that on expiry of his sentence a prisoner was led to the outside boundary of the forbidden area, and told to get going and not come back. If he did so and was re-arrested, it meant six months in jail for returning from expulsion. Chinese judges under the new regime protested that the old Mixed Court judges had exceeded their authority, their argument being that Chinese could not legally be expelled from their own country — which might be regarded as a neat riposte supporting their claim that all foreign areas were unrecognized as such by the Nanking Government.

Abolition of all land concessions in China's treaty ports, signed away by China in the Treaty of Nanking at the end of the so-called Opium War in 1842, was still the major — and

THE RUSSIAN INVASION

unresolved — aim of the new Nationalist Government of China but, as Generalissimo Chiang Kai-shek had told Charlie Sloan and me on that day in March 1927, China was prepared to negotiate for their return. Personally, I don't believe that everyone in the Nanking Government really wanted abolition of these foreign areas. They were too useful as asylums for political refugees, for one thing, and were actually the only reasonably safe and honestly governed cities in all China. When announcing the end of 'expulsion from the Foreign Settlement' as a form of punishment for the Chinese, Provisional Court authorities at the same time vetoed all previous Mixed Court expulsion orders, news which was happily received by several thousand of Shanghai's worst criminals who promptly returned to their old haunts.

4

DAY OF FATE

THIS MAY BE the moment to reveal a Chinese racket which 'beat all' and probably had no equal in history! I mentioned earlier that China reserved to herself the right to execute all Chinese sentenced to death in the foreign courts by foreign judges. This was a matter of 'face' and maintained Chinese sovereignty over the Chinese people. In any case, it was scarcely the sort of responsibility the foreign courts desired to have thrust upon them. The Chinese carried the matter to its logical end, however, and every condemned prisoner handed over to the local Chinese authorities by the foreign courts went through a second 'trial' at which the Mixed Court sentence was 'confirmed' and the prisoner placed in the custody of the Chinese police to await his day of execution. Or so everybody thought!

But police of the two foreign areas of Shanghai were puzzled after arresting armed kidnappers to find that now and then one of their prisoners was supposed to be dead! Checking the fingerprint records confirmed their suspicion and they discovered that well-heeled gangsters were buying their way out of the death-cells. This seemed impossible, for representatives from the foreign police always attended executions of prisoners handed over by the Mixed Courts, a very necessary precaution; therefore they knew that executions had taken place. Who then

DAY OF FATE

had been the victims on these occasions?

It was not long before they found out the answer. Friends of the convicted gangster had paid up and got him 'sprung' and for the 'sacrifice' the police chief simply grabbed any petty thief in the cells on execution day, led him out and shot, strangled or beheaded him according to the fashion at the time, before he had time to yell. And if he did display intelligence enough to know what was about to happen, and holler accordingly, someone hit him over the head with a rifle-butt very smartly and the execution proceeded according to plan.

The foreign police plugged this hole promptly by having their witnesses to the execution fingerprint all prisoners a few minutes before zero hour. A comparison with the records was made on the spot by a fingerprint expert and, from that time on, the native police chief had to look around for other sources of extra income.

My reference to different forms of execution illustrates changes which actually occurred from time to time for the law was very elastic in regard to capital punishment. It seemed that the decision in these matters was left to the Chinese authorities carrying out the sentence of the court, because for similar crimes I saw men shot, decapitated and strangled. When the civil wars around 1924-5 deprived Shanghai of dependable Chinese authority to whom condemned Chinese could be handed over for execution, we had a backlog of seventy-nine condemned criminals in the cells of the International Settlement jail awaiting despatch. We also had a first-class crime wave, as mercenary Chinese soldiers deserted lost causes and returned to civilian life, bringing guns with them to shoot up the town. They held up money-exchange shops, pawnshops, rice-shops and silversmiths with daring regularity. Accustomed as bandits to taking whatever they needed at the point of a gun, they tried to treat Shanghai like any other Chinese town in the interior.

Many of them were good marksmen, too. They took such toll of the police that a hurried order went in for bullet-proof vests for the flying squads sent after them. These were not enough. Many raids on hide-outs found the police at a disadvantage, because in the slums to which they fled the thugs invariably took to the upper floors when the cops arrived.

They had discovered that the steep, narrow and dark staircases in such buildings gave them a top-to-bottom shot at the police coming up the stairs which nullified the advantages of the bullet-proof vests.

Law and order countered this situation by giving a bulletproof shield to every raider to hold over his head going up staircases; and the record still stands to the credit of British sub-Inspector Hinton of the International Settlement police who went in first after a gang of armed kidnappers one day. Hinton found two gunmen at the top of the stairs waiting for him. With scarcely any light to aid him he fired twice, and two bodies came tumbling down the stairs to land at his feet. He ran up the steps as a third kidnapper poked his head around the upstairs door, and though the target was small Hinton got him too, and as he reached the landing saw another man sliding under a bed so quickly brought his score up to four, all dead.

I sat in a sub-station one night drinking beer with several of my police friends in their canteen. One of them got up, buttoned his belt, tested his automatic pistol, and said: 'Well, I've got to get started. It's eight o'clock.' He was a young Englishman, new to the force, and was going out on street patrol in the very heart of the city, among the great, brightly lit department stores of Sincere's, Wing On's and Sun Sun's, where Shanghai's greatest concentration of Chinese night-life in the old wine-and-dine tradition was about to gather speed. Ten minutes later a public

DAY OF FATE

rickshaw trundled into the police station compound. A Chinese constable sat in the rickshaw and 'sitting' on his knees was the lifeless body of the young English policeman. A couple of Chinese armed robbers, taking it 'on the lam', had come fast round a corner, seen the young police officer and shot him dead before he had time to draw. They got clean away.

Anything up to a dozen armed crimes a day was a fair crime-wave for an area of less than 9,000 acres and the police began throwing out nets unexpectedly in selected areas. Cars filled with 'shielded' and 'vested' armed police pulled up and cordoned off a street between two given points. Spreading out they stopped and searched every automobile, rickshaw or pony-carriage and 'frisked' every adult human being in sight—even women, for whom special female body-searchers were on hand. Using women to carry guns to and from the scene of a crime was a favourite gang trick and my gallery of pictures shows one of these female accomplices on the gallows, alongside her male confederates. There were now so many firearms in the underworld of Shanghai that it no long paid smugglers to bring them in. The thousands sold by the Russians from the refugee ships *Okhotsk* and *Mongugai* a couple of years earlier and thousands more carried into the foreign area by soldier-bandits deserting from the civil wars, created a reign of terror inside Shanghai—which was something the civil war raging outside could never do.

The air began to clear around the end of 1925 when Shanghai finally fell into the hands of a military clique—or alliance—which included the Marshal from Manchuria, ex-bandit Chang Tso-lin (the Japs did not bump him off until 193i1), the Shantung giant with the international harem, General Chang Tsung-chang, and a comparatively unknown from Fukien Province, General Sun Chuan-fang. This trio put all opposition to rout and marched into the Shanghai area as complete victors.

As soon as all their antagonists had either gone back to the distant hills or escaped abroad in some foreign ship (using the foreign areas as a refuge and springboard meanwhile) the triumphant trio paid their respects to the foreign community. They invited all foreign ambassadors, consuls and bigwigs of the city, Chinese as well as foreign, to an official reception at the Chinese General Chamber of Commerce. Manchurian warlord Chang Tso-lin could not attend this, but sent along his son, the 'Young Marshal' Chang Hsueh-liang, to represent him. (This was the same 'Young Marshal' who kidnapped Generalissimo Chiang Kai-shek in 1936, but later set him free and apologized for his deed.) The old apple sauce was thickly spread through the speeches from both sides. The victorious bandits assured the foreigners munching the Chinese pastry that a long era of peace and prosperity was about to be ushered in. Assurances of goodwill were exchanged in a variety of languages which kept the interpreters busy. But as soon as the foreigners had taken their departure the Chinese merchants at the party were presented by the conquerors with a hefty bill of costs for the conquest of the city, as well as for the promised era of peace and prosperity. They paid.

The triumphant trio decided to leave General Sun Chuanfang in charge of the city. The 'Young Marshal' was a social butterfly who felt more at home — and safer — in North China, while the Shantung giant, Chang Tsung-chan, could not return to his French, Russian, Polish, Japanese and Chinese concubines quickly enough. So soon as Sun Chuan-fang learned of the current crime-wave in Shanghai he let loose a squad of big swordsmen into the Chinese sections of our city and pretty soon heads were rolling in the gutters or hung from telegraph poles everywhere. When he learned that there were now more than eighty desperadoes in the

DAY OF FATE

foreign jail awaiting execution he promptly agreed to handle the matter on an exhibition basis, guaranteed to knock the ambition out of every would-be gangster within a hundred miles. Not quite sure just what the new 'protector' of Shanghai's peace and prosperity had in mind, the foreign authorities nevertheless consented to hand over a couple of dozen of the condemned prisoners as a sort of 'feeler'.

General Sun then announced a big demonstration parade through all the main streets of Shanghai, including the International Settlement and French Concession, while the Shanghai Municipal Council shrugged its collective shoulders. 'It's too late to back out now,' the chairman told the *Press*. They did, however, draw the line at having a brass band lead this death parade, for it would almost certainly have played 'Dixie', 'Tipperary' and 'There'll be a Hot Time in the Old Town Tonight', favourites at all Chinese funerals.

When word got around — and the native Press saw that it did — crowds streamed towards a Chinese military drill-ground ten miles south of the French Concession. When the two-lane dirt road passed its peak capacity, cars, carriages, cyclists and pedestrians used the farmers' fields beside it until upwards of 25,000 bug-eyed spectators gathered in a circle to watch this revival of early Roman technique. Using the lunch-hour break as the best time for spectator participation, the parade glided through all main streets of the city, the column headed by several open cars containing foreign as well as Chinese police and military officials. The illustration facing p.112 shows part of the *cortège* turning out of Nanking Road in the International Settlement and the photographer who took this picture had his shop in the background.

At the execution-ground two film units had their tripod cameras well positioned atop a couple of outsize native grave mounds, for the Chinese prefer to keep their coffins above ground and pile earth over them rather than dig into the swampy subsoil. That way it is easier to recover the bones in after years when the time arrives to transfer them to the earthenware jar which is their usual last resting-place. A battalion of Chinese soldiers had its hands full keeping the huge crowd formed in a wide circle, but they managed to do so by swinging their rifle-butts with gay abandon every now and then. A great shout went up from the multitude as the trucks containing the prisoners pulled into the centre of the ground, followed by a couple of open flivvers from which stepped the officers in charge of the day's operations. Each prisoner was chained by the wrists and ankles and up from his back protruded a stick carrying a sign proclaiming the nature of his misdeeds.

It was plain that the crowd wanted the prisoners done to death, for public feeling ran high just then over the amount of murder and robbery going about. These men were shot, six at a time. Or should I say they were forced to kneel in sixes but shot one at a time by soldiers, with service rifles at point-blank range, from behind? Most of them had their heads blown to bits and fragments of skull and warm brains went flying everywhere. The movie cameras recorded it all, even to the grave-diggers in the background nonchalantly heaving on their spades and making holes in the mud to bury what was left over from the rifles. Criminals like these did not rate a grave-mound for no friends or relatives were ever likely to come and bottle their bones. No one even knew who they were, save that they had been bandits before they turned city robbers and were probably born a thousand miles from Shanghai. But the thing about those executions which stands out in memory clearer than anything else was the mighty shout of exultation and glee which went up from the throats of the assembled Chinese each time a volley of

DAY OF FATE

shots blew one of the bandits into kingdom-come.

Once was enough for the foreign authorities. They politely begged off from further bloodthirsty public exhibitions and the remainder of the eighty-odd men and women in Death Row were quietly handed over to the Chinese authorities for less spectacular removal.

Unfortunately for the promise of peace and quiet given to Shanghai at that Chinese General Chamber of Commerce reception of previous mention, destiny was lining up a somewhat explosive page of history around now. The day of fate was May 30, 1925, and the time-bomb was set for the middle of the afternoon — a Saturday. Professional agitators, Moscow-trained, had been whipping up mill-workers into a fine frenzy for weeks, So had student agitators, and several of the latter had been arrested for inciting crowds to riot and damage Japanese cotton mills. They appeared in the Mixed Court for a preliminary hearing on Saturday morning, May 30, and were remanded in custody over the weekend in the cells of Louza District police station in the centre of the city; the same whence our young English policeman had sallied forth only recently and been shot down ten minutes later. One thing could be said for the Louza District: it had more people to the acre than any other part of Shanghai, and any sort of disturbance could attract ten, even twenty, thousand rubbernecks in a few minutes.

When the Moscow proteges started shouting for the release of the mill rioters around 2.30 p.m. that day, they quickly gathered round them several thousand idling spectators and others willing to take up the shouts. The station buildings were situated down a drive-in eighty yards from Nanking Road, and a British police inspector named Everson had around twenty Chinese, Indian and foreign policemen to defend it. The police commissioner was in Japan on annual holiday and his first deputy was playing cricket on the racecourse recreation-ground not half a mile away.

At first the situation did not warrant summoning this senior officer, but matters quickly took a serious turn. With the arrival of a few car-loads of key agitators, the crowd of some 10,000 began menacing the police and forcing a passage down the drive-in. The police fell back and Inspector Everson rang for the deputy commissioner. The next couple of minutes started the countdown. With the crowd already half-way to his police buildings the inspector ordered his small force to point their guns at the mob. This gesture had no least effect, and with less than fifty feet left to go Everson shouted 'Fire!' and saved the day. Eight rioters died, four instantly and four later from their wounds. The rest turned and fled.

This sort of thing was just what Moscow had sent its ace agitator Michael Borodin to China for. And down south in Canton it had another ace, General Bleucher, alias Galens, of its Far Eastern army, busily training a young army of hot-blooded Cantonese to march north and take over the country from the bandit-warlords then in control, though their ultimate objective was, of course, the overthrow of foreign imperialists in China, one of their favourite slogans.

Just for the record, here is what actually happened. No sooner had this enthusiastic army of Southern Nationalists set out from Canton under Generalissimo Chiang Kai-shek than Reds seized control of Canton and four days of bloody fighting took place in that great city on the Pearl River before the uprising was put down. One of the casualties was the Russian consul who was caught in the act of dashing round the city in an open car throwing out inflammatory pamphlets inciting the populace to riot. Government troops seized the consul, decapitated him and displayed his head on a bamboo pole in the market-place for days afterwards.

DAY OF FATE

So the Reds dogged Chiang's footsteps all the rest of the way up north, fomenting disturbances at Hankow, Nanking and Shanghai, key cities of China. At Hankow, Reds led mobs over flimsy barricades into the British Concession and forcibly took possession. A few days later England, through British consul O'Malley, signed away her rights to that Concession and the end of foreign domination of China was in sight. At Nanking Reds also led mobs into attacks upon foreigners and Chinese alike, leading the public into believing that this southern army was just an unruly rabble bent on pillage and murder. After a couple of foreigners had been killed, a joint United States and British naval force went ashore under cover of naval guns on the Yangtze River and safely brought out all other foreigners who wanted to leave. Only a handful of diehards remained

We already know what happened at Shanghai. Because of what had happened at Hankow and Nanking, Chiang hesitated to send in his troops to clean up the rabble which, allegedly led by Red China's present-day premier Chou En-lai, had overrun all Chinese parts of the city in the wake of the departure of Sun Chuan-fang, Chang Tsun-chang and Chang Tso-lin. The Reds hoped Chiang would come in after them. They intended repeating their Hankow tactics by forcing the boundaries of the foreign areas and getting Chiang entangled with the international defence force sent there to save Shanghai at all costs.

Chiang, however, left it to his blood-brother, Chief Tu Yuehsen of the Green Dragons and boss of the Chinese underworld, to overcome the difficulty. Tu's men went in, cleaned up the Reds and their hirelings in forty hours and handed Shanghai to the Generalissimo on a plate. For which, in return, he received an open go in any racket his organization could think up.

I have used the world 'government' troops in reference to the abortive uprising of Reds in Canton soon after the Nationalist army set out from the southern city on its northward march. There were, in fact, two independent governments in China at this time, in Peking and in Canton. The latter declared its independence of Peking during the civil war period. The northward march to clean up the civil war and unify all of China under one central government was but a continuation of the revolution launched by Dr. Sun Yat-sen, who first imported Borodin and Galens from Russia and placed his protégé Chiang Kai-shek at the head of the revolutionary, Nationalist army for that purpose.

Sun Yat-sen had already (1911) overthrown the Imperial Dragon Throne of Peking and China had declared herself a republic; but the politicians of Peking who came to power carried on a cloak-and-dagger government which left Sun out in the cold. Government of China, as such, ceased to exist and the warlords launched the civil wars. So Sun Yat-sen tried a second time, turning to Russia for experts, money, arms and ammunition for the purpose, all of which Russia was only too happy to lend. Indeed, the Reds were so anxious to get into the fray that they tried to seize Canton in the manner just described and from then on, right up to 1949 — when Chiang's Nanking Government crumbled — the Nationalist leader, who took over from Sun Yat-sen when the doctor died of a kidney ailment in 1926, always had to fight on two fronts: (I) warlords and Reds, (2) Reds and Japs.

Of Chiang's downfall it has been written that 'a wealthy, reactionary clique moved in and hi-jacked the fruits of his military success'. And that is probably putting it mildly.

Almost from the day the southerners came to town, Shanghai embarked upon an era of whoopee enough to send past emperors spinning in their marble tombs. The pace of the city's world-famed night-life was stepped up out of recognition and the responsibility for this rested almost solely upon Chinese shoulders — youthful ones, for their owners were drawn mainly

DAY OF FATE

Captured criminals and terrorists under death-sentence

SHANGHAI SAGA

China's Lenin
Dr. Sun Yat-sen

The author's curfew pass issued at time of 1927 crisis

DAY OF FATE

from the student classes. It wasn't long before they were crowding foreigners off their own dance-floors, and they were big spenders, too.

Then came the biggest of all changes. As Chinese, they wanted Chinese dancing-partners and that was something Confucius had not provided for. However, a group of smart operators from Canton speedily filled the gap and plastered Shanghai with a rash of new night-spots providing pretty little Chinese hostesses for the big-spending night owls with itchy feet; and keeping up with the current trend Chinese dancing academies sprang up all over the place, converting sing-song girls into taxi-dancers and lazy old opium-smokers into spry jazz maniacs rarin' to go.

Training Chinese musicians to give out with waltzes, foxtrots and tangos was something else again, for here were no possible short cuts. So out went the SOS s to Manila and the United States for ready-made dance bands to meet the new demand. Again the Chinese preference for things Chinese asserted itself, and we who felt it our duty to keep abreast of current changes were startled shortly to hear night-club bands from San Francisco, Chicago and even New York's Harlem district struggling to give their wealthy Chinese patrons Oriental ballads to Dixieland tempo!

But there was worse to come. A Chinese sing-song girl might sound okay after one had downed a quart or two of samshu at a rollicking Chinese dinner-party; the same voice magnified by a microphone on a cabaret rostrum sent one half-way round the bend. Still, from a sociological standpoint, Chinese girls had to thank the cabarets for transforming their age-old lowly status in the community to one of respected opulence. Many a little Cinderella of the rice-pot blossomed into a silk-and-diamond keeper of the family; and down in 'Little Tokyo' it was the same story, with Japanese 'hostesses' arriving by every ship from Nippon to cater to the fast-growing Japanese community and give the local *geisha* a little competition.

Virtually hounded out of their own playgrounds by this tidal wave of native terpsichore, most whites fell back upon a few foreign night-spots which maintained a colour bar, serving up only Russian and Eurasian hostesses for their clientele. One outraged foreign millionaire went so far as to build himself a hotel with a lavish ballroom, where every Saturday night he and his many, many friends let off steam to music provided by the New York Singing Syncopaters, a band of American negroes with several fine vocalists. Before long the owner had songsheets distributed to the guests and, led by the negroes, everyone had a fine old sing-song in the tradition of the barber-shop quartette. But this was no ordinary sing-song, I can assure you. A count of heads on any Saturday night would show upwards of fifty (dollar) millionaires and, making harmony with these, international diplomats, bank managers, judges, three-quarters of the Stock Exchange membership, scores of *taipans*, any admirals or generals who might happen to be in port, civic fathers, visiting Hollywood celebrities such as composer Rudolph Friml (*Rose Marie*) and possibly Two-gun Cohen.

As theatres in Shanghai never started before 9.15 p.m., not until after midnight did these parties get into gear and start to roll; it was usually one or two o'clock before the little negro band leader began his husky renditions under the spotlight in the centre of the dance-floor. At each chorus, this night-clubful of 'diehard imperialists' — as the Moscow-trained agitators branded them — took over under the little negro's baton, and Stephen Foster's spirit really materialized in his immortal melodies which Shanghai society sang week after week in that unique setting. And Shanghai could sing! It had not one, but two, amateur theatrical companies, one dominated by the English, the other by American citizens. Over the years they produced

DAY OF FATE

everything from *The Merry Widow* to *The Front Page*.

A few years later another foreign millionaire decided to build himself a playground for the entertainment of his foreign and (especially) Chinese friends. The late Sir Victor Sassoon, the British capitalist, had just decided to make Shanghai his Far Eastern home, investing heavily in our city with new mills, breweries, hotels, theatres, apartment-houses and office buildings. He built the giant Cathay Hotel on the Bund and dominated that famous skyline until the Chinese Government came along with its new Bank of China, right on the spot where the old German Club brass band used to regale the residents in former, lonelier days. Sir Victor also built the first air-conditioned night-club in Shanghai on the Bubbling Well Road opposite the exclusive and plush British Country Club. He called it 'Ciro's', but the wags of the city soon knew it as 'Sassoon's Sing-song House', a prophetic title as it turned out, for when the depression hit Shanghai it was sold to Chinese interests and transformed into the first air-conditioned Chinese cabaret in China! One never knew whom one might bump into in a Shanghai night-club. Personally, I have bumped buttocks against Madame Galli-Curci, the celebrated coloratura of the New York Metropolitan Opera, in the Little Club and against Anna May Wong, Hollywood actress, in the Vienna Garden, while in various other spots I have competed with Count Ciano for the services of the same Chinese dancing partner and accidentally trodden on the dainty little foot of former actress Betty Compson, friend of New York ex-Mayor 'Jimmie' Walker.

Until the depression hit Shanghai, closing time for the nightspots was when the last customer put on his hat and departed. The only time the dancing-girls got to bed before dawn was when Charlie Sloan ran a shuttle service with the *China Press* flivver throughout curfew in 1927. Sloan's name had become a byword around the cabarets within a few months of his arrival, by reason of the fact that as soon as he entered any of these places he went straight to the piano and spelled the band for more than half an hour with his brilliant piano-playing. The 10 p.m. to 4 a.m. curfew clamped upon the city forbade anyone without a pass being on the streets between those hours and hundreds who tried it ended up in the nearest district police station. Therefore any customer in a night-spot at 10 p.m. had to stay there until curfew ended.

That was all right in places which already held a good crowd at 10 p.m., but if things were otherwise, and fun and frolic died soon after midnight, the girls longed to go home to bed. That was the point at which they remembered Charlie Sloan and his Ford sedan. Charlie covered the girls with rugs on the rear floor whenever a street patrol showed up, though it wasn't long before everyone knew what he had in the back seat, and looked the other way.

The depression caused the city to tighten its business belt, and one way to get a reasonably full working day out of the staff was to shut the cabarets a little earlier so that they might get some sleep before coming to work. A municipal bye-law, passed by the International Settlement, closed all cabarets at 2 a.m. So far, so good. But with the French Concession still running on the old timetable the temptation to make a night of it could be succumbed to by means of a short rickshaw ride, or in some cases by a walk across the street!

Gangsters all over the world find time hanging on their hands, especially around evening. In China's big cities existed a class of social parasites which hadn't quite made the grade as full-time gangsters, who hung around the fringe, scorning to work, picking up small bits of change here and there by making nuisances of themselves. In Shanghai they were known as pi-sehs (loafers) and

DAY OF FATE

they numbered thousands. They could be counted upon to join in any disturbance if only for the chance to gather in a bit of loot. The Chinese cabarets became their 'clubs'. Today it would be this one, tomorrow another. They moved around in small groups, ordering food and drink, often dancing with the professional hostesses, seldom paying for anything. Managements—and girls—knew better than to demand payment. All they hoped for was that some other place would claim their favour in a hurry, for while they remained decent customers stayed away.

Not so with the real gangsters. For them, the red carpet was laid down—especially for 'The Big Fellow', Tu Yueh-sen. As a dancer, the underworld boss was about as graceful as the mythical Green Dragon whom he represented. Yet he stepped out regularly and always appeared to be having the time of his life. But for the extraordinary precautions taken to protect Tu, one would never have suspected this man of heading a villainous organization the very name of which put fear into the hearts of hundreds of millions from Shanghai to Singapore.

Tu's comings and goings round the cabarets were something to see. Before setting out, managements were always advised by telephone of his coming, and they thought nothing of bluntly ordering customers to other tables if they happened to be occupying those needed for the gangster and his numerous entourage. Next a carload of advance bodyguards came and 'cased' the cabaret from kitchen to cloak-rooms, then took up stations to wait for the boss. Tu himself always travelled in a large, bullet-proof sedan, winter or summer, surrounded by more bodyguards, weapons in hand! The United States President had no better protection. Behind the leader's limousine a second carload of bodyguards travelled. Tu never got out until these had surrounded him. Then, with one at each elbow, he ventured to cross the footpath and enter the cabaret, where his men were posted at every door and turn. Inside, while he and his party sat at a front table, guards sat beside and behind, guns in plain view!

Although the gang boss was married he was always picking up new 'chickies', as my friend Tommy Suffolk used to say. Tommy was a weather-beaten old Yank of many summers and also an American institution. No one knew his real age though he often jokingly claimed to have been a bugler in the American Civil War. He was Shanghai agent for America's largest producer of carbon black and I mention his name here solely in order to describe an odd facet of trade relations in this great city. The bulk of Suffolk's buyers were Chinese ink manufacturers and, for those who don't know, Chinese 'ink' consists of solid blocks of almost pure carbon black. A Chinese 'pen' is a brush, and the trick is to dip the brush in water, pass it across the block of ink a couple of times, then apply it to the soft, absorbent rice-paper — from the top right-hand corner down to the bottom, of course, thereafter working over to the left and signing on the bottom, *left-hand* corner.

Once a year Suffolk's up-country Chinese buyers held a convention in Shanghai and in the pre-aerial days of travel some of them needed four months to make the round trip. In the first day or two they dribbled into the American agent's office, paying their respects over endless pots of green tea, and business was never mentioned while these felicitations lasted. They all brought gifts to Suffolk, whose leathery old face cracked into eternal smiles from the first arrival to the last departure. Buyers from silk-producing areas brought fine silks, from tea-producing areas the finest young-bud tea, from famed lacquer or *cloisonné* provinces magnificent samples of their wares. When the last buyer had made town and discharged his obligations to 'the ancient American'; when all accounts had been settled and new orders placed; then and only then did the convention hit

DAY OF FATE

the trail for the city's finest restaurants—Peking food one night, Cantonese the next, over to Foochow fare or some city restaurant specializing in a particular dish.

It is my considered opinion that the Chinese are the world's greatest party-givers and that the only Chinese who does not throw a dinner-party at some public restaurant every few weeks is a dead one. A houseboy who becomes father to a son will throw a bamboo roof over the alleyway in which he lives and turn it into a two-day banquet hall on a come-one, come-all basis. There is no jollier place in all China than a restaurant, once your ears have become accustomed to the sounds of belching and spitting. The latter is an accepted social custom, the former the highest method of praise for the host's menu. He would be very hurt if the rafters did not ring with gastronomic reverberations.

Before the coming of the cabarets, Chinese dinner-parties dragged on into the night with sing-song girls for entertainment on the one hand, and the opium couch on the other. Sing-song girls are—or were—to Chinese what *geisha* are to the Japs. The best of them had their own 'orchestra', a two-string wizard on a Chinese fiddle who followed them around from party to party, tearing the atmosphere apart in those gaps in the sing-song when the girl herself wasn't sending chills up and down the spine. These were possibly the original 'call-girls', for they went from restaurant to restaurant, hotel to hotel, jazzing up parties for the hosts, always in touch with headquarters like radio-controlled taxis. Their glossy private rickshaws dashed around the brilliantly lit central area of Shanghai, among the scores of hotels and restaurants, dazzling headlamps fore and aft, with often a hidden spotlight on the floor lighting up their fascinating little faces, the lotus blooms in their ebony hair and last but not least their glittering jewellery. To protect the gems from possible snatch-thieves, an extra runner always trotted behind, a hand clutching a corner of the pneumatic-wheeled, swift, softly gliding vehicle.

The most popular girls could look big Hollywood stars in the eye from the same income bracket. Their wealthy Chinese fans saw to that. Men like Tu Yueh-sen, for instance. When Tu took to terpsichore he made his favourite sing-song girls learn Western-style dancing, too. He took them around the town two, three and four at a time, all decked out in mink and diamonds; and Old Snake-eyes sure had an eye for beauty. He just loved listening to the gasps of surprise and admiration the crowd threw his way every time he went abroad among Shanghai's bright lights.

Of course there was rivalry between the Chinese cabarets. A new hostess with an overdose of pulchritude could run a ledger out of the red in a few weeks. This was one of the lessons soon learned by the native proprietors, and before the 'no poaching' law came into effect, Shanghai witnessed a classic duel between a cabaret which had two such aces and a cabaret which lured them across the line with unsportsmanlike enticements. Cabaret No. 1 promptly put a dent in the other's business in novel fashion one night, when lights were low. It hired a dozen *pih-sehs* to occupy front tables, masticate several hundred pellets of good, old-fashioned chewing-gum and on a given signal distribute this confectionery all over the dance-floor. The manoeuvre may justifiably be said to have completely gummed up the opposition for that night, which happened to be a big-spending public holiday. With characteristic Oriental patience, cabaret No. 2 allowed several months to pass, waiting for the next big holiday. Meanwhile it had laid the foundation for a cunning reprisal. Undercover 'guests' had established the practice of dipping all lights whenever patrons asked for 'Whistling in the Dark', a popular tune of the time. With the stage thus set, the cabaret crowded to the doors and business booming round the

DAY OF FATE

two runaway hostesses, lights were doused for 'Whistling in the Dark' — by request. The thieving rival got his just deserts in the shape of a sackful of little wriggly snakes let loose upon his floor to slither and slide around the ankles of his cash customers. Matters looked bad for a few moments after the lights went up and the snakes became a reality to the crowd on the dance-floor. Patrons did not stay long, either on the floor or in the building. It was a complete exodus and the score was even. But when they rounded up the reptiles, some fifty in number, all were found to be harmless water-snakes!

One could get a measure of Tu's exalted status in our city merely by being at the same cabaret. To watch the endless bowing and scraping by all who came near him reminded one of Roman Catholics genuflecting at a church altar. But the most sickening sight of all was that of important foreigners toeing the line to this monster, actually crossing the dance-floor to pay their respects to the man known to rule the underworld and control every kind of vice racket behind a façade of philanthropy and posture as a big business man, banker, patron of sport and charity organizer.

When World War II ended in the Pacific area and it was safe to return to Shanghai, Tu Yueh-sen was on the second plane out of Chungking; and when the British Minister to China held a victory celebration at the Embassy soon after, among those going around shaking hands with world diplomats and drinking goblets of victory wine was this same king of the underworld. After all, he had a certain right to celebrate victory. His 'boys' had, right through the Japanese occupation, made the Japs pay heavily for their invasion of China. But not even the power of Tu Yueh-sen could withstand the Reds. When Chiang Kai-shek's army lost the battle of Hsuchow in 1949 he knew the die was cast. Together with most of Shanghai's millionaires he fled to the safety of Britain's Hong Kong, and died there about a year later.

SHANGHAI SAGA

(Footnote on Hong Kong, *Time* magazine, November 21, 1960: 'But Hong Kong night life is hardly wild in the old Shanghai tradition. . . . At war's end (1945), Hong Kong was a wreck. It was saved by its Chinese refugees. Most of them were desperately poor, but among them were Shanghai business men and industrialists.')

5

THEATRE AND DOGS

LET US LOOK at 'theatre' in Shanghai for a while, particularly after World War I.

Before 1914, the locals had to fend very much for themselves and from this shortage grew the amateur theatricals already mentioned. Out of these efforts, in which bankers, brokers, *taipans* and tycoons played Gilbert and Sullivan with more gusto than most groups, grew in turn their own Lyceum Theatre, complete with lavish bar. After World War I came a great and endless procession of world celebrities—Chaliapin, Mabel Garrison, Elman, Kreisler, Heifetz, Zimbalist, the Denishawn Dancers, Galli-Gurci, McCormack, Moiseivitch, Lauder and dozens more. The *entrepreneur* responsible for importing all this fine entertainment was one A. Strok. All of these celebrated artists were satisfied to perform in Shanghai for little more than expenses, knowing of the small foreign community's inability to support a long season. (The 'gravy' was picked up in Japan and the Philippines.) By established custom ticket prices were always $5 (front stalls), $4 (dress circle) and $3 (back stalls).

We Shanghailanders think we may have been the only theatre public ever to have been 'dressed down' over the footlights by an artist of world stature over the prices being charged for admission. Who else but a Scotsman would have had the nerve? For his two weeks' season the late Sir Harry Lauder's advance agent raised prices to $6, $5 and $4. Consequently, Sir Harry opened to a half-filled theatre, which happened to include myself on a free press-pass. After the famous comedian finished his first song he stepped up to the footlights, and in his rich Scots accents lodged a personal complaint to his first-night audience for the city's failure to reward 'the wurrld's finest comedian' (his own words) with a full house. He emphasized that he thought he was worth the higher prices being asked, adding that he had no intention of reducing them. He also wounded local susceptibilities by agreeing to accept chits (I O U s) for tickets if we were short of cash!

His season ended two nights later!

Sometimes the Lyceum Theatre was not large enough for a visiting artist. One of these occasions was for that great Irish tenor, John McCormack; another for Austrian mind-reader and hypnotist Maximillian Langsner, who stirred up a lot of interest by driving around the city's streets blindfolded without accident. The night Maximillian turned them away from the Town Hall he had a white-tie-and-tails audience containing everyone in the upper social bracket plus all the highest diplomatic, consular, military, naval and police brass for miles around. This was the night and place that Bill Cassidy, deputy police commissioner of the International Settlement and habitual drunkard, chose to take on an extra load of liquor and seal his fate as a police officer. The little Austrian had reached a point in his highly entertaining programme at which he was demonstrating his power over birds and animals. He was about to put the quietus on a large White Orpington rooster when, from a side entrance, came the sound of voices raised in argument, plus several juicy British curses. A few heads turned, but Maximillian managed to hold his audience. But once more came the sound of angry voices and now all necks were craned, for the voices were definitely inside the hall.

'Silence!' begged the entertainer, pointing desperately to his

THEATRE AND DOGS

row of hypnotized fowls, but the crowd was more interested in watching Bill Cassidy come staggering down the side aisle, bouncing off the wall every couple of steps and heading for the Town Hall stage and Maximillian. He reached the steps leading up to the stage, stopped and swayed for a few seconds, then began a slow and very unsteady ascent. Ignoring him, Maximillian pointed to the white rooster still sitting contentedly on the stage floor. 'I have put the chicken (!) to sleep,' he cried proudly.

'Thash no chicken,' interrupted Cassidy, pointing down at the squatting Orpington with an unsteady finger. 'Thash a bloody Mongolian turkey!' He turned towards his elite audience and howled with glee at his own wit. Indeed, he waved so vigorously to his many Shanghai friends that he overbalanced and sat down alongside the rooster. At this everyone roared with delight, while the Austrian entertainer went around stroking his hypnotized fowls one at a time to keep the control. Then Cassidy slowly picked himself up off the floor and staggered down the steps from the stage where a police comrade waited to whisk him out of sight.

Poor old Bill Cassidy. It was said of China in those days that a man could go to pieces there faster than anywhere else, and two years after this incident an acquaintance of mine who ran a gambling den in Macao, Portuguese colony on the Pearl River near Canton, reported seeing Bill Cassidy in that 'Monte Carlo of the South China Sea'. He was peddling slot-machines and had a companion with him also previously known in Shanghai — a former public prosecutor of the International Settlement who for many years had been a boon companion and drinking-mate of Cassidy's. Thus are beachcombers born.

When the celebrated composer Rudolph Friml visited Shanghai in the thirties and became a familiar figure around the city's night-spots it was perhaps only coincidental that Hollywood's (and his) *Rose Marie* was being shown. It was interesting to note that a leading Chinese café renamed itself 'The Rose Marie' while one of the top-flight Chinese dance hostesses of the city advised her following henceforth to call her Rose Marie.

After the bludgeoning Shanghai received on Broadway, New York, in *The Shanghai Gesture* we had hopes of our great city recovering its reputation when Friml let it get around that' he had in mind a Chinese operetta. The idea, however, was contingent upon his finding a suitable Chinese girl to play the leading part. He twice visited Shanghai, hanging around the cabarets and other entertainment centres on the lookout for a likely candidate, but was unsuccessful. Much later Rogers and Hammerstein came up with the idea in 1959 with *Flower Drum Girl*.

Now, to live in China and not visit a Chinese theatre is as bad as going to Honolulu and not shooting the breakers on Waikiki beach. Yet there was a time in China when you could not take your wife or girl friend to the theatre. If you did you were sure to have her snatched from you at the entrance and hustled away to an upstairs balcony, where she would be locked up until after the show and released only when all men folk had left the theatre. Indeed, females were so surplus to theatre requirements that all female roles were played by male impersonators.

The Chinese theatre was loaded, even in our day, with what Westerners would call 'strange practices'. As an instance, at legitimate theatres no seats were ever booked in advance on the box-office plan system. Instead, recognized 'scalpers' took up large blocks of tickets and staked out positions in theatre vestibules to await the audience. Chinese drama had its regular followers, most of whom were known by sight to the scalpers, who could always be depended upon to provide the necessary

THEATRE AND DOGS

pasteboards. Patrons and scalpers developed associations over the years to a point where no scalper would have thought of cutting in on a colleague's clientele nor a patron dream of deserting his favourite pasteboard-pedlar, and this mutual-trust system explains why advance booking on Western lines was unnecessary.

Let me try to describe an ordinary visit to a Chinese theatre for a casual, unknown to any scalper. Upon entering the vestibule he will be spotted instantly as a stranger and literally mobbed by a couple of dozen eager scalpers characteristically attired in specially cut long coats, their hands clutching handfuls of seat-tickets. Having been 'claimed' by the scalper who yelled the loudest and, incidentally, having an arm almost torn off in the process, he will be drawn off to one side for the bargaining: a preliminary discussion to discover the customer's desires in the matter of seat position, number of seats required, whether he will be making one or several visits during the season, and so on—especially 'so on', for that means the amount of the tip the casual may be significantly waving around in the air during the discussion, above and beyond the price of tickets. That tip will govern the entire future relationship between scalper and patron should the latter intend becoming a regular and could mean the difference between standing unnoticed in a corner of the theatre vestibule until more worthy patrons have received attention.

If up to now negotiations have been satisfactory to the scalper, the patron gets his tickets and is conducted to the entrance door where the second bandit in the series, the usher, takes over and shows the patron his way to the seats allocated to him. Arrived at the seats the usher hands his patron over to bandit No. 3 in the chain, at the same time pocketing whatever tip his part in the hold-up has been deemed to be worth by the patron. Bandit No. 3 is the seat attendant, who from now on will look after the needs of his customer for the rest of the evening and he is a millionaire in the making. Having seen his patron or patrons safely seated, No. 3 crooks a regal finger at a towel-attendant, or shouts or whistles if necessary, to claim his attention. This worthy rushes up with a basket of hot, steaming, scented towels and each patron gets one to wipe street-dust or sweat from the face, or merely to counteract natural face-oil or B.O. Next a pot of hot, green tea is delivered, with the inevitable saucer of melon-seeds, and set on a small tray which is usually attached to the seat in front.

Most Chinese plays last five or six hours, beginning around 7 p.m. and ending after midnight. No actor worthy of note, however, would ever dream of treading the stage for more than a couple of hours of that time. Understudies keep the audience happy until the star's appearance and patrons customarily send servants along to occupy their seats from opening until around nine-thirty, at which time an audience may undergo an almost complete change as servants file out and master-patrons file in. The script, however, covers the whole evening and Chinese playwrights have to be sufficiently skilful to keep the play's highlights late enough to suit the needs of the star performer.

An audience soon knows when a star is about to make his appearance, for a great commotion sweeps through the theatre. First, the understudies start packing up and quitting the stage. Stagehands begin dismantling scenery and other ancient-looking trappings, sufficient for the servant audience — and the casuals. No one bothers to lower a curtain to hide all these activities. Then in place of the greasy-looking, moth-eaten drapes hitherto used new and gorgeous draperies of rich silk and brocade tapestries start going up, worthy of the stars about to take their place on stage. Such trappings are frequently the gifts of admiring patrons. In former times even His Imperial Majesty bestowed stage decorations upon favoured actors, who derived much

THEATRE AND DOGS

publicity from the fact.

Loud 'Ah's' and 'Oh's' greet the gorgeous fabrics being hung. Stage managers dash back and forth — all in sight of the audience sipping its tea and munching its melon-seeds — shouting directions to the stage crew. Even the orchestra is changed, the newcomers exhibiting due scorn for the second-raters making their noisy exit. For wherever actors in Mei Lan-fang's class tour, they take along the nation's best fiddlers, flautists, cymbal-smiters and operators of the rest of the weird Oriental assortment of stage instruments.

So complete is the change for the imminent appearance of the great one that it includes even those who do nothing more than stand by on the side of the stage (not in the wings!) ready to carry a bowl of hot tea or steaming, scented towel to any performer who suddenly feels the need of either, or both. (While a play is proceeding these menials wander about stage totally indifferent to the audience, placing props in position according to the script, which they know by heart like altar boys in church.)

Then, with almost everything in place, sit-in servants out of the theatre and all true patrons waiting expectantly in their seats for the coming big moment, a hush spreads over the vast theatre. The audience, one might say, has been 'conditioned' by the stage goings-on, which thousands of years of Chinese drama have proved to have sound audience-value.

Suddenly, out of nowhere, while everyone stares with fixed eye at both wings, unsure of the direction of the star's entrance, come a few shrill excerpts from one of the play's musical numbers — then dead silence again. It is a neat, professional Chinese theatre trick which never fails to make an audience turn mental handsprings in sheer ecstasy; sure-fire stuff, guaranteed to bring the house down in thunderous applause. At the height of this, and gauging the moment nicely from long years of experience, the great one steps on to the stage in full view of his tensed fans.

For the next sixty to ninety minutes the audience is mesmerized by truly gifted performances, carrying the script along to that point where the playwright has left the opening for the star's exit. The play is not over. It may have another hour or two to run. But it will have to stagger on to its finish without its star, who bows out to thunderous applause even as the stage crews return to strip the stage of the expensive drapes and throw back the stock scenery for those who intend remaining to watch the show to its end. Stock players pick up the thread of the story, hack musicians file into their seats again. Teapots are refilled, melon-seeds replaced and perfumed towels resume their aerobatics in all directions.

Brief appearances like this have taught Mei Lan-fang and other stage veterans in China that it is good for one's professional reputation (and bank account) to leave an audience with tongue hanging out for just a little more of you. By the same token leading actors never sign long-term contracts. A month is usually considered the limit. Day-to-day arrangements are preferred, thus leaving them free to go from one theatre to another for very limited 'seasons'.

In some old-fashioned Peking theatres, instead of rows of seats, the audience sits at rows of tables set at right angles to the stage, fulfilling the Oriental conception of theatre as something to be heard, rather than seen! It all depends upon the play, and, moreover, most plays contain much pantomime, which has to be watched to be understood. A mountain, for example, is represented in a certain position by a table; a waving oar as a boat in motion. At times, maybe when the budget is low, a 'garden' might be nothing more than a crude sign hung upon the back of a chair stating so.

THEATRE AND DOGS

Elaborate scenery as the West knows it began creeping into the Chinese theatre in the 1930's when producers discovered it to be a draw-card and good for business. Indeed, some actors began complaining that theatres were giving top billing to scenery instead of to them. Not, however, in the case of Mei Lan-fang and others in his class.

One feature of the Chinese theatre unlikely ever to change is the small altar placed out of audience view on stage, to which every actor goes to pay his respects both entering and leaving a theatre.

Once upon a time the Chinese theatre made no effort to warm its customers even in a freezing Peking winter. It told the customers to crowd closer together and warm each other up. Now there was a place for a young man to spend an evening, but for the miserable fact that no females were permitted to occupy seats in the auditorium! In olden times the emperor, and even wealthy patrons, had their private theatres and to be invited to play a 'command' performance in one of these was, naturally, the height of an actor's ambition.

Theatre censors in ancient times had many strange regulations; for example: every new play had to be passed by the censor before public presentation and, once passed, not one word could be changed. 'In case riots broke out,' the censors said. No woman arriving at a theatre unaccompanied by a man was admitted. Those who came with menfolk were detached from the men at entrance doors and taken to a special balcony upstairs from where they watched the show all together. Finally, they had to make their exit from a different direction to avoid all possibility of meeting male patrons.

The organization of these old-fashioned theatres was peculiar in itself. First there was the group which included the owner of the land on which the theatre was built, and the production's backer. Next there was the group handling advertising and seating, of which we already know something. A third group attended to the production and direction of the play, including everything which happened on the stage. This group handled players' contracts, all concessions including ticket-scalpers, door, cloak-room, tea and towel attendants, programme sellers and — a most important person — an audience-checker whose job was to count heads in an audience and check the number against tickets sold, to cut down on 'Annie Oakleys', no doubt.

Groupers handling the play selected the cast, but they had a strange way of rehearsing. Principal actors studied their lines at home and a staff of strict supervisers circulated around their homes daily, checking up on their practice hours and their progress! Stage rehearsals as Western theatre knows them were unheard of since leading actors counted it loss of 'face' to practise their art in the presence of lesser lights in the business. As opening day drew near the script runners doubled up on their visits to the actors, reporting back to anxious managers on the readiness of each to open the show. Supporting players rehearsed in ordinary fashion on stage at the theatre, watched by the group responsible for staging the play, the same being also responsible for prop-shifters, wardrobe-masters, make-up- men and wig-makers.

When air-conditioning first reached Shanghai, where the humidity in summer reaches a point at which three or four changes of clothing a day are necessary, a movie theatre with a fine, comfortable intermission lounge was among the first buildings to have it installed.

Promptly at four o'clock every afternoon one of the city's *taipans* bought an upstairs ticket, pulled a comfortable armchair into a corner and went to sleep for several hours at a stretch, seven days a week. He explained to me that for the first time since coming to Shanghai ten years earlier he was able to sleep

THEATRE AND DOGS

in comfort during summer! Around 10 or 11 p.m. each night he awoke refreshed, drove off to the members' rooms at the nearby Shanghai Race Club, had a grill, then stepped out into the nightlife of the city until dawn, when he returned to the race club to watch his race-ponies have their morning gallop.

Race-ponies!

These were too much a part of life in Shanghai to be overlooked.

When Genghis Khan's warlike hordes overran Asia and parts of Europe in the thirteenth century, they were able to cover vast distances because they rode the backs of sturdy little Mongolian ponies able to carry great weight. Like 150 pounds over a mile in 2.02/4.5 secs., for instance, the Shanghai race record for one of these (13.2 hands) quadrupeds, lassoed on the Siberian steppes and shipped to Shanghai for the pleasure and amusement of its race fans.

On the exact spot where the American adventurer Ward fought off the Taiping rebels and saved Shanghai from disaster in 1861, its citizens later built a luxurious race-track with huge blocks of two-storied brick stables where the shaggy little beasts from the wild North lived in coddled comfort. It can truly be said that the Shanghai Race Club was one of the mainsprings of social life in our city and any young *griffin* wanting to advance himself in a hurry needed but to show prowess in the saddle. As late as 1930 big *hongs* (corporations) like Jardine, Matheson, Butterfield & Swire, Arnold & Company and even the mighty Hong Kong & Shanghai Banking Corporation raced ponies in the name of their firms and the silks worn by their riders represented.

The backbone of pony-racing in China was, however, the private owner-trainer-rider. In other words, the 'gentleman jockey'. For today's equivalent of U.S.$250 any local lad who fancied himself as another Johnny Longden or Steve Donoghue could purchase an untried, half wild Mongolian pony and have a go at it with the Shanghai Race Club's blessing. The S.R.C. actually fostered the set-up. It had professional horse-traders out catching the shaggy wild ponies all year round in Mongolia, shipping the hard-mouthed little beasts twice yearly to racetracks at Mukden, Harbin, Tientsin, Peking, Hankow and Shanghai.

Up in Mukden, capital of Manchuria ruled by ex-bandit Chang Tso-lin, was a British ex-army officer retained by the ex-bandit to teach his troops how to use the deadly trench mortars which previously he had taught Chang Tso-lin to make so well that no one dared invade his territory (except the Japanese, who in 1931 blew up a train containing the Manchurian ruler and annexed the whole of his rich domain).

'One-armed Sutton' they called this soldier of fortune who had lost an arm to one of his own trench bombs. He was another of England's 'mad Englishmen' who go out in the midday sun, dress up for dinner in the jungle or play cricket at the South Pole. Sutton raced and rode ponies and owned Bengal, champion of all North China race-tracks; but was never willing to bring him to Shanghai to meet Warrenfield, Shanghai champion raced by Henry Morris, owner of English Derby (1925) winner Manna at nine to one! Shanghai cleaned up on Manna, urged on by cables from Morris in England. Most of us got the early odds of twenty-five to one and the only Shanghai resident to miss out, it seems, was a well-to-do sportsman and 'man-about-town' who for some strange reason took a set against the Morris horse and laid a heavy 'book' against the favourite. And like the deputy police commissioner and public prosecutor of previous mention, the daring bookmaker likewise ended up virtually 'on the beach'.

(Parenthetically, I should mention that Shanghai had a special fund to aid such men with free passage back to their home country, wherever it might be and no nationality barred. In the

THEATRE AND DOGS

Monte Carlo manner, so to speak. Unfortunately, most of the failures refused to accept the gift, Shanghai was that sort of a place: it was too hard to part from.)

There is something very difficult to describe about racing in which your city's biggest *taipans* and tycoons get up and go for their lives round a race-track against mounts owned and ridden by small business men, bank clerks, even their own employees! One of the toughest riders to beat in a whipping finish was sixty-year-old shipping magnate Eric Moller (Moller Steamships) who turned the scales at 160 lb. and never gave up until he passed the post, frequently in front! But that was old man Moller's character. World War I ruined him when he lost a small but promising fleet of ships. Out of near bankruptcy, it is said, he worked up a second fleet of ships, paid up every last cent and was well established in time for World War II and its fat charter-rates.

Doctors, lawyers, judges, millionaire merchants, *taipans*, tycoons, rode not only at race meetings but at early morning workouts. The mammoth two-storey brick buildings provided by the race club sufficed for everybody's stabling needs and Chinese and Russian *mafoos* (stable-hands) were available for hire as assistant trainers. Part of their job was, naturally, all the dirty work around the stable as well as ordinary grooming and walking exercises. For this member-owners paid a low monthly fee to the race club, and tips to *mafoos* depended in large measure upon the success of one's 'stable'.

This set-up was so unique that it is worth more than passing mention. When word reached the club of an impending new shipment of Mongolian race ponies, for example, the club invited subscribers for them at an average price of U.S. $250. You bought a 'pig in a poke' for sure! And therein was the lure. After all ponies had been vetted and declared reasonably healthy and sound in limb if not wind (!), each pony was branded with a number. On an appointed day about a week later, and in the presence of many hundreds of members, club officials from a lottery barrel drew a pony number against each subscriber's name. That was it. That was your race-pony! You took your number around the club stables housing these *griffin* ponies until you located something probably everyone was laughing at. They had reason to, most times. No thoroughbred of the Western turf which has been out to grass for six months could look rougher or less like a racehorse than the Mongolian *griffins* in those first few weeks. Over the bar every day thereafter owners compared notes on their purchases, reporting progress or otherwise.

The great advantage of the system was that it gave the salaried bank clerk an equal opportunity with the *taipan* of getting his hands on a future blue-ribbon winner. Ex-Cossacks from European Russia and Mongolian horsemen alike were invaluable to inexperienced owners, and expert handling on their part greatly reduced the time needed to get the newcomers into racing shape for the *griffin* races at spring or autumn race meets, each lasting ten days: ten days when all banks and foreign businesses closed from 11 a.m. and Shanghai commerce was virtually dead.

Apart from a drainage-moat and a few buildings here and there the city's racecourse had no barriers to keep out the public at large. Because of this every race meeting saw smart concessionaires erect crude public stands and cash in on the rubber-neck. Needless to say, the aforesaid concessionaires had an interest in laying the odds to anyone so inclined. The strength of mouth of the little Mongolian ponies earned the greatest respect from all who ever tried to ride them; and I have seen more than one bolt twice around a mile track after a false start with its eleven- or twelve-stone rider powerless to stop it. Until the 1930's all race-ponies were known as 'China ponies',

THEATRE AND DOGS

an official definition that meant 'Ponies, fourteen hands or over on measurement after classification (by the club's inspection committee)'. Then, gradually, crossbreds crept in, and to avoid utter confusion these had to be classified as separate racing material.

Chinese hammered hard for admittance at the door of the Shanghai Race Club, and when full membership continued to be denied them they opened up an opposition track in Chinese territory, naming Green Dragon boss Tu Yueh-sen as their patron. There was already in existence an International Racing Club in the outer suburbs which had the full support of both foreign and Chinese race fans. But it irked Chinese owners to be refused membership in the exclusive city headquarters of all Shanghai's pony-racing, and the launching of the Chinese Jockey Club by undergang boss Tu was their way of declaring independence. The public, however, which keeps racing going anywhere, had learned where they got the best run for their money, and the parent organization suffered little from this newcomer to the sport.

As if track-racing were not enough in itself, Shanghai's 'mad Englishmen', aided and abetted by almost as many Americans and sporting Europeans, went in enthusiastically for cross-country riding and paper-chasing. At such times they put on a first-class show for the yokels out in the paddy-fields with their scarlet coats, black velvet caps and white corduroy breeches. The yokels soon knew what to do whenever they saw the paper-layers scampering across the countryside around noon. They congregated around any water ditches on the paper trail and sat patiently waiting for the afternoon's crop of ditch divers. (If you'd ever seen inside a Chinese ditch you'd understand their interest.) They also picked up an odd dollar or two retrieving runaway ponies separated at such points from their riders.

Once there used to be near-riots when the tally-ho parties cut a path through the farmers' crops, but amicable arrangements were made whereby late riders rode the trail assessing damage and paying immediate compensation to any farmer sustaining damage to crops, livestock or poultry.

My friend, Assistant Police Commissioner Springfield (Canton Road opium case), himself a successful jockey and keen cross-country rider, brought back from holiday in Ireland one year a small shipload of trained foxhounds. For these, instead of foxes, they laid an artificial trail of beastly smelling asafoetida. I've got to hand it to the hounds. Getting through the natural aroma of the native countryside to the asafoetida was a tribute to their pedigrees. But they made it.

Cross-country riding differed in several respects from track racing, but the point at which the two met was the inclusion of Shanghai's womenfolk at the foxhunts, and Chinese from the right strata of society. Not Tu Yueh-sen, however. Although he was patron of the Chinese Jockey Club, the day never dawned when the old opium-smoking secret-society leader got up on the back of a pony in China — racer or hack. The betting system in use was the pari-mutuel, whereby all investments were pooled, 10 per cent drained off the gross as the club's 'take', the remainder being divided according to a standard percentage formula, win and place money remaining separate throughout.

The all-powerful stewards of the club gave generously to charity throughout the year, and I doubt whether there ever existed another list of public bequests like that which they compiled twice each year. Every six months the club donated over $175,000 to foreign and Chinese charities out of its average $2,000,000 take from the annual public investment of around $20,000,000.

The city's race-track was more than just that. It was our

THEATRE AND DOGS

principal recreation-ground as well. Where the gallant American adventurer Frederick Townsend Ward fought the bloody battle of Muddy Flat in 1861 and drove off the Taiping rebels, in later years the people of Shanghai played their Rugby, soccer, baseball, polo, cricket, hockey, bowls and golf. In summer the grassland was subdivided into a hundred tennis courts, and temporary bamboo clubrooms went up for the season of outdoor barbecues and hot-weather entertainments. In 1927, when Chiang Kai-shek's southern army advanced upon the city and none knew what the morrow might bring forth, the defence army used the area as an aerodrome for scout planes borrowed from an aircraft-carrier in port.

Now that the Reds have taken over, the clubrooms have become 'houses of Chinese culture and museums', the giant concrete stands regularly fill with Chinese citizens for hate sessions against the 'enemies of China', while the sixty or more acres of recreation-ground have been over-planted with trees and re-designed as a native parkland. And over in what used to be the French Concession, the once magnificent 'Canidrome' greyhound race-track has also been turned into an instrument of anti-foreign hatred. This fine concrete amphitheatre became a people's tribunal when the Reds first took over. Fifty thousand Communist stooges daily poured into the Canidrome — what an inspired name for a dog-track! — to watch the daily denunciations of 'capitalist landlords' and 'foreign stooges'; son against father, employee against boss.

It was the 'People's Court' and it sentenced thousands to death while the campaign of terror lasted.

Shanghai always did things differently! Even with its dog-racing. It was typical of the spirit of its citizens that even when the future looked so black in 1926 after passing through the crisis of the May 30, 1925, affair at Louza police station, followed by a crippling general strike and months of anti-foreign riots, there were those who planned to introduce a new sport just then gripping England — greyhound racing. Unbeknown to each other because of the policy of secrecy, three separate companies were formed to open dog-tracks in Shanghai — two in the International Settlement, one in Frenchtown. And just as a matter of interest the man behind Luna Park (one of the international tracks) part-owned the Majestic Hotel of which I have already written, and was responsible for our Saturday night songfests under the baton of our little negro from New York.

In the race to open first, Luna Park won by three months and claimed the all-important Saturday night for its own. Second to open in the International Settlement, the Stadium entered upon a sure market, for Luna Park had already proved itself as an investment. Indeed, the Chinese had gone greyhound crazy!

Unlike other countries where the dogs race, China had no owners, breeders or trainers of its own. Thus came into being the first scheme of its kind in the world under which the track itself provided kennels, trainers and veterinaries. All that was left for an owner to do was pay a monthly bill for the lot.

As with the ponies, so with the dogs. Club membership was wide open. To become an owner one had first to become a member. The first shiploads of greyhounds, from England and Ireland, went into the lottery barrel like the ponies. The clubs played no favourites. No owner ever touched his dog except for an occasional pat at kennel soirees every Sunday morning when the club rolled out the barrel under a giant marquee. Six trainers, all English importations and each with upwards of fifty dogs in his care, keenly competed for their 10 per cent of stake money won by the animals they handled.

Six months after starting both tracks were holding two meetings weekly and packing the cash customers in, with free

THEATRE AND DOGS

ice-cream and hand fans given away on hot nights and unlimited complimentary tickets on application. A 25 per cent dividend went to Luna Park stockholders at the end of the first year's operation, 50 per cent the second!

After running a form sheet for my newspaper covering Luna Park dogs, I was invited to become a permanent at the track, with a multiple assignment embracing the starter's job, publicity and a continuation of the form sheet. I took it. Six months later the racing manager, an English importation, went out, his second in command moved up and I went in as his assistant, keeping all the old assignments, but adding to them the occasional task of handicapper.

By now Saturday nights in Shanghai were 'Luna Park nights', white-tie-and-tails affairs at which Mr. and Mrs. Everybody made a point of being present. As an added attraction we invited visiting celebrities to make presentations of trophies, and made sure that there was at least one special prize at every meeting. Among the many who performed this chore for us were the great golf champions of the 1920's, Walter Hagen and his wizard showman companion, Joe Kirkwood Snr.

Our membership list resembled a Who's Who in diplomacy, with an impressive collection of foreign ministers plenipotentiary, consuls, judges, as well as every *taipan*, foreign or Chinese, in the great city.

Sir Victor Sassoon, fresh from India on a Far Eastern business survey, held a strong kennel at Luna Park, his dogs being identifiable by 'V.S.' names, such as Veiled Secret, Very Soon, Very Slippy. We did not know it then, but the wealthy cotton magnate was over from India laying plans for a wholesale transfer of capital from British India, which occurred a couple of years later. (By that time, unfortunately, Luna Park had ceased to exist!)

One day the Luna Park management received an ultimatum

from a mysterious source. The new Nanking Government, the directors were informed, not recognizing any foreign concession in China, proposed taxing the two dog-tracks in the International Settlement as though they were in Chinese territory, and the assessment mentioned was a staggering sum. But, secure in the belief that its written franchise from the foreign-controlled municipal council of the Settlement would be honoured, the directors of Luna Park rejected the Chinese overtures, which they termed 'blackmail'. The Stadium, second track in the International Settlement, followed suit. Within a week of these refusals, the Chinese Press opened a campaign against the two foreign-owned tracks, accusing them of 'fostering gambling among the Chinese people'. For several weeks the native editors sailed in under the cracking whips of some unseen force, crusading against the dog-tracks. Someone with a sense of the dramatic planted unsuccessful dog-race tickets on some of the dead bodies to be found every morning in the river or on the streets of Shanghai, insisting that these were suicides because of the dog-track losses!

We knew that the Western powers had granted tariff autonomy, returned the Mixed Courts, opened parks to Chinese and enlarged the city councils to include Chinese members. Nevertheless, we were shocked to learn that they were seriously considering closing down the dog-tracks because of this outrageous campaign being fought by the native Press on behalf of someone in Nanking. And this in spite of written franchises! Our directors were men with their ears close to the political ground, and in my own case I was given a personal tip from the highest source to unload any dog-track shares I might be holding—pronto!

The authorities closed Luna Park by force, little more than two years after its opening, barricading all roads which led to

THEATRE AND DOGS

the track on the night of the next meeting. The Stadium, so built that its back stretch overlapped the Settlement boundary into Chinese territory, was put to death by the Chinese themselves simply placing a squad of local gendarmes over the back fence and taking up a position across the grass track. The bottom fell out of the greyhound market on the Stock Exchange, $25 shares diving from their peak of $75 to $1 overnight.

The two victimized tracks joined in a lawsuit against the Shanghai Municipal Council for breach of contract, plus damages, naming a sum approximating U.S. $1,000,000 at the prevailing exchange rate. Naturally, the case never reached the courts. The plaintiffs finally decided not to send good money after bad, realizing that the only 'court' allowed under the existing treaties to try such a case would comprise judges from among the foreign consuls — the Consular Court; the very same men — or body — which had decided the case beforehand by bowing to the demands of the Chinese. A classic example, one might say, of throwing away the lifebelts to lighten the sinking ship!

Frenchtown had its own dog-track operating by now, of course, a luxurious affair of concrete stands with 50,000 capacity, vast kennel-space and training ground. A syndicate of Frenchmen, Britons and Chinese purchased what had been the private riding-track of millionaire Henry Morris, (Manna 1925, Derby winner) in the centre of Frenchtown. On this they built the Canidrome. Its main grandstand contained the very latest in members' amenities, with spacious dining-rooms and ballroom atop the big stand, glass-fronted to permit a view of the racing.

Another member of the syndicate was Mexican Carlos Garcia, operator of Shanghai's principal roulette establishment, 'The Wheel', later to be the scene of some excitement also. Garcia put up the bulk of the money and remained the principal stockholder for years, but used a 'straw-man' on the board of directors, to whom he delegated his authority.

The difference in treaty positions between the International Settlement and the French Concession could not be better revealed than in this Chinese effort to close all dog-tracks in Shanghai for their failure to pay up the 'squeeze' demanded. When the two international tracks turned down the proposal, the Chinese put on 'squeeze' of another sort, as I have stated, and closed the two tracks whose directors later admitted their mistake in not agreeing to pay the blackmail. The French track, on the other hand, conscious of its own 'sovereign' position, answerable only to Paris through the French Minister to China, told the Chinese to go peddle their papers and that was that! The Canidrome continued to operate, and most successfully, from its opening in November 1928 until the Japanese took over the city in the Sino-Japanese war, promptly on the day after Pearl Harbour was bombed, December 7, 1941.

With the closing of Luna Park I went back to newspaper work, and one of my colleagues for this new spell was Demaree C. Bess, now foreign editor of the *Saturday Evening Post*, famous American weekly.

Meanwhile Carlos Garcia, operating what was known as The Wheel at 151 Bubbling Well Road, secure in the knowledge that as a Mexican he was immune from prosecution for running a roulette establishment, was about to have the rung pulled from under him.

The Wheel was conducted on lavish lines though Garcia, either through a sixth sense or from force of habit, always 'screened' customers through the standardized peephole in the door as though, deep down, he anticipated trouble some time or other. His clientele included the highest of high society. White, yellow, brown, black or brindle made no difference; the city's biggest gamblers included all races, and their money looked alike to the

THEATRE AND DOGS

soft-spoken Mexican. Telephone, and one of The Wheel's fleet of limousines was at your door in ten minutes to carry you there. Turkey dinners, wine and cigars were always 'on the house', for no doubt Garcia found that recklessness invariably accompanied intoxication. The small Portuguese woman who sat wrapped in her shawl playing small stakes to a system every night received the same treatment as the *taipan* dropping thousands. She invariably won, too.

After what had happened to Luna Park and The Stadium the method employed to get rid of Garcia and The Wheel came as no surprise to Shanghai. Without warning, and acting on instructions issued through the 'consular crowd' to police of the International Settlement, Garcia's place was suddenly barricaded shortly before midnight one Saturday while gambling was at its peak. Instead of breaking in, police officials placed a table and chairs at the main entrance, other exits being covered. At the table sat a deputy police commissioner with a Shanghai directory, notebook, pen and ink and a hurricane lamp to light up proceedings.

When word reached players in The Wheel of downstairs happenings, a steady exodus began. Every person leaving was asked for proof of name, address and nationality. The city directory was there to check up on all information and to deter any 'Davy Crocketts' or 'Li'l Abners' from registering. Then, for the first time, Garcia discovered the awful truth — that Mexico had abandoned extra-territoriality suddenly and without warning and by doing so had stripped him of his only protection. He was, and had been for at least twenty-four hours, virtually a Chinese citizen. He had even been permitted to go on breaking the law unknown to himself, and extenuating though this circumstance was it did not save Garcia from a twelve months' jail sentence!

As a sequel to The Wheel episode, more than sixty British

patrons of the casino caught in the net that night appeared in the British Consular Court subsequently. All were let off with a caution as to the consequences of a second appearance for a similar offence.

I had not been long back at newspaper work before the Canidrome offered me a position involving multiple duties similar to those which had first taken me to Luna Park. First, they required a starter with experience. As there were only two in the Far East, and as the second necessary qualification was 'experience in publicity', the field narrowed down to me. Before long I was, in addition to starting, also handling the track's advertising, producing a weekly dog-race magazine distributed gratis among the fans, and acting as steward at all trials and race meetings. The aggregate return for these manifold activities was very gratifying: especially the lack of regular office hours which, in a place like Shanghai, with its alluring night-life, made the job a sinecure among sinecures.

Nevertheless, when my friend Tetsu Kusakari, a former Luna Park member and greyhound enthusiast, came to me in 1933 and asked me to help him start a dog-track up in Dairen, chief port of the Kwangtung Peninsula at the top of the Yellow Sea, I gave him a good hearing. Kusakari was a member of that exclusive Shanghai clan known as 'exchange brokers'. Its social status in the community can, perhaps, best be gauged when I say among its most active members was Henry Morris, mentioned earlier as owner of English Derby winner Manna, and a dozen other 'gold' dollar millionaires.

These brokers bought and sold foreign currency by the million and they were easily picked out of the razzle-dazzle city traffic, because they dashed around the banking district in low-slung, four-wheel carriages dragged by snappy little cast-off Mongolian racing ponies. Quaintly dressed Chinese coachmen

THEATRE AND DOGS

wearing imitation mandarin hats sat high on the driver's seat, but the broker invariably stood up in his carriage with one foot hanging over the side ready to drop off and dash up the steps of the next bank of call, even before his carriage stopped. Time being the essence of their every contract, exchange brokers found this the speediest means of getting round the city, closing deals which could swing from profit to loss in a matter of minutes.

Kusakari's own 'office' was a peach. It was a boarded-up section under the back stairs of a Japanese bank. But it was on the ground, and saved Kusakari precious minutes every time he had to dash from bank to bank signing, buying or selling contracts for foreign exchange. He had no less than sixteen direct telephone lines hooked up under the stairs and three assistants to help in the foot-running business which followed every deal started on the telephone. In that fast and furious trading no one recognized any contract which was not in black-and-white!

There were Japanese mats on the floor of this 'office' and on these sat his three assistants (when they were not out on the run with a contract!). Only the boss himself rated a table and chair and even he had to get down on his knees at times to use a telephone low down under the stairs which formed the ceiling of his headquarters.

But Kusakari was a wealthy man. He also raced ponies and was a member of the important Shanghai Race Club. He lived Western-style in a large French-owned apartment house, his son was a health officer in the Shanghai Municipal Council and his charming daughter attended a foreign school. The dog-racing bug bit him badly when he saw the phenomenal success which met its introduction to Shanghai. He quickly rustled up a syndicate of influential Japs in Tokyo after Luna Park closed and between them they started wooing the bigwigs of Dairen.

Dairen was but another name for Port Arthur of unhappy

memory since the Russo-Japanese war of 1898, when Admiral Togo and his 'barbaric' fleet sank the mighty Far East squadrons of the Tsar. The Japs renamed the warm-water port of the Liaotung Peninsula Dairen. It was the great port through which Japan poured men, materials and munitions into that part of the Asiatic mainland known as the Kwangtung Leased Territory. The Japanese military ruled the territory and permission for any kind of commercial activity had first to be obtained from the Japanese military governor of the territory.

When Kusakari approached me so excitedly one night at the Canidrome—a little the worse for liquor I might add—it was to confide in me the long-awaited information that a licence to open a dog-track in Dairen had finally been issued to his syndicate. I then appreciated his condition the more. Would I, asked Kusakari, go with him to Dairen and help him run his dog-track? He promised me *carte blanche* on the racing side of the business, a long contract and most attractive terms. I asked for forty-eight hours to think it over and in that time I went to see my Canidrome boss who was, of course, Carlos Garcia's 'strawman'. He agreed that it was an unusual opportunity, but warned me to hold out for a percentage of the gross turnover, which had been the means of making him a millionaire at the Canidrome, small though his percentage was.

A month or two later I turned over my Canidrome job to my successor, and sailed for Hong Kong. There, I had to pick up the Osaka Shosen Kaisha's s.s. *Melbourne Maru* for Australia, where I was supposed to buy all the greyhounds required for starting business at our new track in Dairen.

For seven months Kusakari kept me hanging around in Sydney and his cash remittances were tardy in coming and smaller than expected. An occasional letter spoke of 'difficulties' and I soon got the feeling that all was not as it should have been.

THEATRE AND DOGS

Meanwhile I had more than a couple of hundred greyhounds 'on a string', with deposits paid, owners being permitted to race them until call-up day. Then Kusakari cabled me to dissolve all commitments and return to Shanghai; but there was no mention of any funds, or how I was to get back. Fortunately I found a ship sailing for China in a couple of days. I quickly sold my car and bought my own ticket, advising Kusakari accordingly.

On return to Shanghai the old fellow was apologetic and very despondent. It appeared that there had been a change of military command in the Kwangtung Leased Territory and the governor to whom they had paid their 'licence fee' had already returned to the mainland of Japan with the fee, leaving Kusakari's syndicate to start negotiations all over again. I gathered that most of the money had come from his own pocket and that it had made quite a dent in his bankroll. To aggravate the situation, the incoming military governor had a reputation which foreboded ill for anyone wishing to introduce gambling in any shape or form. In short, Dairen was out.

Fortunately for me, my successor at the Canidrome city job was of that ilk which favoured Bacchus and the management were relieved when I agreed to assume my old 'burdens' once more. The race-track, I discovered, was facing stiff competition on the gambling front from a Latin-American organization offering *hai-alai* to the public seven nights weekly with matinees every Sunday. *Hai-alai*, for the uninitiated, supposedly originated among the Basques of Spain. It is played on an indoor court using the floor (wood) and a three-sided, concrete court. Spectators occupy the fourth side, the galleries being protected by strong wire netting from floor to ceiling, some fifty feet high. The two end walls of the court are faced with a special concrete-and-cement mixture of secret formula so that the ball, similar to a baseball in appearance and size and covered with specially treated goatskin, rebounds with terrific speed after being hurled against them.

Players wear a *cesta*, or long, curved hollow basket strapped to their throwing arm. Teams line up, and on a signal from the umpire opponents alternately gather in the ball and hurl it back against the right end wall, leaving an opponent to gather it in, either direct or on the first bounce, repeating this operation until a player falters. For thrills and excitement there is nothing better than a night among the *hai-alai* gymnasts.

In Shanghai, *hai-alai* headquarters was in their own auditorium, mentioned in my introduction as the place where Californian Four-Square Gospeller Aimee Semple McPherson tried to convert Shanghai—unsuccessfully. To combat *hai-alai* competition and keep the attention of Shanghai's gamblers constantly focussed upon the greyhounds, the Canidrome stepped up production to four meetings weekly in addition to Sunday afternoon matinées.

The policy of inviting prominent visitors to Shanghai to attend the Canidrome and present trophies—initiated by Luna Park years earlier—had never been allowed to lapse and the Frenchtown track had its share of celebrities. I well remember the night Frank ('Bring 'em Back Alive') Buck came to the Canidrome. His host was Australian surgeon 'Doc' O'Hara, one of the city's biggest gamblers and a friend of mine. As soon as O'Hara and his distinguished guest entered the members' enclosure, the 'Doc' spotted me sitting in my usual seat in the official box and he accosted me, race-book in hand.

'I want a few tips,' he grinned. 'Gotta friend with me.'

I grinned back. 'You ought to know better than to come to me,' I told him. 'From here, every dog has a chance to win.'

'Well, put it this way, you bloody high-and-mighty,' 'Doc' persisted. 'I know nothing. That makes you better than me, or

THEATRE AND DOGS

you wouldn't be sitting up there. Right?'

'Okay,' I said. 'But remember, I'm only saving your face because of your friend.'

Now this one is worthy of Ripley. I scanned the entries and one of the first names to attract my notice was The Buck, a dog entered for the fifth, or next, race.

I ran my eyes over the opposition and thought the dog had drawn too bad a starting-box to justify the kind of support the 'Doc' usually gave to his fancies.

Nonetheless, I told O'Hara: 'Number three in the fifth might claim your attention. But it's only a hunch.'

The 'Doc' studied his book for a few seconds, read the name, then looked up at me and grinned amusedly.

'He'll do,' he said, and walked off.

The result is obvious, or I wouldn't be telling this. The Buck appeared to have little chance as the field came around the last turn, but with an electrifying final burst the big red dog pushed through a tightly packed field in a finish of heads and short heads to get the decision, at four to one. So, of course, I had to accept the 'Doc's' invitation to get out of my box, go down and join him and Frank Buck, big-game hunter en route to the Malay Archipelago to bring back more jungle animals — alive.

Then we had Madame Wellington Koo, wife of the distinguished Chinese Ambassador (London, Washington) step on to the track and make a presentation one night: Betty Compson, Hollywood star, and other celebrities on other occasions also.

But suddenly big changes occurred at the Canidrome. In 1936 Ike, the managing director and my friend, told me that he was quitting. The French directors were getting under his skin and he was even then negotiating a 'severance settlement' from his contract.

Within a month everything had been settled. Ike left the

Canidrome and joined the board of an American company which had just taken over management of China's largest fleet of merchant ships, the China Merchants' Steam Navigation Company, with more than thirty coastal and Yangtze river boats. In reality, the American company was but a 'front' for the Chinese shipping company and a ruse to gain foreign protection in the event of any future upheaval, whether domestic or international. The shrewdness of this move was shown the following year when the Sino-Japanese war began and all ships under the Chinese flag became fair game for Japan's bombs and guns.

I had had just about a year of peace and prosperity in my new post of racing manager and business was really booming — when Black Saturday suddenly struck Shanghai.

That was the day bombs fell into our city: into the foreign areas themselves, bringing death and disaster.

6

JAPS, DOLLARS AND RICKSHAW COOLIES

FOR TEN YEARS the Japanese had been watching the new and vigorous Nationalist Government of China grow in strength and solidarity, and what it saw it did not like.

Baron Tanaka's blueprint for conquest of all Asia under the Rising Sun had been drawn up at a time when China was a leaderless giant, torn with internal strife and official corruption, a no-account nation unable to prevent grabs such as Japan had been making on the mainland for several decades, the last being Manchuria in 1931.

Even as early as 1927 Generalissimo Chiang Kai-shek had been too friendly with Manchurian dictator Chang Tso-lin to please the Japanese, who long had eyes fixed on the vast agricultural and mineral resources of the Three Eastern Provinces, as Manchurian territory was sometimes known. So Japan removed Chang and annexed Manchuria.

When the Nanking Government announced its intention of recovering the lost territory at some future date, and actually began assembling the first air force in China's history, Japan took time by the forelock and launched the 1937 Sino-Japanese war. This was done, it will be recalled, by staging one more 'incident' at the Marco Polo Bridge, far into North China where Chiang Kai-shek not only had no troops worth mentioning, but where he wasn't popular with the peasants anyway, being from the South.

So as not to be drawn into the Japanese trap, Chiang began bringing large numbers of his crack troops into the Shanghai delta region, and under the guidance of several German military experts prepared strong fortifications for the expected Japanese attack.

It wasn't long in coming. In its frame of mind at that time, the Japanese military command was ready to thrash the impudent Chinese commander even on ground of his own choosing. The pretext for opening hostilities this time was furnished by sending a small party of Japanese plain-clothes military spies out to the Chinese military airfield on the outskirts of Shanghai. The Chinese discovered them (as was intended), there was some shooting and a couple of the Japs were shot. It is not without some significance that while these events were taking place, Japanese consular police and S.S. men were dashing all over Shanghai ordering all Japanese to report to the Japanese consulate-general immediately. They knew, of course, just where to find everyone. No Jap lived in Shanghai without registering every change of address.

While the Japanese military authorities played for time by pretending to 'investigate' the incident they had so thoroughly stage-managed themselves, fast Japanese ships were loading all Japanese women and children and ferrying them across to Nagasaki in Japan at top speed. Only male Japanese were allowed to stay, and these were being allotted their military duties even before negotiations 'broke down' and hostilities commenced.

Chiang Kai-shek's best battalions were pulled into the Chapei district on Shanghai's north side and, remembering how close 'Little Tokyo' came to being overrun in 1932 by Chinese troops incensed over the Japanese seizure of Manchuria, the Japanese commander took no chances this time and started hostilities.

JAPS, DOLLARS AND RICKSHAW COOLIES

The day was Thursday, August 12, 1937.

That night we called off the race meeting at the Canidrome and went up on the rooftops to watch the battle of Chapei in progress.

The historical books on the subject tell of traditional jealousy between the Japanese army and navy, of the non-arrival of reinforcements from Japan, of a passing typhoon which held up the reinforcements and of deep penetration into Little Tokyo by Chinese regulars and guerillas. To do them justice, the greatly outnumbered Japanese defenders put up a mighty battle in defence of 'their' territory and literally held the fort until heavy Japanese military reinforcements finally arrived.

Tied up at a Japanese wharf less than 100 yards from the Japanese consulate on the fringe of the Hongkew district was the *Idzumo*, flagship of the Japanese naval forces in Chinese waters and headquarters of the Japanese naval commander. The Chinese air force set out to sink the *Idzumo* and there are some 1,500 dead Chinese who wish they hadn't. Those are the ones killed by a Chinese bombing plane which took part in the *Idzumo* attack but veered off course, bombs intact, after tracer bullets from the *Idzumo* scored several hits. The other planes pressed home the attack, but no bomb got closer than 500 yards to the cruiser. Some fell into the Whangpoo River but two crashed into the International Settlement.

One of these went through the roof and top floors of the Palace Hotel at the corner of the Bund and Nanking Road; another hit Nanking Road at the main entrance to Sir Victor Sassoon's luxury Cathay Hotel, opposite the Palace. About eleven people were killed and scores wounded. Damage to both buildings, to the road, to parked automobiles and to dozens of native rickshaws, threw the area into confusion and temporarily diverted attention from the *Idzumo*, which emerged unscathed. About half an hour

SHANGHAI SAGA

later the damaged Chinese plane, still circling over the city while its pilot figured out how to get rid of his bomb load, finally came in low towards the Shanghai racecourse.

The Chinese version of this affair gave out later that the pilot, finding himself losing height, flew around looking for a suitable place to let go of the bombs and picked on the wide open space of our race-track. He had a huge audience when he came in for the drop. On the fringe of the track was the huge Chinese amusement centre, Great World, where for some strange reason thousands of Chinese refugees from the fighting area had come to a halt and packed all surrounding footpaths. One minute the crowd was cheering the overhead aviator, the next it was screaming in terror and death.

These pilots seemingly had had no training. The others let go their bombs half a mile too soon over the *Idzumo*, this pilot let go his lethal cargo from about a thousand feet even before he crossed the boundary fence of the race-track. I should know. I watched the bombs fall, just as half an hour earlier I had watched the attack on the *Idzumo* from a position on top of a high building on the Bund, next door to the Palace Hotel. Two bombs fell, one behind the other, death and destruction were widespread at Great World corner that Saturday afternoon. When the smoke cleared there was a crater at the junction of Avenue Edward VII and Tibet Road fifty feet wide and about twelve feet deep. Not so large, perhaps, in these days of H-bombs, but the 1,500 dead and seven or eight hundred wounded tell their own story.

Traffic was running east and west across Tibet Road at the time and two lanes of automobiles were burned out by the blast for a distance of half a mile. A Chinese traffic cop perched in his overhead control box less than fifty feet from where the bombs struck was never seen again, and a veritable hail of human parts spun through the acrid air to a circular distance of half a mile

JAPS, DOLLARS AND RICKSHAW COOLIES

from the double bomb-blast.

The Chinese held on to the Shanghai area for three battle-weary months, during which the Japanese destroyed the entire Chinese air force. From then on the Chinese were sitting ducks for the Japanese airmen, who used them for target practice and brought off some commendable pinpoint bombing by any standards. Nonetheless, the prolonged resistance of Chiang Kai-shek's men got so much under the skin of the arrogant Japanese War Office that it demanded, in the name of the Berlin-Tokyo axis, that Hitler recall the German experts attached to the Chinese army.

When the Chinese positions became untenable shortly after the departure of the Germans, Chiang ordered withdrawal from the Chapei (north) area to prepared positions. In view of the fact that the Japanese rode the skies with impunity this was a risky business, but the Chinese solved the problem. One morning Shanghai woke up to find Chapei completely enveloped in smoke cloud to a height of nearly 1,500 feet. The dead calm atmosphere allowed the dense clouds to rise straight up and stay there for the rest of the day. This was the beginning of Chiang Kai-shek's 'scorched earth' policy, and was the means of extricating his best battalions from the swarm of dive-bombers with which Japan from then on harried the Chinese defenders. One curious incident resulting from hostilities involved the Shanghai 'bastille', commonly known as Ward Road Jail. This big International Settlement prison was situated on an important eastern district thoroughfare named Ward Road in honour of the man who saved Shanghai from the Taiping rebels. Fighting between the Chinese and Japanese was never far from Ward Road and the huge prison was frequently in communication with the rest of Shanghai by telephone only.

After Ward Road Jail had been pierced by upwards of a dozen

shells in an artillery duel between the Chinese and Japanese forces, members of the Shanghai Municipal Council held an emergency meeting. With more than 6,000 Chinese prisoners on their hands, and the jail taking a pretty good shellacking from gunfire, it was decided to grant release to all the 'minor' prisoners and transfer several hundred of the worst types to new premises closer to the heart of Shanghai. Word was passed to both Chinese and Japanese headquarters and a period of truce arranged. The Shanghai General Omnibus Company — a foreign-owned public service — sent its whole fleet of single- and double-decker buses to the jail, loaded up the 'pardoned' prisoners, carried them across the city to the open fields on the south side of Frenchtown, and turned them loose!

Few stranger sights can have been seen. Bewildered by the sudden and unexpected freedom thrust upon them, but glad to be out of the target area, the vast majority of the ex-prisoners immediately began to change from prison garb into their own garments which had been re-issued to them before evacuating the prison. After a period of mental adjustment and searching for friends and relatives, the release having been widely publicized for that very purpose, night came on with the merest handful still squatting around, uncertain of their next move.

The entire entertainment world of our city was thrown into confusion by the war. Ten o'clock curfew was calamitous to a city where high jinks were just beginning at that hour. But with something like 20,000 dancing-girls needing to make a living out of the cabarets, and the overheads of the latter going on in spite of differences between China and Japan, the period of inactivity came to an end with the introduction of five o'clock tea-dances lasting until 9.30 p.m. when the lights went out suddenly and the scramble for home was started to beat the ban.

Taking our cue from this, we at the Canidrome also

inaugurated evening race meetings, beginning at 5.30 p.m., and some idea of the effect of war upon the populace can be gained from our first night's business under the new conditions. The attendance was poor, as was to be expected. Whereas we had been doing a gross turnover on fourteen races of $350,000 and more, three and four times a week, our total for our first race meeting held during hostilities amounted to little more than $20,000 for eight events! After several weeks of this our French directors went to the French consul-general, 'sovereign ruler' of Frenchtown (by the grace of Tu Vueh-sen), and laid our plight on the official table. We asked for—and got—15 per cent of the public investment henceforth, a rise of 50 per cent on our previous rake-off.

My official position entitled me to occupy the company's house adjoining the training kennels, which were situated on the very boundary of Frenchtown and Chinese territory on the south side of Shanghai. It was a sumptuous residence, having formerly been a select gambling-house operating under licence, unlike The Wheel of Carlos Garcia in the International Settlement, which could not have obtained a licence in that quarter under any circumstances. The Canidrome purchased the house because it was divided from the main kennels only by a wooden fence and a gate was soon let into this. Such proximity made my work of supervising the kennels, kennel staff and training so much easier.

A point about those kennels. They were built upon a piece of land acquired from several different Chinese vegetable farmers, and one of them stubbornly refused to sell until the Canidrome guaranteed (in writing) not to disturb the family grave-mound rising like an earthen blister on the edge of his plot. The architects had to design a semi-circular bend in our ten-foot-high brick wall in order to pass behind the grave. We had also to enclose

SHANGHAI SAGA

the grave-mound against possible vandalism, since the family meant to move to another farm miles away. Respect for gravemounds was not a Canidrome monopoly. Even the racecourse of the International Settlement had half a dozen large mounds dotted across its centre field, which in time came to be used as grandstands by spectators at football matches, polo or whatever was going on.

The Hung Jao Golf Course, headquarters of Shanghai's golfing elite, had to face a similar problem when under construction, but its designer, J. B. ('Ben') Ferrier, father of Jim, American golf pro., neatly met the situation by utilizing the mounds as golf 'hazards'. When Walter Hagen and Joe Kirkwood Snr. toured the world in 1929, this was the course on which they played their exhibition games.

Slowly but surely we drew the crowds back to the Canidrome, and their numbers increased in direct ratio, it seemed, to the distance the Japanese drove the Chinese forces away from Shanghai into the hinterland. Within a month or two of the scorched earth evacuation of Chapei by the Chinese forces, the Japs had pushed the latter so far back from Shanghai that we no longer heard the sound of gunfire. But for the first time our city suffered from the impact of war, inasmuch as farmers from that area were prevented from supplying Shanghai with its usual daily quota of fresh vegetables, fruit, poultry, eggs and other foodstuffs. Native fishing fleets were continually being harassed by Japanese naval units, and there was an ominous shortage of the staple food product—rice. Not content with these restrictions, the arrogant little Japs made things as difficult as possible within the foreign settlement by throwing cordons frequently around this or that city block, denying everyone entry or exit whilst they searched for imaginary spies. Because of the international nature of the Settlement the Japs claimed the right to enter it at

JAPS, DOLLARS AND RICKSHAW COOLIES

will and held frequent parades through main streets to impress the populace. Not so in the French Concession, where the French consul-general stood on his rights and made them apply for permission whenever they wished to enter the Concession or cross it to gain the Chinese territory beyond.

We pulled business back into our dog-track through one spectacular after another and to catch the early evening trade opened a large restaurant serving hot meals to hungry punters right through every meeting, combining Chinese with foreign food.

We staged the first 1,000-yard races for greyhounds ever held and hired a Cantonese animal trainer with a team of monkeys which were trained to ride as jockeys on the backs of some of our older and best-tempered dogs.

The picture facing p. 160 gives some idea of what that set-up looked like to our fans. The whole show was a riot.

Our turnover climbed past the $200,000 mark which, at the new discount rate of 15 per cent, was almost pre-war business.

There is little doubt that, but for the continued presence in Shanghai of American and British troops in comparatively large numbers on a permanent basis, Japanese control of the city would have tightened. Because of hostilities in Chapei and other northern parts of Shanghai there had been large-scale evacuation of those areas, even by non-Chinese residents, and any of the latter wanting to return to their homes after the fighting shifted to the southern sector found Japanese soldiers both truculent and brutal. For a start they demanded that everyone passing their sentries bow deeply in Japanese fashion. Up in North China cities such as Tientsin they were, of course, doing better because of the lack of uniformed opposition. There they were stripping foreign men and women down to their underwear and socks in winter weather on the pretence of searching for weapons.

Through it all the Shanghai civilian volunteer in uniform never lost his sense of humour. This body of men of many nationalities which manned the barricades at every crisis comprised, as has been said, leading business men, judges, lawyers, even retired millionaires.

One unit had the job of guarding a sector of the perimeter of the International Settlement where ordure boats assembled daily to remove the great city's huge night-soil cargo. This went up on the flood tide by the many canals and creeks of the Yangtze delta for distribution among thousands of farms a hundred miles or more beyond the city. Thousands of iron 'honey-carts' roamed the unsewered sections of Shanghai in the early hours of every morning, their crews padding barefooted up the backstairs of homes in order to empty the bathroom 'thunderboxes', as the locals termed them. The native barges waited at the loading stages, in a creek between wharves in the International Settlement harbour area. Like every other harbour creek it had to be guarded, and the volunteer unit which drew the black marble for duty positions at the start of the crisis decided, when martial law was lifted, to immortalize their spell of odoriferous civic duty by handing each participating volunteer a medal and citation.

One of the most unfortunate aspects of the Sino-Japanese conflict of 1937 developed from the depreciation in the value of the Chinese dollar, which was the main reason for most of us being in China in the first place. Indeed, the Chinese dollar is worth a whole chapter to itself.

The 'oil for the lamps of China' was once paid for in solid silver dollars, 5,000 per box, and collected by the ton from dealers all over the vast country where Standard Oil and Shell Oil (Asiatic Petroleum) distributed their product. Similarly, the giant British-American Tobacco Company sent its armed

JAPS, DOLLARS AND RICKSHAW COOLIES

collectors into dangerous, bandit-ridden territory to bring back the boxes of silver bullion which was the only form of acceptable payment. Why was this so? Because silver had a certain intrinsic value whatever its source or origin. Silver dollars minted in far-off Szechwan Province were still silver dollars on the Shanghai market, though perhaps at a slight discount.

But paper dollars — uh-uh!

Of the ten or fifteen types of banknotes circulating in the Shanghai area, only those of the foreign banks and two or three Chinese banks were trusted by the mass of natives. It was not a criminal offence to print and circulate banknotes anywhere in China before the coming of Chiang Kai-shek. Only the public — and the money-changers — determined the fate of a banknote issue, and rumour could do amazing things to the notes of *any* bank.

Shanghai must have been one of the few places in the world where one could walk up to the counter of a money-changer and buy the currency of any country one cared to mention. Within the boundaries of Shanghai's two foreign areas were more than 2,000 money-changing shops scattered far and wide, those in the outlying areas supplementing business with sales of cigarettes, toilet articles, tea, incense or general merchandise. On every counter of every money-changer's was a grooved tray containing the 'break-up' for dollars for those in need of quick change, say, to pay off a rickshaw runner. The 'break-up' might vary from day to day but its rate was fixed at 10 a.m. daily when Way Foong, the big British Hong Kong and Shanghai Banking Corporation on the Bund, opened for business and issued the daily rates of exchange. Though nominally 100 cents, the Shanghai dollar was always worth more than that in terms of 'small money', more often fetching six twenty-cent pieces, one ten-cent piece plus between ten and eighteen copper cents.

SHANGHAI SAGA

President Chiang Kai-shek tried to change all that. He wanted the currency on a 'big money' basis, with the dollar fetching two cents. But old habits — and too many small coins — die hard. Business deals, ledgers and restricted currency operations went over to the big money, but to the very end the counters of the money-changers continued to display their little grooved trays of small money for those wishing to change a dollar.

As part of his plan to create a Chinese air force to fight Japan, if and when necessary, President Chiang Kai-shek called in the nation's silver dollars. The United States Treasury agreed to buy these at a price based upon their silver content. Chiang obtained gold dollar credits in exchange and Two-gun Cohen used some of this credit when purchasing aircraft for him. Chiang shortly thereafter minted and circulated brand-new silver dollars (of debased content) with appropriate subsidiary coins of 'big money' value. Mostly, however, the Nationalist Government's 'small coinage' consisted of paper units.

Chiang was still exporting silver dollars to the United States after the outbreak of hostilities in July 1937. Hundreds of millions of dollars had been shipped before this, but the Japs naturally wanted to prevent their enemy from obtaining further credit abroad. For this reason the Japanese prevented the Pacific Ocean liner, the 24,000-ton *Robert Dollar*, from leaving Shanghai towards the end of 1937 until the vessel had discharged several million silver dollars back on to the dock at Shanghai. It was, perhaps, merely coincidental that the Dollar boat was later bombed 'by mistake' by Japanese planes in South China waters.

The currency of a nation finds its own level on world markets and from a quite respectable position vis-à-vis the American dollar in the early 1930's, the Chinese dollar began to slip badly by 1937; and the situation was not improved by rumours that Madame Chiang Kai-shek had secretly taken off for South

JAPS, DOLLARS AND RICKSHAW COOLIES

Monkey jockeys at Shanghai dog-track

Burning Brithish ship abandoned by pirates in Bias Bay. British naval tug from Hong Kong is alongside putting out fire while British warship (foreground) stands by. Kidnapped hostages from native junk are returning to merchant ship in rowing boat

China coaster burnt out by pirates

JAPS, DOLLARS AND RICKSHAW COOLIES

America with a heavy load of gold aboard a giant military transport airplane.

Mr. Tung, Canidrome *compradore* and friend of gang boss Tu Yueh-sen, was one who was beginning to find the currency position more than a trifle irritating, because he ran the cabaret attached to the Canidrome's membership section and employed therein an all-American negro orchestra direct from Chicago. Having contracted this band when the American dollar exchanged for Ch. $2.50, Mr. Tung saw only disaster ahead as China's trade declined under Japanese military invasion. The native dollar had already passed the four-to-one ratio and Mr. Tung's negro entertainers were on a gold dollar contract. He therefore took the band contract along to a shrewd lawyer and inquired what might be done about it. The lawyer studied the contract closely, especially the small type, and presently smiled a smile of satisfaction which shortly enveloped Mr. Tung also.

A night or two later, after a dog-race meeting, there was a big crowd in the Canidrome ballroom. I was sitting in my usual corner with the other officials; the band was playing; the floor was filled with couples dancing; the leader of the band, a small, dapper negro, was waving his wand and, like other members of the band, no doubt feeling very happy at the declining rate of exchange and the prospect of more and more spending money.

Suddenly the dapper little negro found himself rolling on the floor with a white customer in a smart dinner suit bending over him and shouting, 'Get up and fight, you bum!' Anyone could see that the negro was no match for his husky aggressor. He looked imploringly towards his comrades who, of course, had already stopped playing in surprise. Then the big white man grabbed the little negro again and lifted him to his feet so as to punch him to the floor once more, whereupon the other negroes dropped their instruments and piled into the big white man, administering what is known as the 'grandfather of a hiding'; not, however, escaping entirely unhurt themselves. The ballroom immediately became a scene of uproar, ending only when the intruder had been literally thrown out; but the interlude lasted only twenty minutes and was forgotten in an hour, Shanghai being accustomed to meeting such situations.

Next day, however, Mr. Tung served dismissal notices upon every member of his negro orchestra, invoking a clause in their contract against creating disturbances or doing anything 'likely to injure the business of the ballroom'. The ex-sailor who had been hired for the job pocketed his $500 (local currency) which Mr. Tung considered cheap at the price, and next night a Filipino orchestra was installed.

As a footnote to this affair, I must mention that the ex-sailor hired by Tung was shortly after this himself rounded up by U.S. Federal agent Nicholson as an escaped convict from the United States, wanted for a felony. Little 'Nicky', one of the United States Treasury's smartest operators in the Far East, stood but 5 ft. 2 in. high and was therefore no muscleman in his job. All the same he brought Nemesis to bear upon numerous currency forgers and narcotic agents in the course of his stay. His was the tip which broke up a gang operating out of Shanghai around 1937-8 described by Harry Anslinger, former United States Customs commissioner, in his Saturday Evening Post memoirs some years ago and involving several deaths.

In that affair a gang used a Eurasian nurse from a Shanghai hospital to transport a trunk containing a large quantity of narcotics to California. When the nurse was picked up there (after once escaping and being re-captured) Shanghai police also picked up the dead body of a male Eurasian on a vacant lot in the French Concession. Government investigators believed the man had been murdered to keep his mouth shut. The second death in

JAPS, DOLLARS AND RICKSHAW COOLIES

this case occurred aboard an ocean liner on the way from South America to New York, when a passenger named Brandstatter hanged himself in his state-room. The official theory on this was that Brandstatter knew the game was up as a result of the arrest of the Eurasian nurse on the Pacific coast. He expected to be arrested on arrival at New York and so took his own life. Brandstatter was one of two brothers, twins, who 'graced' the night-spots of Shanghai for several months around that time. Tall and very handsome, the twins foolishly drew attention to themselves by going everywhere at night in beautifully cut full evening dress, rendering themselves extremely conspicuous and, inevitably, claiming the attention of little Nicky, whose job it was to observe such strangers as the Brandstatter boys.

The highest point ever reached by the Chinese dollar was around three and a half to the pound sterling during World War I; the lowest shortly after the Communists took over in 1949 when an ordinary letter from China to overseas countries required stamps to the tune of more than Ch. 1,000,000!

There were two sounds to which Shanghai residents became as accustomed over the passing years as residents near an airport become used to the screech of jet planes. One of these was the sound of silver dollar clinking against silver dollar as minor assistants in money-changing shops tested the coins for counterfeits. Their deft fingers and sharp ears all day long and deep into the night banged dollar against dollar listening for the dull tone betraying the dud. It did not always mean a counterfeit; often merely a coin from a distant province carrying less silver content than the 'master dollar'. That difference in tone meant a difference in several cents to the seller. To the uninitiated buyer, however, the shop was always ready to forget that any difference existed. The dollar had a cousin known as the tael, which bore about the same relation to the dollar as does the English guinea to the pound. That is, it was sort of 'snob currency'. Its value was, roughly, one-third greater than that of the dollar. That was the common tael; for use by professional men such as doctors, lawyers, livestock auctioneers and real-estate agents in line with practice in England and elsewhere in sterling areas. The Haikwan (Customs) tael was still another unit of 'currency' and although one never cast eyes upon a Haikwan tael, one could see, feel and even possess a common tael.

To find out how this mess all came about, one must recall that before China was blasted open for foreign trade by British gunboats around 1843, its monetary system was not based upon the dollar, which came along in the wake of the gunboats when some convenient medium of currency was sought acceptable to both Chinese and foreign traders.

The common tael existed before the gunboats and was a small shoe-shaped ingot of silver, bearing the chop (stamp) of the maker, who thus guaranteed it. Its value was based upon its silver content, subject to fluctuations in the value of silver and, therefore, rather unstable. To counteract this instability the Chinese Imperial Customs introduced the mythical Customs (Haikwan) tael based upon 'gold units', which is about as far as I need take the reader.

Customs staff members were always paid salaries in Haikwan taels, of course, and the strength of the Customs tael was revealed to us by the eagerness of money-changing shops to cash our pay-cheques for us each month. One's pay-cheque consisted of a small piece of coarse, absorbent Chinese rice-paper approximately four inches by six. On this was 'brushed', Chinese fashion, an order for payment on the Customs bank of so many Haikwan taels, and for the benefit of those 98 per cent members of the staff who did not read Chinese script the amount of salary being

JAPS, DOLLARS AND RICKSHAW COOLIES

paid was also sketched in plain English figures in one corner by the same brush-writer. What made the toilet-paper so valuable, however, was the huge Customs chop in indelible Chinese red ink, completely dominating the document; a chop known to almost everybody living in Shanghai and anywhere else along the seaboard of China, not to mention the vast hinterland. In other words, the Customs chop was possibly the best-known among all the millions of chops abounding throughout trading China.

As the money-changers always gave Customs employees a high rate of exchange, it was to them that we always took our monthly pittances and we even shopped around among them until we found one offering more than his competitors. The main reason for the good standing of Haikwan taels was the fact that whereas banks might go bust — as one American institution did soon after I arrived and another shortly before I left — the Customs had behind it not only all China's Customs revenue, but a sound organization handling such finances. Every loan made to China by a foreign nation looked to Customs revenue — and nothing else — for repayment. Well, what else was there to look to, in the time of which I write? Any taxes which were collected were done so at the point of a gun, usually, by some bandit or ex-bandit turned provincial governor, and such collections were hardly ever for the populace at large! So much for the Customs tael. It was but a book entry in the nation's finance.

The common tael was scarcely more, although it was, at least, represented by that little boat-shaped silver ingot. One certainly never paid one's doctor in silver ingots! At most, some of us collected a silver tael as a curio and placed it among other curios on the mantel or on a sideboard. It was as rarely seen as the golden guinea piece of England. Gold, too, had its curious sidelights. Though — save for Customs gold units, another book entry—the currency of the nation was by no means based on a store of gold in some deep vault, there was probably more actual gold in circulation in China during the period of which I write than in any other country in the world! And I don't mean represented by the rings, bracelets, ear-rings and other trinkets worn by Chinese womenfolk.

The Shanghai Gold Bar Exchange was as notorious in the Far East as Monte Carlo is famous in Europe. But the daily gambling turnover of the former made Monte Carlo look like a dabble in peanuts. Towards three o'clock in the afternoon on any trading day at the Gold Bar Exchange the scene resembled Wall Street on that fateful occasion in October 1929 when the bottom fell out of the market. The bottom fell out of the market for someone nearly every day in gold-bar gambling and it was because of the pernicious effect of this gambling centre upon Shanghai's commercial life that the exchange was closed under pressure from President Chiang Kai-shek who had, as a youth, once worked there as a junior clerk.

Blood-brother or not, Chiang's financial advisers discovered that Tu Yueh-sen, the underworld king, was manipulating the gold-bar market to such extent that even the gold units upon which the Haikwan tael was based were being affected. Gold bars, the precious yellow metal, really existed. Any speculator could demand his gold-bar credit on twenty-four hours' notice if it happened to be a large amount, immediately if a mere hundred bars or so. Quotations on the Gold Bar Exchange fluctuated so rapidly at times that no clerk with a stick of chalk could keep pace; so they installed an electric sign to wipe out investors that much faster. Hence the daily panic as the clock headed towards 3 p.m. each day. In Shanghai, just as one might inquire of the weather forecast for next day, one heard on all sides from 3 p.m. onwards, 'What did gold bars close at?' Chiang did well to close

JAPS, DOLLARS AND RICKSHAW COOLIES

the Gold Bar Exchange.

But another, possibly less-known, form of gold speculation held pride of place among China's middle classes and went even deeper down into the poorer servant class, for the instinct among Chinese to gamble is very strong. The art of the gold- and silversmith in China is still very much alive today. Scores of such establishments flourished all over the old Shanghai, and many of these had been driven to the shelter of the foreign-controlled cities of China by bandits in that period of unrest between the abdication of the emperor in 1911 and the coming of Chiang Kai-shek in 1927. I do not pretend to understand why, but the price of gold, like silver, fluctuated constantly throughout China and this fact led to the introduction of what might be called a form of harmless, 'long-term' speculation by moderate-minded Chinese, and not a few foreigners.

The gold—and silversmiths made available finger-rings of pure, soft gold, which bore the chop of the establishment, and could either be worn or put somewhere in safe keeping. The daily (buying and selling) price of such rings was displayed on a small blackboard on the counter of every such shop. There was only one simple rule to follow when trading in them—buy them when gold was cheap, hang on and sell when the price rose. Sometimes it meant 'hanging on' for six months or more. But sooner or later someone on the Gold Bar Exchange would send the price soaring or tumbling, and that was the signal for a vast horde of gold-ring speculators to re-activate their holdings, one way or the other. The shops dealing in such rings were honour-bound to exchange for cash immediately on demand, and did so without demur as soon as they had verified their own chop. This gold-ring market was a form of speculation within reach of houseboys, amahs and even rickshaw coolies.

Many well-meaning people have, over the years, raised a

great song-and-dance at man's alleged inhumanity to man in permitting, or condoning, the use of rickshaws, based on the mistaken belief that rickshaw-pullers lead some sort of dog's life. Some people—not many—have even refused to ride in a rickshaw, unable to witness such human suffering! Maybe if they had seen the rickshaw-puller's family suffering from lack of food brought on by lack of business they would have second thoughts. There is also widespread belief that pulling a rickshaw is so strenuous that no puller ever reaches the age of fifty and is past his prime at thirty! It is not denied that pulling a rickshaw can, at times, be strenuous work, but if I had to choose between that and some of the other physical tasks done by Chinese of the coolie class, I'd settle for the rickshaw any time.

Compared with trundling a wheelbarrow or hauling a handcart for instance, rickshaw-pulling is a pushover and usually twice as remunerative; yet one has never heard any protests on behalf of either a wheelbarrow or a handcart coolie. The latter, most of the time, is called upon to put about four times the poundage per square inch into his daily toil than that required of a rickshaw coolie when plying for hire. The wheelbarrow-pusher, on his part, raised steam to the tune of six or seven times that of the rickshaw coolie, and no wild guesses go into that statement for the evidence was always all too plain for everybody to see in the streets of Shanghai any day of the week. It was a common sight to see a long line of wheelbarrow 'taxis' transporting as many as eight plump Chinese mill-girls—four on each side—to and from work morning and evening—and glad of the business.

Added to the avoirdupois involved was the wheelbarrow-pusher's need to *balance* as well as push his load, for Chinese wheelbarrows had this in common with Western ones—each had but a single wheel! As for the Chinese handcart, it was simply a platform on a pair of cart wheels, with the axle across centre.

JAPS, DOLLARS AND RICKSHAW COOLIES

Jutting from each corner of the platform was a short shaft, or handle. Iron ringbolts were affixed to both sides, both ends. Back and front look alike. Propulsion was by means of ropes attached to the rings on the pulling end, with a 'helmsman' steering by the short shafts at the rear end. A handcart crew consisted of from six to eight rope-pullers, depending upon the nature and weight of the cargo. These handcarts conveyed merchandise by the ton. At times the loads were piled so high there was no visible communication between pullers and steerer. Nor were there any brakes! If braking was suddenly necessary, pullers hastily rushed to the rear with their ropes and hauled backwards. Nor did it always work out, especially on the down side of an arched bridge. The only thing to do if one of these overloaded handcarts got out of control on a downhill run was to obey the frantic yells of the helmsman and crew and go for your life. So heavy were handcart loads at times that special stone 'rails' were let into the macadam roads on prescribed routes to prevent their wheels becoming embedded in the soft tar during the hot summer months!

Rickshaw-pullers, by comparison, got off easily. Although their licensing conditions compelled them to accept any fare in ordinary circumstances, they had ways and means of rejecting overweight prospects who might possibly rupture their stomach muscles. If such a potential fare was foreign, no problem existed, for rickshaw-pullers in all of China's seaports and cities preferred them to their own kind; they paid more and, if over-sized, could usually be depended upon for something extra. If Chinese, however, the heavyweight was taken care of by means of the established custom among the natives of making a contract before embarkation.

All that a rickshaw-puller wanted to know from his foreign patron was — 'Where go, marster?' A Chinese would-be passenger, on the other hand, had to state his destination almost to the exact yard, and sometimes the travelling directions required plenty of clarification before the puller would commit himself. He required a clear mental picture of the spot where his fare intended to alight. Having got this he then named his fare, and the next few moments generally developed into a walking argument along the kerbside until one or the other gave way. Only then did the journey begin. But let there be any misunderstanding between the parties concerning the destination; let the rickshaw-puller discover that he had let himself in for more labour than he imagined, and the fun started.

'You said this is where you wanted to go,' he would say to the fare, emphasizing the remark by dropping the shafts of the rickshaw to the ground.

The fare most probably countered by retorting: 'You're mistaken. It's another couple of blocks further on.'

'I'm not mistaken,' the coolie would splutter back. 'You cheated me.'

'I didn't cheat you. You're probably some country bumpkin who doesn't know this city very well.'

'I'm a third generation rickshaw-runner in this place and I don't like being cheated.'

'You're a fool. No one is trying to cheat you. You haven't yet reached the place I told you.'

'Don't call me a fool! This is as far as I'm taking you for the twelve coppers we agreed upon. So hand me my money and let me get about my business, or shall I call a policeman?'

'I'll pay you when we reach the place I said.'

'Well, I'm not taking you a yard further for twelve coppers. If you want to pay fourteen coppers I'll take you two more blocks. If not, pay up and let me go.'

The argument might proceed to the point of bodily assault,

JAPS, DOLLARS AND RICKSHAW COOLIES

or the customer might cave-in and cash up. The rickshaw coolie was far from being the under-dog many people imagined. With his own people he made a contract beforehand, to be on the safe side: with the 'Imperialist barbarian' he accepted on trust, sure of a square deal. Time and again when on the lookout for a public rickshaw I came upon one in the throes of arranging a contract with a Chinese. In a flash all negotiations were broken off and the rickshaw placed at my feet with a grin and a 'Where to, marster?'

Public rickshaw coolies and the Chinese and Indian members of Shanghai's police forces were at constant loggerheads. The latter regarded the rickshaw-runners as a ready- made source of income in times of acute financial stress — meaning when they needed a little extra pocket-money. On the slightest pretext — even a fabricated one if need be — these coppers seized the seat cushions from rickshaws coming close enough. This immediately put the rickshaw coolie out of business (a) because he had to have a cushion for passengers to sit on; (b) because his vehicle was only hired and it would take more than a day's takings to replace the cushion. A third good reason why he had to recover it was that all public rickshaws were hired out on a twenty-four-hour basis, with two coolies dividing the day; thus loss of a cushion affected both of them.

Well aware of these difficulties, many Chinese and Indian policemen made a daily practice of purloining as many cushions as possible during hours of duty. Victimized coolies had no choice but to pay the twenty or thirty cents' ransom demanded in order to get the cushion back pronto and make up the extra as fast as possible. I have seen as many as ten or fifteen cushions stacked at the feet of a traffic cop at a busy intersection, all of them belonging to rickshaw coolies alleged to have committed traffic offences. Hundreds of rickshaw coolies were 'booked' daily in this manner all over Shanghai and the standard ransom for all such minor offences was a fifty-cent fine next day at the police station concerned. Knowing this, it was seldom very difficult for the 'squeezing' traffic cop to extract his twenty- or thirty-cent on-the-spot fine and give the cushion back immediately.

To rickshaw-runners of quite ordinary physique, trundling a rickshaw offers very little hardship. It is merely a matter of 'balance', as I have tried and discovered. I once lost an election wager and by way of payment had to drag a newspaper colleague the full length of Nanking Road by rickshaw in broad daylight, wearing an opera hat and holding a twelve- inch cigar in my mouth all the way. Once the shafts have been raised, the weight of a passenger is transferred to the wheels and, after a good heave and a trot, the rickshaw runs itself on level ground. And in most of China's great cities, particularly the treaty ports, the ground is very level. Shanghai's highest 'hill' was merely an arched stone bridge in the centre of the city across the celebrated Soochow Creek, where there were always strong Chinese urchins waiting to grasp the shafts and help haul your rickshaw over the hump for a couple of coppers.

One of the greatest enemies of the rickshaw coolie was the weather. When the typhoon season came around, with the wind howling through the streets at eighty to ninety miles an hour and the rain lashing everything round about, with water knee-deep in the streets, the rickshaw coolie would cheerfully carry you pick-a-back from front door to rickshaw, or vice versa, to keep your feet dry.

Visiting seamen knocked out by the famous 'Hongkew Whisky' were carried in their thousands over the years back to the waterfront and handed over to officers of the watch by public rickshaw coolies. The hooch sold as drinking liquor in Hongkew (Little Tokyo) and imbibed so freely by strangers was before its time. It might well have been used getting modern missiles

JAPS, DOLLARS AND RICKSHAW COOLIES

into orbit. Its properties were never fully known, but at least one judge in the British Consular Court steadfastly refused to penalize any man brought before him if the evidence revealed that he had been quaffing this stuff distilled and humorously termed 'whisky' in Little Tokyo. I once came face to face—in the old Mixed Court—with a Chinese who blandly testified that his work consisted of refilling non-refillable whisky bottles bearing world-famous labels. He described the method employed and the court asked that it be not divulged for the safety and well-being of whisky-drinkers the world over. As to the contents of the concoction used for the refill, the man knew nothing. But everyone who lived in Shanghai knew the consequences of swallowing it.

It is perfectly true that unwary rickshaw passengers abroad late at night were waylaid, robbed and sometimes beaten by rickshaw coolies or their confederates. A very small percentage of pullers used the rickshaw merely as a criminal instrument and the role of rickshaw-runner as a cover for their crimes; but these were few in number and public rickshaws taken as a whole bore a good reputation.

Then there were the rickshaws of the Shanghai sing-song girls—those brilliant, gay, illuminated vehicles seen dashing through the brightly lit streets of the down-town entertainment district. They were 'the most' in rickshaw elegance, lacquered to a mirror gloss, each with a pair of huge, chromium-plated, battery-fed headlamps as well as a third lamp dangling below from the axle.

Leaders of this profession invariably announced the fact with an extra spotlight operated by one tiny, satin-slippered foot, while the other stamped upon a little bell attached to the floorboards underneath the thick animal-skin rug. From hotel to hotel and restaurant to restaurant, these little butterflies of

SHANGHAI SAGA

Oriental song dashed through the milling crowds of this allnight up-and-doing city, responding to calls with all speed, in order to collect as many appearance fees as possible in a night's entertainment. Sparkling with many thousands of dollars' worth of real jewellery on fingers, ears, wrists and adorning their ebony hair, they were protected from snatch-and-run thieves by husky runners who trotted at the rear of their rickshaws, clutching the back of the vehicle. Following at a respectful distance behind, but headed for the same destination, the private fiddlers of the songsters made their nightly rounds also, fiddle in calico bag slung over shoulder, eyes half closed, snatching sleep as they went along.

Every sing-song girl had her headquarters, usually at one of the leading Chinese hotels. To there she headed at starting-up time to check for customer calls. Party givers were not bound to summon the sing-song girls who happened to be registered where the party was being given. What's more, the man-abouttown giving a party did not require to know anything about headquarters. Even if some very special girl were requested by a guest, all that was necessary was for her name to be furnished to the head waiter and he did the rest.

It might be that several girls were needed to brighten up a party. Special invitation cards were always ready. Favourite names were written thereon and the hunt began by telephone to locate the wanted ones. While the wine flowed, or the dinner got under way, replies began to come in with information regarding the availability or otherwise of the asked-for singsong girls. Sometimes they were fully tied up for the night — and sent their regrets. Others could come within a certain time while some might even be immediately available. In cases of complete writeoffs, other names were chosen and further efforts made until a full complement of entertainers had been assured.

JAPS, DOLLARS AND RICKSHAW COOLIES

Like the Japanese *geisha*, the Chinese sing-song girl was supposed to be an entertainer and good conversationalist. Many were successful in their profession because of their beauty rather than their talents, as I knew well after sitting through many dinner-parties at leading Chinese restaurants listening to songs strangely discordant to Western ears. On the other hand several had delightful voices, and there were also a couple of old fiddlers with precious two-string native violins that gave out velvety tones of which Stradivarius himself might have been proud.

7

REDS, RACKETEERS AND PICKPOCKETS

IN HIS FASCINATING book Shanghai Conspiracy Major-General C. S. Willoughby, intelligence chief attached to General Douglas MacArthur's staff in World War II, opens by drawing a pen picture of Assistant Commissioner of Shanghai Police (International Settlement) T. Patrick Givens.

Pat Givens was in charge of the Political Division and Willoughby reveals a much-harassed police officer, pleasant and mild-mannered withal, yet faced with the tough assignment of coping with the activities of some of the cleverest and most diabolical characters ever to slink across the world stage — agents of Moscow engaged in spadework for the eventual capture of China by the Reds.

Givens was on my beat during one of my several periods of attachment to a Shanghai newspaper and I watched the genial 6 ft. 5 in. Irishman grow from inspector to assistant commissioner and blow out at the same time from a tall, gangling 180 lb. to something in the neighbourhood of 235 lb. — mostly, I should say, through the aid of a giant-sized thermos flaskful of malted milk which always stood on his desk during working hours. Looking back, I see clearly now the difficulty of Givens' task as well as the great success he and his staff achieved against unnatural odds, for few realized then the full extent of the Red plot against China.

REDS, RACKETEERS AND PICKPOCKETS

Prodded by the government of President Chiang Kai-shek, who was one of the few fully conscious of the threat, Givens and his men managed to round up several of Moscow's best agents, thus throwing the Red timetable out of gear and seriously delaying plans for the overthrow of Chiang, a programme which World War II was to delay by several more years.

Chiang had already dismissed and expelled from China Michael Borodin, propaganda expert, and General Galens, military aide, and Moscow responded by despatching Dr. Fortunatoff, a subversion expert, who was arrested and searched upon his arrival in Shanghai. The search was carried out at the Hongkew police station by two White Russian detectives, of whom there were many employed by the police of both the International Settlement and the French Concession. Inside the lining of a book in Fortunatoff's baggage, they discovered a secret Communist Party certificate identifying the bearded doctor as the new head of the Far Eastern Department of Agitation. That same night the two Russian detectives were contacted by someone who offered them Ch. $10,000 to admit that the certificate was a forgery, planted by them in the doctor's baggage.

Dr. Fortunatoff, meanwhile, was free on bail of Ch.$ 20,000 pending investigations. An Austrian lawyer with an imposing record of legal successes in Shanghai had been retained for the doctor's defence. As a Russian, the latter naturally came under the jurisdiction of the Mixed Court, that queer and possibly unique tribunal which claimed jurisdiction over all foreigners in Shanghai who did not enjoy the benefits of extraterritoriality, as well as all Chinese residing within the foreign areas of the city. But when the case was called Dr. Fortunatoff failed to appear. His counsel denied all knowledge of his whereabouts, but police declared they had information he had skipped to Peking and was even then hiding in the Soviet Embassy there. So another

197

20,000 Red dollars went down the drain as the court ordered the bail to be forfeited.

The importance of getting China into the Red camp was emphasized shortly afterwards by a steady flow into Shanghai of Communist leaders from England, America, France, Germany and even India, and Willoughby's book tells in great detail of Pat Givens' unceasing warfare — and remarkable successes — against the enemies of the Nanking regime.

One of the major aims of the new Nationalist Government established by Chiang Kai-shek was to recover control of the two Mixed Courts which functioned so well in the two foreign sections of Shanghai, so let us look at the picture of one facing p. 177. This picture was taken on the occasion of a farewell presentation to one of the United States of America 'judges', Mr. W. E. Jacobs. Cast your eyes over those assembled. Save for one or two police officers (and myself) the others on the floor of the court are legal practitioners who made regular appearances and obtained most of their income from practising in this legal gold-mine.

Note the gentleman with the thick black beard. That is Dr. O. Fischer, the Austrian lawyer for Dr. Fortunatoff. The woman in the picture is Dr. Flora Rosemberg, a woman lawyer occasionally making an appearance here also. As for the remainder, they include American, British, French, Italian, Scandinavian, French, White Russian and Chinese but the last-named, although often better qualified to practise than some of the others, were employed mostly in the preparation of cases and as interpreters for their foreign partners. Indeed, their most important role was the bringing in of clients, the vast majority of whom were Chinese. The foreign lawyers were regarded more as mouthpieces of the Chinese solicitors, for the Mixed Court was ostensibly foreign-controlled.

Hulls of Chinese nineteenth-century war-junks

Group of captured Chinese pirates handcuffed together

Note the positions of the two judges seated on the Bench in this picture. Judge Jacobs sits on the right and the Chinese magistrate on the left. These so-called foreign 'judges' were not fully legally trained, and were always addressed as 'Assessor'. Usually they were vice-consuls, with some legal training, attached to their respective consulates. Almost without exception they also spoke Mandarin Chinese and so were able to converse intelligently with the Chinese magistrates, who were there under the written constitution of the court to help administer the Chinese civil and criminal Code of Law. Relations between assessors and magistrates were invariably excellent. They always conferred before giving judgment and in my experience all judgments were unanimous.

Not so after the Nanking Government pressured the Western powers to grant semi-autonomy in these courts to China. First they changed the name from Mixed to Provisional Courts, an interim title and an ever-present reminder to the powers that the courts' changed status — with their continued foreign supervision — was but temporary and eventually would be abolished when China assumed total control. From the day they became Provisional Courts, positions on all Benches were reversed and the Chinese magistrates changed seats with the foreign assessors. Incidentally, the former were no longer magistrates but full judges from the High Court of the Province of Kiangsu, who took to wearing cap and gown, the cap strongly resembling that worn by the LL.D.s of England, a wide, shapeless, flat and circular piece of black velvet trimmed with official yellow around the outer brim. The gown was also slightly lined with the same yellow material.

The most important change, however, was in the administration of the law. Foreign assessors were not even given equal status with the Chinese judges, but were merely tolerated on the Bench as observers. They might disagree with

REDS, RACKETEERS AND PICKPOCKETS

Gathering of international lawyers

a judgment but they lacked power to interfere beyond entering a written protest—which had not the slightest effect upon anybody. Foreign lawyers were barred from appearing to plead for any save foreign clients and thus, with one stroke of the pen, China cut off the main source of income from three-quarters of Shanghai's foreign lawyers.

There were about eight courts in the Provisional (Mixed) Court of the International Settlement during the years I 'covered' them for newspapers. Most of the cases were criminal ones, and from these each day's best copy usually came. Something of a world record must have been created on the day the old Mixed Courts handed out a total of forty-eight death sentences, twenty-five life imprisonments and 387 years of jail life during a crime wave. It is true that in some of the capital cases there might have been a single preliminary hearing, at which the police asked for a remand to gather up some odds and ends of evidence. On resumption, however, all cases went sailing through to a fast finish, unquestionably the swiftest disposal of capital cases anywhere outside of a dictatorship country.

Let me take you briefly through the trial, say, of a gang of a dozen or so armed robbers, or kidnappers—for ransom, naturally. (There is another kind of kidnapping rampant in Eastern countries, but it comes under the headings of 'slave trading' and 'white slavery'. These are regarded as lesser offences.) Observe once more that picture of the Mixed Court. There are two witness-boxes, one on each side of the Bench. That on the left of the picture was generally used by foreign witnesses and police, the one on the right by Chinese. Then observe the numerals painted inside (and also outside) the prisoners' dock. This method was used to assist judges in identifying prisoners who were, wherever possible, placed in the dock in positions corresponding to their numerical order on the police charge-sheet.

REDS, RACKETEERS AND PICKPOCKETS

We are set for the resumption of the trial of a gang of desperate killers, probably ex-soldiers from the civil wars who, having been on the losing side, discarded their uniforms, entered the city of Shanghai and tried to make a few fast dollars at the point of the gun. As the case re-opens, there is a lot of shuffling at the back of the court and a good deal of loud shouting of names as Chinese police sergeants summon the next batch of defendants from the smelling, spitting, wheezing, restless jungle which is the prisoners' waiting-room.

When all the prisoners have taken their proper places in the dock the police prosecutor rises and reiterates briefly the basis of the charges, then summons the senior foreign police officer, who led the arresting police party, to give brief evidence identifying the prisoners before the court. This evidence is usually substantiated by one of the Chinese detectives who took part in the arrests.

While the evidence is being heard, likely as not a policeman on duty within the courtroom may suddenly dart in among the public benches and snatch a cigarette from the mouth of an offender, or walk over and cuff on the ear another who has retched and expectorated on the floor in true native style. Foreign assessor and Chinese magistrate seldom make any notes during a trial, though a foreign and a Chinese clerk each keep a brief précis of proceedings for the record.

The prosecution is a collective one, against the gang as a whole. The municipal advocate (prosecuting attorney) pauses every couple of sentences to permit translation from English into Chinese for the benefit of the Chinese magistrate and it is to be noted that English was the first language of the court while it remained the Mixed Court, Chinese after it became 'Provisional'. There is no swearing-in of witnesses. They are assumed to be on oath as soon as they enter the witness-box. Foreign witnesses usually give evidence first and in the case under review that of the leading witness might go something like this:

'Inspector Watson, your Honours, from Gordon Road police station. On the afternoon of September 4, about four o'clock, I received word that a gang of armed kidnappers had holed-up at No. 123 Chusan Road and I proceeded with a party to that address. After exchanging about fifteen shots with the gang we arrested the ten defendants and rescued a Chinese boy who was being held for ransom. We returned the boy to his parents. One of his ears had been cut off during his captivity. Two other kidnappers were killed while making the arrests. The persons we arrested are those in the dock.'

Sometimes a Chinese detective goes into the Chinese witness-box to confirm that he shot the two dead kidnappers.

The two judges then confer for a minute or two, after which the Chinese judge addresses each prisoner individually, by name. As each accused responds the judge asks if he has anything to say, having heard the evidence just given. If the answer is negative, the judge then asks the accused for an admission of his guilt and very rarely is the smooth flow of the case halted by a refusal, though occasionally I have heard prisoners make a bid for leniency by a statement such as, 'I didn't want to do this. The others made me.' Once a prisoner raised loud laughter (and even the judges smiled) by declaring that he thought he ought to get less than the others because his pistol jammed and he didn't get a chance to do any shooting! Now and then, also, I have seen prisoners argue with each other in the dock and even come to blows.

After each prisoner has admitted his guilt—and any women accomplices have learned to their dismay they are just as guilty as the men—the two judges confer again, then start entering judgment on the charge-sheet, the one in English, the other in Chinese. A hush descends upon the courtroom as the Chinese judge once more addresses the prisoners. Everyone knows fatal words are about to be uttered. Each accused again is made to respond to his name so that his individual doom may be personally addressed to him. Sometimes a prisoner is seen whispering to another and I often wondered what had been said by a man who had just been condemned to execution.

For some reason or other, wives of condemned men in court wait until the judge has completely finished before giving vent to the spine-chilling wails of anguish which inevitably follow in the wake of such capital trials. The court allows a reasonable amount of this, depending on the experienced courtroom staff to remove the causes as speedily as possible. Yet between the start of this trial until the last of the condemned has passed out into the heavily guarded prison van waiting at the back door, may be no more than thirty minutes!

At one time while covering this court for my paper, I owned what was possibly the second-best collection of opium pipes and opium-smoking utensils in the world! What I regarded as the No. 1 collection belonged to an American assessor attached to the court who had a predilection for collecting Oriental curios. In the International Settlement section of Shanghai it was an offence to smoke opium or to possess it and the law was quite frequently enforced there, though seldom in the French Concession where, as we have noted, Green Dragon boss Tu Yueh-sen kept large stocks of the drug and more or less openly sold it through a chain of retail outlets.

At least once a month the Traffic Division of the Shanghai (International) Municipal Police managed to stage a major raid upon one of the city's many posh opium-smoking clubs. Whenever it did so there was usually a fine collection of opium-smoking paraphernalia to set before the court as evidence, apart from the twenty or thirty drug addicts standing in the dock.

SHANGHAI SAGA

The curio-collecting American assessor invariably indicated to the prosecuting sergeant of police which items among those seized in the raid he desired for his collection—their confiscation and destruction being a foregone conclusion—and these were instantly set aside at the end of the case. It was my practice to follow the paraphernalia out of the court at such moments, and by arrangement with the sergeant take second pick from the loot. The sergeant, incidentally, had no instinct for collecting, otherwise this incident would never be recorded. Wherever that American assessor's collection of opium pipes now happens to be I am without information, but I do know that it contains some magnificent pipes with jade, ivory and gold-encrusted mouthpieces, while some of his supplementary implements such as opium-containers, lamps, trays and ash-dumps were exquisite examples of the gold- and silversmith's art, worth many thousands of dollars.

Among the hundred or so different types of opium pipe which fell into my hands was one captured from a Chinese merchant who travelled regularly between Shanghai and Chungking, the World War II capital of the Nanking Government, some 1,200 miles up the great Yangtze Kiang River. It was made to fit into the false bottom of a silver teapot which fell out at a twist of the wrist, revealing a full set of opium-smoking implements. For a pipe, however, there was a mouthpiece and (bowl) burning end, both made of Canton blackwood, while the rest of it was a rubber tube, curled around the base of the teapot! I have ever been grateful to the prosecuting sergeant for not drawing the attention of the assessor to that particular item.

If there is one impression, more than any other, which sticks in the mind after watching hundreds of Chinese criminals on trial for their lives, it is the fatalism with which most of them faced up to the grim situation. Always about such cases there was the

REDS, RACKETEERS AND PICKPOCKETS

same indifference to death which one encountered in every other walk of Chinese life. This, one can only assume, comes naturally to a people used to watching death at work every day of their lives somehow, somewhere for floods, famine and disease on the grand scale carried off millions every year. Every day, municipal handcarts in Shanghai gathered up several dozen corpses from doorways, alleyways or gutters where they had fallen asleep and failed to wake up again from various causes — cold in winter, heat in summer, starvation or plain unwillingness to go on living. On the Whangpoo River, or along the numerous creeks and canals branching from this river into the delta region around Shanghai, members of the Water Police Body Recovering Squad patrolled in special sampans daily on the lookout for floating bodies. Sampan-men or others living on the water hailed them to point out another 'floater', some new, others bloated from a long and undetected stay in the water. To each the river policeman attached a hook and rope, towing his 'catch' back to the disposal jetty near the city mortuary at the end of his shift.

In between the annual national disasters netting millions and the daily pick-ups, banditry, violent crime and other uncertainties of life must have contributed towards the nonchalance displayed by most Chinese towards death. For millions of them the margin between life and death was very slender; how slender one or two examples of an unusual nature may help to show.

Take the 'Burlington Berties' of China; Burlington Bertie, for those who may not know, being a London character who went around picking up cigar and cigarette butts dropped by extravagant smokers who left sufficient to make stooping worth while. A small army of butt-gatherers roamed Shanghai's streets on fine days armed with long, metal-pointed skewers with which they deftly gathered up all cigarette butts over half an inch and dropped them into a tin slung around the neck. The harvest was added to as long as the sun shone. On wet days all 'Berties' stayed home and went to work on the stockpile of cigarette butts, slicing away the burnt ends, separating paper from unburned tobacco. Deft-fingered assistants, possibly other members of the family, then hand-rolled this harvest into new cigarettes. The final step was to sell these home-made cigarettes among the portable restaurateurs who in turn sold them to rickshaw coolies, wharf coolies and other lowly labourers whose habit was to purchase and smoke one cigarette at a time.

The streets of Shanghai offered other evidence of man's struggle for existence, making it easier to understand why so many Chinese were willing to give up the fight. No large firm in Shanghai (perhaps in all China) possessed what in the West is known as a staff canteen or cafeteria. Instead, managements contracted with one or other of the city's many restaurants to supply so many *tiffins* daily and the caterers went all out after such contracts. Thus, around 11.45 a.m. each day, from out the kitchen doors of hundreds of restaurants scattered throughout our city, poured a small army of delivery cooks and coolies, bearing at the end of stout bamboo poles large wooden containers of steaming hot food with appropriate utensils for its consumption by bank clerks, shipping clerks, shop assistants and what have you. All that customer firms provided was the dining-room, tables and chairs' and possibly the ubiquitous teapot and hot, green tea which is as much a part of Chinese business as the elevator in the big department store.

However, on the return journey every restaurant delivery coolie had to run the gauntlet of half a dozen tattered, filthy and possibly diseased beggars who knew almost to the minute what time they would pass. Woe betide the coolie who denied the beggars the opportunity to scrape out the returning food-containers. From bitter experience most of them had learned

REDS, RACKETEERS AND PICKPOCKETS

that co-operation was preferable to vituperation. For in the early days, before the restaurants learned their lesson, the beggars had a way of bumping into the delivery coolies and scattering all over the road the hot, steaming food of those who on their return journey had failed to slow down and allow all food remnants to be taken from the carry-alls. A few such disasters soon brought the restaurateurs to heel, although one or two had to be nudged still further into putting extra rice into the rice-container over and above the needs of the consuming staff. After all, such surplus merely had to be added to the contract price next time and in this regard every restaurant found itself in the same boat.

Perhaps the only other sight comparable to this noonday rush for leftovers was on the harbour, where 'beggar-boats' attached themselves to incoming ships by means of long bamboo boathooks. The No. 1 position was the gutter from the galley, from which all food scraps made their exit. Over this the beggar-boat which had secured the inside running strung a sieve-bag, with mesh of a gauge enough to allow all liquids to escape but still retain the food. Some ships regularly on the run, whose cooks were wise to the ways of the beggar- boats and also to the hardships of their occupants, divided the kitchen refuse between the galley outlet and hand deliveries to other boats not so favourably placed, thereby earning for themselves the praises of the entire beggar-boat fraternity and, no doubt, a good mark in heaven. Truly, there was a reason why the seagulls long, long ago had given Shanghai away as a place where the competition was too fierce to earn a living.

The street beggars of Shanghai will probably be remembered very vividly by every tourist who ever saw them. Like beggars the world over, Shanghai's mendicants knew all the tricks of extracting money from pedestrians. There were those who picked up the corpses of abandoned girl babies off the vacant lots each morning, slung them across their bare chests and used them as decoys for the soft-hearted. They changed them only when the presence of the dead little innocents began to offend the nose. There were those who displayed fearsome 'wounds' or 'diseases' aided by clever applications of pig's blood, mud and other make-up. There were, of course, the true professionals, the deformed, made thus in their infancy by professional beggar parents. There were the unfortunates without hands or feet, victims of crude, swift 'justice' for some crime or misdemeanour in the eyes of some official.

It was said that in the old Imperial days rope coolies who slipped whilst towing the Imperial barge over the rapids in the Upper Yangtze Gorges lost their feet as a punishment. And all old China hands from Shanghai will remember the rolling, howling Beggar of Chapei, a monstrosity without hands or feet who rolled along the ground into the International Settlement daily from some hovel in Chapei. The inhuman sounds he uttered while rolling along the footpaths in all weathers gave the jim-jams to so many nervous women that he finally had to be gathered up in a truck and dumped 100 miles into the country — unofficially, of course.

Green Dragon boss Tu Yueh-sen was credited by some with having as many as 50,000 working for him in and around Shanghai and if one includes the beggars that estimate might be nearly correct, for they were a vast army in a city of comparatively small area. One found them everywhere, but those in the know said that only the beggars operating in the two foreign areas of our city were on Tu's payroll, while the vast majority of those working the Chapei and Nantao (both Chinese-controlled) districts were independents.

According to the best information in my possession Tu's beggars operated only on allotted beats, and in return for

REDS, RACKETEERS AND PICKPOCKETS

this protection performed a variety of duties for the big boss. Protection being one of Tu's rackets, beggars were frequently used to bring any reluctant storekeeper to heel by means of picketing. Mostly, however, they were used as lookouts, as decoys, as guncarriers if any of Tu's boys had a big job to do, also picking up and getting rid of any weapons tossed away by the boys when they had finished with them. There was plenty for them to do while Tu was struggling to reach the top and to make known his wants to Shanghai's business men. Long before I left Shanghai, however, the mere mention of the head gangster's name was sufficient to make the affected public run to headquarters with the monthly ante, without waiting for the collector to call.

In his rise to supreme overlordship of the Shanghai Basin with its 200,000,000 population stretching through the Yangtze valley, Tu Yueh-sen had but one rival after Generalissimo Chiang Kai-shek came to power in 1927. This was Loh Likwei, fat, jovial chief Chinese detective of the International Settlement police and a one-time gangster himself, like almost every other Chinese detective on any of Shanghai's police forces. 'Lolly' Kwei was one of the best. A good mixer, he was always to be found at the end of a day's work drinking beer with the men in the police canteen at Central Station, immediately opposite to the American Club on Foochow Road. Tu Yueh-sen may have held honorary rank as 'chief of detectives' with the French Concession police force. Lolly Kwei was more than an 'honorary'; he actively filled his role and went on many raids after armed desperadoes within his own territory.

Frequently, as many of us with an ear to the ground knew, investigations by police took them up paths which seemed to point in the direction of Green Dragon headquarters. Wise cops usually began to lose the trail as this fact dawned upon them. Now and then an over-zealous policeman kept going, and

SHANGHAI SAGA

Detective Inspector James Cruikshank, in charge of Armed Crime Suppression for the International Settlement police, was one who failed to heed the red light during an investigation in the late 1920's. My first inkling of Cruikshank's mistake came from a chance visit I made to the canteen of the Central Police Station one morning before eleven o'clock. To my surprise I found two assistant commissioners of police there, with several other high-ranking officers, all drinking. The sight was so unusual that I sensed something out of the ordinary was up and beat a hasty retreat, though not before I had overheard one voice say:

'Mind you, I don't blame you a bit, Jim. You are a pretty big target, you know.' At which they all joined in laughter.

It subsequently transpired that Lolly Kwei had passed on a friendly tip to the ace crime sleuth to get out of town, fast. He had, Lolly told him, trodden on the toes of the Frenchtown underworld boss once too often and word had gone out to 'get Cruikshank'. The huge, 245 lb. Scot didn't waste any further time. Like everybody else in the police force he knew that no safety precautions were of any avail once the order had gone out to 'get him', so he sailed for Britain within forty-eight hours. The alternative? He would probably have been 'bush-whacked' by one of his own Chinese detectives on the next armed raid upon some kidnappers' den.

The only other occasion known to me of a high police officer fleeing from the wrath of the gang boss of Frenchtown was when a deputy commissioner of the International Settlement police took off within twenty-four hours of being ambushed in his car when leaving home for his office at 8.30 a.m. one day in 1938. He dodged death by throwing himself to the floor of his car while his chauffeur stepped on the gas and got out of range. This officer, too, had failed to heed the red light when making some investigations, and this time there was no Lolly Kwei to warn him, for the Chinese himself had been ambushed, together with two of his bodyguards, when leaving a restaurant around midnight about two months earlier. No doubt Tu had considered the time ripe to clear all likely opposition from the local stage.

Shanghai had never previously seen a funeral like that given to roly-poly Lolly. It required four hours to pass a given point and included every professional Chinese musician and mourner in the city. There was a band playing mixed Western and Chinese music every 100 yards. The death of this friendly old fellow somehow sent a shiver through the rest of Shanghai, and from then on the supremacy of the chief of the Green Dragon Society was acknowledged everywhere, even in the innermost diplomatic circles of the Western powers.

The only known instance of a clash between the underworld boss of the Chinese mainland and President Chiang Kai-shek of Nationalist China occurred in 1947, when the latter was striving manfully to stamp out black-marketing in an effort to stabilize the nation's currency. Chiang Ching, the President's son by his first wife—married when Chiang was an unknown countryman—had been given the job of ferreting out black-marketeers. Young Chiang set about this task so ruthlessly that he was soon nicknamed 'Tiger' Chiang. He uncovered one enormous stock of black-market goods in a godown belonging to the Yangtze Development Corporation, situated within the International Settlement, and seized the goods in spite of the fact that the Yangtze Development Corporation belonged to, or was controlled by, Dr. H. H. Kung, brother-in-law of the president.

Investigations are alleged to have shown that Dr. Kung's son, David, owned the black-market goods and that he sent an urgent appeal to Nanking for intervention to prevent the huge cargo being confiscated. Almost immediately Madame Chiang Kai-shek left Nanking for Shanghai, and the story goes that upon her arrival she 'went for' her stepson in no uncertain terms, berating him 'for unwarranted interference' and 'overstepping his authority'. It is also claimed that Madame Chiang accused young Chiang of 'attacking the Kung interests'. Whatever truths or falsehoods were among the many rumours abroad at the time, the incident was regarded in Shanghai as 'a great scandal' and less than a week after the newspapers picked up the story, David Kung sailed from Shanghai for the United States of America.

Scarcely had this incident closed before Tiger Chiang's agents ran headlong into some agents of Tu Yueh-sen operating black-market goods and young Chiang refused to let go a second time! Indeed, he hung on to this new discovery so hard that Tu Yueh-sen himself had to make a hurried trip to the capital to set matters right and he and the President are said to have exchanged harsh words. Nonetheless, young Chiang had to let Tu's agent go with a nominal fine and release the seized black-market goods!

Every large city has its rackets and Shanghai had a couple worth disclosing if only because they may have been unique. I have already mentioned what happened each time one changed a dollar into small money at a money-changer's; but I failed to explain that each of the twenty-cent silver coins received in such an exchange would, if converted entirely into copper coins, bring between thirty and forty coppers in return, so that a dollar, if exchanged entirely into copper coins, would fetch anything up to 250 coppers!

Now let's go back a few years and clamber aboard a Shanghai tramcar (or street-car). It has 1st-, 2nd and 3rd class compartments. The first two are in a divided lead-car, the other in a rattling trailer, wherein a second conductor usually battles with coolies, servants, wet vegetables, live poultry, eels, lobsters and snapping crabs. The trailer conductor sees no future in his job until he graduates to the leading carriage, where real good pickings are

REDS, RACKETEERS AND PICKPOCKETS

to be had. For example, all fares are listed at so many coppers per section. If, therefore, a passenger tenders a twenty-cent silver coin and asks for a twelve-cent ride, the conductor gives him eight coppers in change. A little arithmetic will show that the conductor profits on this single deal by no less than fifteen coppers, if we work on an average basis of thirty-five unofficial coppers for that twenty-cent coin. The tramway company gets twelve coppers, the passenger eight coppers change, the conductor the other fifteen coppers!

For that reason Chinese passengers always tried to have the correct fare — in coppers! — before boarding a tram in Shanghai.

Those foreign passengers who bothered to follow this Chinese custom had to suffer a torrent of foul abuse in the local dialect from the conductor, who regarded every such thrifty passenger as a pickpocket, with himself as the victim. However, all foreign passengers were contributors to conductor income in some way, although not many of them were aware of the fact. Only one that I am aware of managed to beat them at their own game and he was well known by choice names to every Chinese tram or bus conductor in the city. He was a multi-millionaire, but of a nationality known for its carefulness. He rode to office daily by tram and invariably had the correct fare in coppers ready. One day, however, he found himself short of the required number and as the conductor approached him he held out a silver twenty-cent piece and inquired, 'What exchange are you giving today?'

The conductor blandly asked him where he was going (as if he didn't know!) so that he could make a calculation, and upon being told answered that he would be exchanging at the rate of twenty coppers only. Speaking fluent Shanghai dialect, the millionaire called him the most insulting names and demanded to be put down at the next money-changer's shop, so that he could change his silver coin and thus be able to tender the correct fare in coppers!

That same millionaire built and equipped a first-class hospital for Chinese in the International Settlement during his lifetime, and at his death left millions of dollars for the building of other charitable institutions, as well as a school building for girls of British nationality with accommodation for many boarders from the 'outports' of China, as all coastal cities outside Shanghai were usually called.

Drivers of Shanghai street-cars occupied an open platform, and frequently two of them would brake suddenly, pull up alongside each other, ignore all banked-up traffic and indulge in several minutes of bitter insult and foul language, often delivering the 'clincher' with a rasping throat-clearing and a mouthful of sputum tossed at the other driver before throwing the power handle and jerking away again. Expectoration was also the favourite method drivers employed for helping tardy native pedestrians get out of their way in crowded streets.

Pickpockets were omnipresent in Shanghai. They operated extensively on all public transport, jostling among the 1st and 2nd-class passengers, relieving them of wallets, watches, and other detachable articles worth carrying to the nearest pawnshop. Apparently there was collusion between them and the tram crews, for the traffic manager of the Shanghai Tramways Company once gave me the free translation of a Chinese letter he had received from the Tramways Pickpockets' Union, complaining against his conductors. Here it is:

Shanghai, 20th October, 1299

The General Manager,
Shanghai Tramway Co.

REDS, RACKETEERS AND PICKPOCKETS

Dear Sir, We have the honour to draw your kind attention to the misconduct of your point-boy No. 33 stationed at Nanking Road and the Bund.

We confess that we are doing pickpocketing business which is illegal and dangerous. We are, most of us, living in a strange place and have no other means to maintain our living. The money we obtain with difficulty cannot, therefore, be shared by others.

The said point-boy demands his extra every day, otherwise he would board the car and find fault with us by shouting to the passengers – 'Beware of pickpockets!'

Thus, our business is spoiled and we would run the risk of being found out and fined.

We have been extorted several tens of dollars already by this point-boy.

We earnestly hope that you will investigate and punish him accordingly.

Yours faithfully,
The Shanghai Pickpockets' Union.

Usury is such an ancient financial practice that a city like Shanghai was bound to have its quota of Shylocks, but it may surprise the reader to learn that those with the worst record throughout China were the Indians. They never issued receipts for any instalment repaid on a loan, general practice being to issue one only after full liquidation of the debt. This fact was brought to light in the British Consular Court where many moneylending claims were lodged by the Indians against clients who all told the same story.

There were different factions among the Shanghai Indians, including, of course, the black-turbanned fraternity avowedly anti-British and the cause of many disturbances. In the old

SHANGHAI SAGA

American West, sheriffs made the parking of guns mandatory upon entering a courtroom. Likewise, in Shanghai, Indians were compelled to park their loaded canes upon entering court; heavy bamboo rods some five or six feet in length with ten inches of lead pipe attached to one end. It was not an uncommon sight to see a couple of hundred turbanned Indians slugging it out on the lawns of His Majesty's consulate-general at the end of a particularly bitter case involving the moneylenders. Eventually, the court handed down a wise ruling to all clients of Indian moneylenders: to repay all loans through the court, which agreed to act as intermediary to save the unwary from the unscrupulous usurers.

Of all Shanghai's many moneylenders, none grew richer or was better known than Silas A. Hardoon, who had reached Shanghai from Baghdad, a penniless immigrant, at the close of the nineteenth century. In the early 1930's he died, leaving behind a synagogue for Jewish residents and a fortune in the region of Ch. $400 million, most of which was represented by large blocks of choice real estate in the down-town sections of the International Settlement.

Beginning as a humble night watchman on the wharves, Hardoon lived frugally and saved. He married a shrewd Chinese woman and together they grew rich. Silas and his native wife began lending small sums of money, then larger and larger sums, and as soon as he had several thousand dollars saved up his wife insisted that he buy land. In a fastgrowing city this was a sure-fire road to riches and at the end of World War I the Hardoons not only owned large portions of Shanghai real estate in the business section, but marked off for their own residence an entire block scarcely more than a mile from the waterfront which eventually became known as Hardoon Gardens, a real showplace mentioned in the tourist guide-books.

REDS, RACKETEERS AND PICKPOCKETS

With no children of their own, the Baghdad Jew and his plump Chinese wife of humble stock began adopting waifs and strays and eventually had about thirty living in the great rambling house inside Hardoon Gardens. They were of various nationalities, including Chinese, Russian, Eurasian, French, Italian and Portuguese. Instead of sending them to school Hardoon set up his own school at home, and employed foreign teachers to call daily and conduct regular classes. Believing that his wife had brought him all this good luck, Hardoon bowed to her every wish and no one ever said that he looked at another woman. He spent all his time either in his sparsely furnished office or at home and never attended social functions.

One could set one's watch by the ancient French automobile which clattered down Nanking Road every morning and back home in the evening, a thing of gleaming brass headlamps from the 1915 production line. Hardoon, the fat man with no visible neck, rode alone in it. Although he owned property worth millions of dollars he never went in for insurance, because most of the buildings were old and could one day be replaced with what he had saved on premiums.

Within three or four weeks of his death, relatives from the Middle and Near East began pouring into Shanghai laying claims to the vast fortune about which world newspapers had run headlines. A few weeks later most of them returned to their homes when the British consulate-general made it clear that Hardoon's affairs might take a couple of years to reach the point of probate. The only ones unperturbed by the descent of the unknown relatives from afar upon Shanghai were Hardoon's widow and the Buddhist priest from the Bubbling Well Temple nearby, a close friend of the family and said to be their financial adviser.

8

Pirates and Secret Societies

IN MY TIME there was still piracy of a kind on the China seaboard which takes in the coastline from Singapore to Vladivostok. My story concerns such goings on only so far as Shanghai was involved, and let me say at the outset that the day President Chiang Kai-shek withdrew all silver dollars from circulation was a sad one for China's pirates and the big bosses behind them.

Where commerce is lively, money has a habit of banking up in some quarters and thinning out in others, so leading banks in the principal cities of Shanghai, Hong Kong, Tientsin, Swatow, Amoy or Foochow from time to time sent or received millions of silver dollars packed in wooden boxes, 5,000 to a box, to rectify such situations. It was for the purpose of hi-jacking these valuable cargoes that most of the big piracies occurred between 1915 and 1930.

But, declared the leading British newspaper in China of that period:

'The Chinese pirate of the twentieth century is not the romantic figure one usually associates with tales of the Spanish Main. He has none of the magnetism of Morgan or Gunn, or Brangwyn's handsome buccaneers of the seventeenth century.

'Rather does he represent a class of low-down swabbery, of cut-throat thieves, wharf-rats of the Canton River and the fever-

PIRATES AND SECRET SOCIETIES

haunted creeks of the Fukien seaboard; a type of creature which although human in shape can, and will if occasion arises, behave like a jungle beast.' (*North-China Daily News*, March 13, 1924.)

The group of captured pirates aboard a British warship shown in the illustration facing p. 176 may not appear to give full support to that press description, for the captives are a sorry-looking lot. But hopped-up with drugs and carrying guns they were far from the cringing cowards this picture shows. It was because of such gangs that even Canadian Pacific Co.'s ocean liners up to 27,000 tons had to carry special military guards drawn from the British garrison at Hong Kong at one stage of their activities. It was because of their brutality once they had taken over a vessel that Chinese travellers became afraid to travel in their usual small coasting ships and paid the higher rates of the big foreign liners like the *Robert Dollar* and the *Empress of Canada*; and even these, as stated, carried guards with orders to shoot any unauthorized person attempting to approach the bridge.

The British Admiralty, charged (through its Far Eastern Fleet) with protecting British vessels, tried one method after another, but the pirates went on capturing the ships and getting away with the bullion. The British authorities at Hong Kong and the Chinese authorities at Canton even launched a joint amphibious attack upon Bias Bay, notorious pirate stronghold, just north of the British colony. The pirates knew of the plan before it got started and all the raiders found at Bias Bay was some packing from recently looted cargo. As a gesture of authority or reprisal the leader of the expedition burned down several fishermen's huts and destroyed several sampans, regarding same as part of the pirates' equipment, as undoubtedly they were, for on a subsequent raid a much wanted pirate leader was found in one of the remaining huts.

This fellow, trapped in bed one night, his hut surrounded by

SHANGHAI SAGA

British sailors and Chinese soldiers, came nearer to the heroes of the Spanish Main than any other before or since. Called upon to surrender, with several searchlights focussed on his humble dwelling, the pirate tried to make a dash for it into the dark woods nearby, shouting defiance as he ran out of the door with a blazing pistol in each hand. He fell, riddled with bullets, at the end of fifty yards as the searchlights followed his flight and gave the sharpshooters in the party an easy target.

Because the special regulations on piracy prevention called upon the crews to resist all pirate attacks, the China Coast Officers' Guild and Marine Engineers' Guild, representing all foreign crew members on China coasting ships, instructed members to refuse to put to sea until the regulations were changed. Moreover, they demanded that all armed guards be removed from ships!

Why? They argued — and even sent a representative to press the point with the British Admiralty in London — that wherever resistance had been shown to pirates seizing a ship there had been bloodshed, loss of life and damage to the vessel. On the other hand, where no resistance had been shown none of these things had happened. Under a flood of protests the Hong Kong Government eventually gave back to ship captains their right to decide when to fight and when not to fight the pirates; and in so doing they may have been influenced by the wholehearted support given by the Chinese shipowners to the two guilds in their stand against the government.

The Hong Kong Chamber of Commerce was asked for its ideas on how to stop piracy, and in answer suggested installing wireless on every ship plying the danger routes, as well as installing special iron grilles to make it hard for the pirates to reach vital parts of these ships. The chamber's continued support for the armed guards, however, was condemned by the two guilds, at least so far as the Indian guards were concerned, it

PIRATES AND SECRET SOCIETIES

being alleged that these were not only untrustworthy but useless in a fight. A suggestion that 'convoys' be employed on the danger routes was also rejected as 'impractical as well as beneath the dignity of the British Government in peace time'. The chamber's best suggestion for combating piracy was to raid Bias Bay, the escape route for ninety-nine out of every too pirates operating on the China Coast.

The popularity of Bias Bay as an escape route for pirates after abandoning a captive ship was due to several factors. In the first place deep water ended well out into the bay so that pursuing craft, such as British warships, were unable to follow them very far for, as a general rule, pirates were well out of range of capture by the time any rescue vessel arrived upon the scene. Secondly, the pirates always had flat-bottomed sampans or junks waiting to take them, their loot and hostages off as soon as they entered the bay. Every expedition was highly organized, and there were always accomplices ashore in the bay to help them unload the loot and to cover their tracks. Finally, Bias Bay territory was in itself somewhat bleak and uninhabited. It gave easy access into the thickly populated interior and that was where pirates sped with all possible haste.

To raid Bias Bay in the hope of catching a nest of pirates, or to regard it as a 'pirate stronghold', was, therefore, to ignore the facts. The pirates themselves were drawn from many different communities, and Bias Bay merely the centre to which they reported at the end of a job, before resuming their ordinary work elsewhere as farmers, labourers, artisans or even shop assistants. Only a hard core of experienced professionals permanently existed as seagoing buccaneers, and these alone had access to the wealthy principals of the organization living it high in Hong Kong and Shanghai all the year round. This was revealed by a high Chinese police official of Kwangtung Province, who tried to convince the Hong Kong authorities of the futility of staging amphibious raids on Bias Bay and later had the satisfaction of being able to say 'I told you so'.

Although silver dollars while still in circulation were the prime objective of pirates, occasionally they went after a shipment of banknotes, and it was one of these shipments which ultimately led to the exposure and undoing of a highly respected citizen. Despite every effort at secrecy it was common knowledge that someone very close to the heart of things was betraying closely guarded secrets to the pirates, and one of the big foreign banks laid a trap in the hope of catching whatever big-shot in the Chinese Customs service was sharing secrets with the pirates.

Several million dollars in banknotes were set for transfer from Shanghai to Hong Kong and every precaution taken to hold the information down to three or four persons in the bank concerned and in the Customs, for no such large amount of money could be shipped without first getting Customs clearance. The bank concerned figured that only two Chinese in the Customs knew details of big money shipments. But which one was in league with the pirates?

The money was booked out on a British coasting vessel — favourite prey of pirates — and both Customs officials informed. However, the bank performed a last-minute switch of ships, transferring the money to another British vessel leaving at about the same time. But they informed only one of the Chinese officials of their action and obtained his signature okaying the switch, which was sufficient to make it legal and authoritative. The second official knew nothing of the plan. The switch occurred two hours before sailing time, yet a gang of pirates managed to board the ship and obtain passage 'tween decks where almost all Chinese passengers travelled. After two days at sea the gang took over the vessel — and the bank knew its suspicions had been

PIRATES AND SECRET SOCIETIES

in the right direction. The man was denounced to the Customs administration and thence to the Nanking Government. His execution was reported shortly afterwards. But one never knows in China. Execution is usually reserved for the poor.

The final touch to the story is this. The huge haul of banknotes taken by the pirates on that raid was quite useless. The notes had a signature missing, and widespread publicity was given to this fact to prevent their use.

Very rarely were pirates captured. Those shown in the illustration opposite p. 176 were unlucky. Here is the story.

On November 15, 1926, the British coaster *Sunning* (2,555 tons) was seized by a large gang of pirates, forty in all, en route from Shanghai to Hong Kong. They collected a large shipment of silver dollars as well as many thousands of dollars' worth of jewellery and furs from the native passengers. Everything had gone so well that the pirates became quite friendly with the foreign officers and allowed them an unusual measure of liberty to move around the deck. Guards with drawn guns followed them everywhere, but did not object to them having conversation between themselves, or with the handful of foreign passengers in the first class, including one Norwegian woman. Consequently a couple of the officers saw a chance of recapturing the ship from the pirates, and worked out a plan which was put into operation at midnight, some hours before she was due to reach Bias Bay and her rendezvous with a pirate junk. Taking the pirate guards on the bridge by surprise and flattening them with concealed bludgeons, the plan got off to a good start, but went slightly astray when sounds of the scuffling reached the alert ears of a lower-deck pirate who came running up to investigate. The second officer, an Englishman named Hurst, quickly grabbed a gun from one of the felled pirates and shot the advancing man dead. The shot sent the whole pirate gang into frenzied action within seconds and the bridge was besieged for the rest of the night.

Part of the plan had been to have all foreigners come running to the bridge on a given signal, but the early shooting made emergency moves imperative and the saloon skylight immediately under the bridge was used to get everybody on to it, including the plucky Norwegian woman. The pirates then attacked the bridge in wave attacks from both port and starboard sides for several hours, being repelled by good shooting from the officers and engineers on the bridge, all now bearing rifles and pistols taken from the bridge armoury. Seeing the tide of fortune turning against them, with increasing numbers of their gang lying dead or severely wounded around the deck, the pirates hastily broke open the ship's stores and hauled several drums of kerosene and oil forward, placing them in position beneath the saloon and bridge. They suffered more casualties in doing so, but seemed willing to take every risk in their desperation. With an exultant yell they set fire to the oil and the central section of the *Sunning* was soon a blazing inferno.

This fact undoubtedly saved the ship and those on board from total disaster, as the fire was seen by a passing ship whose captain guessed rightly, from the burning vessel's proximity to Bias Bay, what was happening. He sent an urgent wireless message to British Naval headquarters at Hong Kong and several fast warships were quickly on their way to the scene.

Meanwhile the wind had suddenly shifted, swinging the *Sunning* round, so that the fire took a direction towards the section of the ship occupied by the pirates and several hundred of the Chinese deck passengers. With the flames already licking at their feet, some of the pirates launched a lifeboat and tried to get away from the burning vessel. They were still pulling hard for Bias Bay when the warships arrived, one of which picked them

PIRATES AND SECRET SOCIETIES

up. One or two pirates jumped overboard to escape capture and of course drowned. The rest threw away their guns when they saw the game was up and tried to mingle with the passengers, who later derived great satisfaction from pointing them out to the rescue parties clambering aboard the Sunning, while fire crews soon had the fire under control. The captured pirates were returned to Hong Kong for trial and it is noteworthy that they staged an unsuccessful jailbreak in the Colony lock-up while in custody awaiting judgment.

This marked the first occasion of a captured ship being recovered from pirates, but unfortunately was followed, next time the pirates struck at a British ship, by some of the most brutal and callous treatment ever handed out to foreign officers on the China Coast, resulting in the slaying of her captain and chief officer and the serious wounding of two other officers and a couple of passengers.

I shall mention but one other case, a bloodthirsty affair carried out, not by Chinese this time but by a group of foreigners, in what was probably the worst piracy in modern times.

Frequenting Shanghai's lower-class dives and dens about 1934 was Prussian ex-captain Hugo ('Tubby') Taudin, brooding over the fact that his master's ticket had been taken from him on account of continued drunkenness. Once he had been a popular skipper along the China Coast; too popular. Now he had no ship, no job and practically no money. He spent his days in low-down dives of Hongkew district, quaffing the brew already described as 'Hongkew Whisky', alternating with *samshu*, the cheap Chinese wine which the coolies drank when opportunity offered.

Among Taudin's cronies who met daily for mutual rumination and sympathy were Heinrich Westerman, former prosperous butcher-restaurateur until he took up gun-running as a sideline and ended up a broken-down ex-con; Artur Gautschi, German ex-hardware salesman; Walter Mueller and Hans Schroeder, the last-named being a Swiss. Because they all spoke German they grew by association into a closely bound quintette, sharing each other's possessions and secrets; and in his more sober moments Taudin formulated a last desperate plan to get himself off the beach and back on to the bridge of a ship, which was the only kind of living he could make, or wanted to make.

On June 26th, 1934, these five were in the North China port of Tientsin. How they managed to get there I do not know, but Taudin had a Russian friend there who skippered a small Chinese coastal ship plying between Tientsin and other North China ports. He knew that Captain Vikhman possessed a kind heart and that is how this gang of murderers managed to get aboard the *Sheng An* (1,358 tons) on the pretext of wanting a free passage to Shanghai! The chief officer was Nicholas Azarieff, another Russian, and his Latvian bride of four months. These were the only foreigners on board. The vessel carried Chinese engineers, the total crew numbered fifty-eight, and on this trip the *Sheng An* carried 100 Chinese deck passengers and a full cargo of soya-bean oil.

At first Captain Vikhman had refused passage to the beachcombers, for they bore all the signs of having been on the bottle for a considerable period; but under a persistent barrage of backslapping and reminders of their comradely past, the soft-hearted White Russian yielded and took his non-paying passengers aboard. He knew that only an appeal to the local Chinese authorities could have got the men away from the *Sheng An* and he did not wish to go that far. For his kindness Captain Vikhman paid with his life.

The Taudin gang, fortified by further shots of native wine, suddenly appeared on deck around dinner-time on the second evening out. All carried pistols, which they flourished unsteadily

PIRATES AND SECRET SOCIETIES

as they stealthily approached the captain's cabin. Peering through an open porthole, Taudin saw the captain and the wife of the first mate, who was on bridge watch, having their dinner. The giant Prussian pushed his arm through the porthole and fired pointblank at Captain Vikhman, killing him instantly. He then turned the gun on Mrs. Azarieff and slew her with his second shot. The sound of gunfire brought the chief officer running down from the bridge and the moment he hit the lower deck Taudin shot him dead also.

Meanwhile, Gautschi and the other three members of the gang kept lookout for other crew members, and first to come upon the scene was Captain Vikhman's cabin-boy, bearing a tray of food for the captain's cabin. Gautschi fired twice and killed him. Attracted by the shooting, two Chinese sailors, two quartermasters and two firemen then came running up from below straight into a hail of bullets from the murderous drunken Teutons. All fell wounded and Taudin calmly strode up and finished each one off in turn.

No one else came running.

When satisfied that he had the crew and passengers thoroughly cowed, Taudin shouted at them in 'pidgin' English. He first bellowed for some sailors to come and dump the bodies of all the dead overboard. This done, he called for crew members to come forward and ordered all passengers below deck. The drunken German then outlined, in the well known 'pidgin' phrases common along the China Coast, what he intended doing with the *Sheng An*. All passengers would be put ashore at some quiet spot along the coast. The *Sheng An* would then sail for Valparaiso (South America) where the soya-bean oil would fetch a good price. The ship would be sold also and Taudin said he reckoned on getting about U.S. $80,000 for the lot. This money he promised to divide equally among them and it would be sufficient to buy passage back to China for those who wished to return. First, however, he would take the *Sheng An* to the Japanese port of Dairen, there to take on extra fuel and provisions for the long voyage across the Pacific.

'Any objections?' demanded Taudin, brandishing his big, black pistol.

He received no answer so took over the bridge and re-set the ship's course for Dairen, at the same time shouting for a cabin steward to bring up a bottle of whisky with which to drink to the success of their venture. But years of drink, drugs and dissolute living had impaired Taudin's navigation to such extent that the *Sheng An* failed to reach Dairen, and piled up instead on the rocks of Hoshigaura Beach, just south of the Japanese port. Frantically he tried every mariner's device for refloating the little coaster, but she stuck fast and he soon realized, drunk though he was, that his South American dream had come unstuck. He told his fellow pirates that there was nothing else to do but abandon ship and either take to the distant hills or try to lose themselves in the dives of Dairen.

First, however, Taudin and his companions herded all on board, crew and passengers, into one of the holds and nailed them in as well as locking them up. They then lowered one of the ship's boats and rowed round the rocks towards the nearby beach, having agreed to split up and head for Dairen by different routes as soon as they landed. Unfortunately, they reckoned without the vigilance of a Japanese coastguard. Observing the party come ashore the Jap decided to follow Taudin, biggest of the five, and he trailed the Prussian into the brothel quarter of the city.

Less than two hours later Taudin found himself surrounded and disarmed by a party of Japanese gendarmes. He was giving them a fairly plausible account of himself when another gendarme

PIRATES AND SECRET SOCIETIES

arrived to inform the lieutenant in charge that some Chinese had escaped from the *Sheng An* and told quite a different story at police headquarters. As a result, Taudin was locked up and patrols went out to comb the area for his missing companions, all of whom were subsequently brought in, Westerman and Mueller being discovered in an opium-den in a far corner of the city, Gautschi and Schroeder hiding in the hills.

'Hard times drove us mad,' Mueller admitted after his arrest. 'We were crazy to do it.'

Taudin also confessed soon afterwards, but protested that other members of the gang threatened to kill him unless he went through with it! He admitted, further, that the murder of so many in cold blood was part of a deliberate plan to cow the rest into submission. Yet the German consul at Shanghai, when apprised of the facts, described the Prussian as 'gentle, refined, educated and philosophical'.

Japanese police naturally took jurisdiction over the prisoners, despite lengthy protests from the German consular authorities, and they came to trial at Dairen on April 26, 1934. As the acknowledged ringleaders, Taudin and Westerman were sentenced to death by strangulation. Gautschi and Mueller received life imprisonment. Schroeder, who apparently merely 'tagged along', received ten years' jail, and all immediately appealed against their sentences. This they were allowed to do, but at the re-hearing, while the death sentences on Taudin and Westerman were confirmed, Gautschi and Mueller were ordered to share the same fate and the sentence on Schroeder was reaffirmed.

Piracy really needs a whole book to itself, but for the moment it is enough to say that nowadays Chinese pirates have gone all modern. As it is no longer possible—owing to lack of foreign shipping—to carry on by the old methods, they have gone back to the ancient style of overtaking and boarding likely looking craft, using fast, diesel-engined light junks for the purpose, manned with machine guns and plentiful supplies of Tommy guns. Once, as a variant, some of them boarded a passenger plane to accompany some wealthy Chinese gamblers returning from Portuguese Macao to Hong Kong. An attempt to force the pilots to change course somehow misfired and the plane plunged into the sea with all on board in shallow water near the British Colony. Police were satisfied that it had been an attempted kidnapping of wealthy hostages for ransom.

Kidnapping, of course, continues. It has been practised in China for many centuries and some idea of its extent may be gleaned from the fact that a voluntary organization formed by well-meaning Shanghai citizens of different nationalities, in the first twelve years of its existence rescued 3,782 persons, mostly children, from kidnappers. This quasi-missionary body, which bluntly termed itself the Anti-Kidnapping Society of China, had men and women agents spread all over China but maintained headquarters in Shanghai. The agents gave of their own time in all weathers to watch incoming and outgoing trains, ships and other means of communication, intercepting those who dealt in the lives of children both for white slavery and for industrial slavery. No child was safe from their clutching hands. Children of wealthy parents identified themselves usually by having a bodyguard and such children as these were kidnapped for ransom. Mostly, however, children were taken and sold to factory-owners in distant cities and it was this traffic which the Anti-Kidnapping Society sought to stop more than the other.

On one occasion, on a tip given to police, a factory in the French Concession was raided and thirty-one missing children discovered chained to the wall, working with their small hands making cheap kitchenware out of tin. They lived their lives in

PIRATES AND SECRET SOCIETIES

chains and the only link with fresh air was a small row of open ventilators high above their heads. Light for their work came from cheap oil-lamps. Their little bodies bore marks of repeated whippings and one who had attempted to escape showed signs of cruel torture. Their working hours were from daylight until midnight, their food chiefly rice, cabbage and occasionally a little fish. If they died their bodies were removed in secret and dumped into a nearby alleyway. The proprietor admitted having purchased the children from kidnappers at five Chinese dollars each, or the equivalent of about eight shillings sterling. The Frenchtown court gave him fifteen years in jail and sold his factory to help educate the children. Widespread advertising throughout the country reunited thirteen of them with their parents, but the remainder had to be placed in an orphanage.

For the purpose of keeping these back-yard factories constantly supplied with cheap labour there existed a Kidnappers' Guild whose members were specialists in child abduction and the enticement of children away from homes or guardians. The Anti-Kidnapping Society, whose record of almost one rescue daily for twelve consecutive years speaks volumes for its zeal, claimed that with more members it could easily have doubled that figure. They also admitted that many more remained undiscovered than were ever rescued. It goes without saying that abducted female children were sent to brothels, but in all cases it was usual to put as many miles as possible between the scene of abduction and the point of sale. It was due to this that only thirteen of the thirty-one children rescued in that Frenchtown factory were claimed by their families.

Another, and probably more important, factor was that the parents of such children were bound to be illiterate and only chance conversation might lead them back to their children.

Another queer organization very active in Shanghai in my

time was the Shanghai Benevolent Society, which concerned itself principally with collecting corpses off the streets, deserted alleys and vacant lots of the city. Although, as stated, the municipalities provided staff and collecting vehicles for this purpose and the river police picked up bodies found floating in the Whangpoo River and adjacent creeks, the Benevolent Society went looking specially for new-born babies which were dumped anywhere wrapped in old newspapers or rags, when not wanted by the mother, the father, or both.

The kind-hearted Society took extraordinary steps to aid any abandoned infant found with a lingering spark of life. These were rushed off to the nearest orphanage for immediate medical treatment and hundreds of useful lives were thus saved.

The Shanghai orphanages had special baby-receptacles at their main entrances for receiving unwanted children. Anyone with a baby to dispose of yet unwilling to murder the child by dumping it in the open could place the infant in this receptacle, which revolved. By ringing a bell they could summon an attendant and witness the safe transfer of their child into official hands from a secluded spot, no questions being asked of anyone, by anyone. These orphanages contained children of many other nationalities besides Chinese.

How busy the Benevolent Society could be is shown by these figures (both foreign areas) for one twelve-month period:

Adult corpses collected. ..1,231
Infant corpses collected. ...6,864
Jars of human bones collected.70

During the same period, the figures for Chinese-controlled areas of the city were:

PIRATES AND SECRET SOCIETIES

Adult corpses collected....3,612
Infant corpses collected....4,627
Jars of human bones collected.88

All bodies so collected were given a coffin and decent burial.

As a rule, Chinese desire strongly to be buried in their native district, close to their birthplace. Most overseas shipping companies on the China run in pre-Red days carried a stock of coffins with plenty of embalming fluid, and there was an understanding between Chinese passengers and the companies which ensured return of dead Chinese to China instead of being buried at sea.

This business of returning home to be buried was regarded so importantly by Chinese that in Shanghai, where one met Chinese from such remote areas that they could not understand each other's language, many guilds were set up, one purpose of which was to arrange such interments. These provincial guilds existed for numerous purposes, though their origin may have been to push the products of their native district like chambers of commerce. Later they extended their aid to fellow provincials in distress right up to the point of death. For this eventuality they kept a plentiful supply of coffins in their private godown and arranged 'boxing' and home transport for all members whose fees had been paid up.

Guild members had their own secret signs for identification and it was not an uncommon thing for a visitor from, say, distant Szechwan Province, 1,200 miles away, to go in search of a 'compatriot' in the city's teahouses. By placing his empty teacup in a certain position, anyone from Szechwan could signal that he was from the old home province and would join up for a cup and a chat if the other cared to. If, however, the cup was placed in another special position, a knowing observer would

235

recognize it for a signal of distress and be honour bound to go to the rescue. If, for example, a slick Shanghai pickpocket had relieved the man from Szechwan of his bankroll, leaving him flat and far from home, it was but a matter of time before help arrived. China has more teahouses per square mile than the West has milk bars. The strandee might have to consume many cups of tea and spend many hours hunting for a compatriot, but it is the sort of occupation a Chinese enjoys and success was certain in the end.

On the subject of secret societies and guilds a London newspaper published this account of them, written by one with a deep knowledge of his subject:

'First, and paradoxically, the Chinese are the most union ridden and faction-split folk in the world. Second, wherever his countrymen are in any number, the Chinese finds it difficult to escape the influence of the *Kongsis* (trade societies), or of the *Tongs*.

'Thirdly, the individual Chinese abroad, who makes money and wants to keep it must stay away from China. The *Kongsis*, *Tongs* and, above all, the *Triads*, link him with China. The intricate network of *Kongsis* interlaces Chinese society, which is separated by trades and varieties of race.

'There is a greater difference and opposition felt between Chinese from different provinces than between people of different countries in Europe — Hylams, Cantonese, Hokkiens, Fukiens or Manchus are a few, for instance, of the distinctly different types of Chinese who don't mix.

'As the *Kongsis* swallow and control the labouring classes, or form rings in trades, so the *Tongs* bind, or are used by the more prosperous Chinese and envelop the *Kongsis*. The *Tongs* are more political than provincial in the racial sense and more commercial in motive, than political.

PIRATES AND SECRET SOCIETIES

But engulfing all is the mysterious *Triad*, the all-powerful and wealthy secret society. It intervenes and inter-weaves. It pulls strings and demands services. And, over all, it exacts heavy monetary tribute.

'Ask any "Westernized" Chinese to explain or even discuss the *Triad* and he will become evasive or embarrassed; but he has to acknowledge and obey it. The *Kongsis* organize the emigrant Chinese hundreds, even thousands, of miles outside his own country and so widely and thoroughly is the collection net spread that even the native rickshaw-pullers contribute their few cents to the *Kongsis*, while hotel-boys and other servants in all their sub-divisions of duty pay part of their wages into their different societies, to be pooled.'

The name *Triads* appears in very early accounts of piracies in Chinese waters, as far back as the sixteenth century. Actually, they were the forerunners of our twentieth-century gangster boss Tu Yueh-sen but soon after the Red Government took over in China (1949) it seems that its leaders, in their great need for foreign currency, encroached upon the functions of the *Triads*. The then President of the United States was even moved to tell the Peking Government to lay off putting the 'squeeze' on Chinese residing in the United States. Many thousands of them had been compelled to remit large amounts in gold dollars to China to prevent relatives living in that country from bodily injury. In many cases aged Chinese parents wrote to American relatives requesting sums of money quite beyond their capacity to pay, and in many cases the old people, as threatened, were imprisoned, tortured and even put to death.

In September 1952 there was a message from Singapore stating that a wealthy Chinese of that city, in a funeral ritual at the Malayan city of Kuala Lumpur, swore vengeance against the Chinese Communist Government for causing the deaths of his aged parents. In a 2,000-word scroll addressed to his dead parents, Yap Foo Thou made his pledge before a crowd of 100 friends and relatives. He told them that his parents jumped into the sea with their hands bound after repeated demands made upon them by the Peking Government for money from their son in Malaya. They wrote telling him they would be tried before the People's Court and executed if the money were not sent. Yap declared that his parents despaired of ever receiving the money and so decided to end their lives before their final trial.

On the subject of death, and coffins, it is interesting to note that considerable business is done by coffin manufacturers in miniature coffins for the fighting crickets of China. As the bullfight is to Spain and Mexico, or the cockfight to the Philippines, cricket-fighting is to China, where pedigreed battlers from underground are the medium of huge wagers among the more old-fashioned types of Chinese.

The warring cicadas slug it out in ingeniously constructed bamboo cages with glass tops for public viewing. When the money is down and the glass partition between the champs withdrawn, it is usually a knockdown and drag-out affair, bets being paid on the cricket first to gnaw the other's head off. District champs receive more pampering and fussing than a fighting-cock in Manila, but the coffin industry profits from the losers, who are never written off entirely. Cricket lovers are a superstitious lot and believe that, by giving a fallen idol a decent coffin and burial, there is a better chance of some day discovering another champion possessing the reincarnated fighting spirit of the deceased. Stocks of coffins for the crickets are always readily available. They measure but a couple of inches in length and are painted either chestnut or black. Some outstanding battlers have been held in such high esteem that their lamenting owners have honoured them with luxurious little crates inlaid with silver and

PIRATES AND SECRET SOCIETIES

gold and silk-lined. Even jade has been known to be used to ornament coffins of some ex-champions, in times when the sport flourished more than nowadays.

Coffins have been used for other and more sinister purposes in various parts of China. There was, for instance, the occasion when a professional opium-smuggler wished to get a cargo into Shanghai via one of the numerous creeks which join up with the harbour of the metropolis. He first started a rumour of his intention and made sure that it reached the ears of the barrier police whom he would have to pass.

They waited for him.

In due course the smuggler sent a cargo boat down the creek, bearing a large coffin. The police officer in charge was torn between respect for the dead and an itch to get his hands on the reported opium shipment. In the end, despite a great show of indignation by the coffin party who threatened all sorts of reprisals for desecrating the dead, the officer broke open the coffin. To his great horror he found a dead body inside — and nothing else.

The 'family' of the deceased immediately filed a damage suit against the district police officer, and while this was waiting to be heard sent a second barge through the creek with two more large coffins containing, of course, a full load of opium. Despite a very urgent desire to inspect the inside of these two coffins the barrier police feared to do so, and the smuggler got his dope through to the big city!

9

'Squeeze' and Chits

ONE HAD TO learn to live with more things in China than bad smells; 'squeeze', for example. ('What's in it for me?' is the Western equivalent.)

No employee, particularly a house servant, could keep his self-respect in a job which paid no percentages and if one wanted a contented household one—whether foreign or Chinese—had to bow to 'custom' and close an eye to the rake-off system.

The tailor who called to measure you for your new suits knew he must pay his toll to your head boy to gain admittance to your home. He then added this to the cost. The cabinetmaker who delivered a piece of new furniture could not get it past your front gate without the inevitable sweetener. Your provision merchant 'kicked back' a fixed percentage of your monthly bill to your cook in return for your continued patronage—or else. Every servant below the rank of head boy chipped in a bit of his or her wages to the major domo or soon the latter was recommending someone's discharge on trumped up charges.

If opportunities for extra cash were few, compensation was taken out of your possessions. One of your best pairs of socks, for example, was reduced one day to a single. You could yell for its mate until the Great Wall of China collapsed, but there would be no sign of the second sock. You tossed the lonely sock to one side

'SQUEEZE' AND CHITS

and in a few weeks had forgotten about it, even though it was a good sock and cost you several dollars. Very soon it went too to join its mate in the servants' quarters. From then on the pair might either be sold outside or worn by your head boy on his night off. Likewise your underwear. The servants all ate at your expense, but what you probably didn't know was that you might be keeping a couple of boarders as well. At one stage of the Sino-Japanese war in 1937-8 I counted twelve beds in my basement on the first and only occasion I had to pay a visit there to check the coal supply. In high places all this was termed the 'perquisites of office', or just plain 'perks'.

Even official floggers and executioners attached to the yamens of every district had ways and means of supplementing their income. Indeed in most cases they paid a premium to get the job! Take the flogger, the wielder of the bamboo. A prisoner sentenced to be caned was invariably given a chance to speak to the court flogger. If he had the necessary money he received a light, face-saving punishment. If without means he 'got the works'. A skilled flogger could lay the strokes on with every appearance of strength, yet a prisoner who had paid up would feel little at which to complain. A favourite method of causing regret to prisoners unable to purchase surcease was to dip the cane in brine before each stroke and draw the weapon swiftly across the body upon contact, thus tearing the skin apart and letting the brine through.

Even a headsman knew how to grow rich out of his victims. A swift, full-strength blow on the nape of the neck separated head and body of those who had paid for the privilege. For those who had not done so—and this I saw on the occasion when the pictures facing p. 97 were taken—the executioner became a butcher, removing the head by slow, torturing stages accompanied by blood-curdling yells from the victim.

As with floggers and executioners, so with everyone else holding government office; 'squeeze' was whatever the incumbent could actually wring from his position.

The first new word I picked up on my first day ashore at Shanghai was *tiffin*, an Indian word used throughout the Orient meaning lunch. The second was chit. Frequently they went hand-in-hand inasmuch as permanent residents signed chits for everything, including to. Thus, from India the Chinese borrowed *tiffin*, from the Portuguese *compradore* and from — who knows? — that most useful word, chit.

One lived by chits in China. There were several different kinds. There were even chit-boys attached to every business house, whose job was to carry chits from person to person, with a book for the signature of the receiver. Chit-books so used often figured in lawsuits, and a chit coolie could become an old, respected and ultimately superannuated member of a firm. To get so far meant that he had proved his trust. Between business houses, especially banks, a trustworthy chit coolie was an important link. Contracts were dispatched by him, and office managers checked chit-books on important matters to verify safe delivery. The chit coolie who let himself be drawn into an alleyway gamble while on official business could easily be detected by the time entry in his delivery book upon return and there was someone in every office whose business it was to make such checks.

Most business houses (*hongs*) had a series of chit-books bearing names of banks and other firms with whom they did regular business and these, of course, were the ones used when the time came. Most old China hands lived on the chit system, at least until air travel reached the Orient. Up till then most foreigners were trusted to discharge their debts before leaving the Far East, but air travel made a quick getaway possible, and from then on chits were accepted only from persons well known

'SQUEEZE' AND CHITS

or with their names in the city's hong book. This was a rare if not unique publication. Most large cities have their directories. Shanghai went beyond the usual with one or two sections not generally found in other directories, including the *position* in a firm occupied by everyone listed. This was most important to the Chinese. It affected one's credit rating very considerably. A newcomer to Shanghai desirous of starting to live on the chit system had, of necessity, first to make sure that his name and position with his hong were properly entered in the hong book which was issued annually with a supplementary edition in June of each year. The Shanghai hong book was the bible of business for the great Eastern city, and if you were not listed in it you were definitely *non persona grata* in the eyes of Chinese business men, whether merchant or brothel-keeper where, it was widely reported, chits were also acceptable.

No doubt the origin of the chit system was to counterbalance the custom in that part of the world of paying salaries once a month. For the ordinary worker that meant a long time between pay-days. No doubt also there were those who felt in the early days that lack of patronage was brought on by lack of ready cash. Chits filled the breach. In the days of sailing ships, when everybody knew everybody else and comings and goings were widely heralded, the idea, or possibility, of anyone skipping the port without first honouring their chits was just not considered. Indeed, right up to the end in 1949 it was an old Shanghai custom for persons departing from Shanghai to publish the fact in the business notices of the daily Press. Such notices merely gave the name of the departing ones in a half-inch column advertisement with the letters 'P.P.C.' in the bottom corner. In local parlance that came to be known as 'Please Postpone Calling'; in other words, 'I have left Shanghai', for the notice invariably appeared on the day after departure.

SHANGHAI SAGA

Because of the deep well of trust between Chinese and resident foreigners it became virtually unnecessary for any Shanghai resident to carry any money, save perhaps some small change for rickshaws or tips. But, just as Chinese New Year was crisis time, and settling day for Chinese to liquidate outstanding debts, so Number One Day of every new month meant the same thing for foreigners and their accumulated chits. Indeed, not a few hard drinkers actually had to wait until their chits arrived to discover where they had been spending their time during the past month! (A series of 'lost week-ends'.)

Of course when a man got himself into such a condition that he was unable to account for his movements, was it to be wondered that he frequently faced extraordinary liabilities on Number One Day — such as forged chits alleged to bear his signature and others carrying items of expenditure which only the proprietors presenting them for payment really knew whether or no he had actually received? But then these proprietors were no doubt merely recouping losses thrust upon them by foreigners who went about signing for champagne and other forms of whoopee as 'George Washington' and 'John Rockefeller', and got away with it, in spite of the *hong* book.

The first five years in the Far East (especially Shanghai) were unquestionably the hardest for any young *griffin* just arrived from home, whatever his country of origin. For this reason most of the big firms inserted a clause in first contracts forbidding the employee to marry. It was so much easier for failures to be shipped home when they had no legal ties or responsibilities in the Orient. Once past the five-year hurdle they were deemed worthy of their hire, a renewed contract after a spot of home leave and, of course, freedom to enter into matrimony.

I recall one instance, however, of a young Englishman who went so wild in his first six months that it was simply too

'SQUEEZE' AND CHITS

expensive to ship him home in the time-honoured manner. He had amassed a veritable mountain of chits from every conceivable house of entertainment and whereas it was customary for the understanding old Chinese *compradore* of his firm to act as go-between for the others with the monthly collectors, this debt staggered the old fellow and he went to see the *taipan* of the firm in the interests of the new and obviously irresponsible newcomer. The upshot was a severe carpeting for the *griffin* and compulsory impounding of his monthly salary. The *compradore* was empowered to pay his board and lodging and issue a mere $25 monthly for minor expenses such as rickshaw fares and cigarettes. The rest of his salary was apportioned among his creditors on a *pro rata* basis following a 'creditors' meeting'. Even on this basis the young *griffin* in question was literally mortgaged to the eyebrows for the next twelve months.

Whether for a noggin of rum or a night of love, the chit was the Open Sesame for anyone listed in Shanghai's *hong* book and it needed a strong mind for the resident of modest means to keep one step ahead of the collecting shroffs who called around every Number One Day. Even staying sober was not enough to stave off disaster in the gyp joints. It was necessary to write the amount of a chit in plain, unalterable words, as I learned after discovering certain alcoholic beverages of a kind which I never drank added to my soberly signed chits during my own *griffin*-hood.

At the pony and dog-race tracks there was a cashier always on hand to lend a few hundred dollars to any backer of good community standing who had the misfortune to go broke, and a chit solved the problem.

My own native tailor worked out a system for himself which I considered qualified for the title of high finance. About twice a year he dropped into my home with a large bundle of samples of what he termed the latest suit patterns and though I was perpetually 'into' him for a couple of hundred dollars, it suddenly dawned on me that these visits occurred when I appeared to be on the verge of liquidating the entire debt and thus removing myself from his clutches — which, believe it or not, was the very last thing he wanted!

So he dropped in smiling with his big bundle of latest spring or winter suitings, as the case might be. He then urged me with a flood of flattery and fairly good sales talk to invest in several more suits, even though he knew that my wardrobe was already choking with spring, summer, autumn and winter clothing, not to mention a large collection of silk, satin and camel-hair dressing-gowns and heaven knew how many pairs of pyjamas. One day, when we got to know each other better, he confessed. If, he said, he allowed me to get out of his debt I might be tempted not to get into it again. Or my own houseboy might try to introduce me to some other tailor, at a higher commission than he was then receiving from my tailor. By keeping me on the hook with several new suits he knew that I was worth an average of $25 monthly remittance on each Number One Day. By persuading a dozen or so of his other reliable clients to accept a few more suits, he thus had consolidated revenue to the tune of something like $300 each month, more than sufficient to meet his own overhead expenses. Anything past that figure gave him the working capital which I observed him regularly investing in the pari-mutuels at both pony and dog-races, year after year.

Chinese seldom signed chits in the same manner as foreigners unless they were of that small clan who frequented foreign clubs or bars, as did ill-fated Loh Li-kwei, ex-chief detective of the International Settlement. Should a signature be required Chinese gentlemen carried for the purpose their own private chop; a small piece of jade or ivory, the end of which was carved with native characters bearing their name. Such chops were carried

'SQUEEZE' AND CHITS

in a tiny case, less than half the size of a cigar holder, with a small compartment at one end containing special red paste or ink into which the carved end was dipped before affixing the seal. These were obtainable from any ivory carver. Sold blank, like metal keys, they were carved to the customer's order and usually splintered around the edges afterwards as a means of preventing forgery for it is very difficult to duplicate a chipped edge, as a microscope would readily reveal.

'Squeeze' was by no means confined to Chinese, and indeed it was due to this practice on the part of a certain French member of the Chinese Customs service that I barely escaped with my life during my first month of night patrol on the wharves. Totally unaware of events earlier in the evening, I passed along the wharves of the lower section of the river shortly after 1 a.m. on this occasion. My job was to visit every ship, as explained earlier, and no sooner had I set foot on a certain Yangtze River boat than a couple of Chinese ran up to me, looked hard into my face, then turned and ran along the deck, shouting as they went. I was, of course, wearing my Customs uniform. Within seconds an angry mob had surrounded me, but at that stage of my career I knew insufficient of the local dialect to understand their behaviour.

A Chinese quartermaster belonging to the ship was standing nearby, and knowing that all quartermasters spoke some English I asked him what the trouble was all about. He struck an unfriendly attitude which puzzled me, as Customs officers invariably commanded respect. I finally got from him the fact that earlier in the evening I was supposed to have put all passengers on this ship — which was soon due to cast off for upriver ports — through the wringer and they were fighting mad about it. The situation became so ugly that the quartermaster advised me to get off the ship as fast as I could. I could not make any of them understand that I had just come on duty, and I then realized with a start that I strongly resembled the Frenchman who had just gone off duty on these wharves.

At the age of eighteen, in the small hours of the morning, surrounded by yelling Chinese, 10,000 miles from home and with no other white man in sight, one does not try to argue oneself out of a situation like that in pidgin English. I went at the lick of my life down the gangway and the mob took up the chase. As soon as I reached the wharf upwards of 100 wharf coolies, half of them bearing thick bamboo poles for lumping cargo, took up the chant, whatever it was, though I could see by the look on their faces lit up by overhead arc lamps that it was not of the friendly variety. One or two of them swung their poles at me, but I dodged and kept going. Which was about the worst as well as the best thing I could have done, for a Customs officer on the run was something they had probably never seen before and it kindled their mob instincts. In a few seconds the entire wharf gang joined up with the pursuing passengers and I was going like the wind about thirty yards in front.

I knew that if I followed the regular road out on to the public street I would meet many other coolies who would be sure to heed the cries of my pursuers and stop me, so I headed for the big, twenty-foot-high fence dividing the wharf from a dockyard next door. The Customs service had an arrangement with this dockyard company permitting Customs officers to use a small gate in the fence when on patrol duty and, fortunately, a large bolt was on the *far* side of that gate. I knew this but my pursuers did not and, thinking they had me cornered, I heard a triumphant note in their yells as soon as they thought they had me trapped. In a flash I had the small gate open, went through and secured the heavy bolt. That was that.

The same afternoon I returned to the wharf and made some inquiries. My continental colleague, I learned, had gone through

'SQUEEZE' AND CHITS

the native passengers imposing summary fines upon opium-smokers, whose presence was easily detected by the sickly fumes emerging from their staterooms. He had also combed through the luggage of deck passengers and invoked the export regulations upon every small pretext, collecting 'fines' of one or two dollars from anyone having anything at all over and beyond personal clothing, and threatening confiscation if passengers refused to pay up. He apparently made a good though illegal haul, and for my unfortunate resemblance to him I almost got knocked senseless with a bamboo pole and dumped into the Whangpoo River.

Naturally, I got hold of the foreman of the wharf coolies and explained to him that, as I had just started my patrol, it could not have been me who 'squeezed' their countrymen.

He and his men agreed and grinned sheepishly, and I might add that they were the same coolies who had chased me but a few hours earlier, for coolies attach themselves to a wharf and work every ship docking there.

It always amazed me how much Chinese, even of small means, were prepared to spend on marriage, birthday and similar occasions, millions of them going through life saddled with an almost impossible debt due to inescapable native tradition. It was therefore with something like the impact of unveiling Turkish women that China's Nationalist Government soon after assuming office in 1927 introduced, through Mayor Wu Teh-chen of the Greater Shanghai Municipality, marriage at bargain rates. Mayor Wu invited young betrothed couples to come and be wed under licence at the administration building for as little as $27, which included two seats at the official wedding breakfast, a bouquet for the bride and two certificates of marriage. In cold cash, this meant a saving for each couple of more than $1,000 and after the first batch of seventy-five nervous young couples came through the opening ceremony with nothing worse than mild jitters mass marriages grew in popularity, as did the new fashion of young Chinese couples choosing their own mates.

On the doubtful side, however, was Chiang Kai-shek's 'New Life Movement', another innovation designed to divorce the populace from old and unwanted habits. Chiang appealed to Boy Scouts and Girl Guides to help put this new idea over. The Nationalist leader was not only down on opium-smoking and had made it a capital offence, but also wanted to abolish Western cigarette-smoking, notwithstanding the fact that only recently his revenue officers had taken up stations at the exits of all foreign as well as Chinese cigarette factories to collect internal revenue on every outgoing case of cigarettes. To Chiang the New Life Movement was apparently more important, for his corps of youth went out upon every highway, snatching the cigarettes from the mouths of every smoking Chinese passer-by. Bewildering as this seemed to many, it was as nothing to the ancients who found themselves suddenly grabbed by a couple of Boy Scouts still wet behind the ears, who cut off their queues (pigtails) without so much as 'By your leave'. In the new democracy any reminder of the ancient, grovelling China at the feet of the Manchus had to be removed! For the Manchus, after 300 years, had been forced in 1911 to abdicate the Dragon Throne of Peking.

China had not merely been returned to Chinese control, the nation was now in the hands of the people from the South, more progressive, more energetic and much more nationalistic than the Northerners who had been running the country for several thousand years. Different in many respects from each other, they were alike in the common propensity for 'squeeze', as witness what happened to precious supplies of food, medicines and clothing sent to China immediately after World War II ended. These supplies passed through official hands on to the black

'SQUEEZE' AND CHITS

market at scandalous prices, dealers not even bothering to remove the Red Cross and other relief-organization wrappers.

10
END IN SIGHT

THE END OF my Shanghai sojourn was in sight from the day the Japanese began making route marches through the International Settlement after driving the Chinese army out of the Shanghai area.

As war in Europe seemed a foregone conclusion, with Hitler in charge of Germany and the Berlin-Rome-Tokyo axis operating, I began to think of getting out. I had learned sufficient of Japan's methods to foresee the likely course of events in Shanghai should war in Europe become a reality. Her expansion hitherto had always been based on opportunism and a European war seemed the logical moment for putting into effect the next stage of the Tanaka Memorial—all Asia under the Rising Sun. Japan had tried to achieve this ambition during World War I with her infamous Twenty-one Demands, but had finished up with little more than the ex-German territory around the fine Shantung Province port of Tsingtao. When the new Nationalist Government of Chiang Kai-shek seemed on the brink of making peace—and union—with the warlord of Manchuria, Marshal Chang Tso-lin, Japan disposed of the latter and seized Manchuria, knowing that in the depression years around 1931 no country in the world was likely to undertake any costly military action to help China. Now in 1939 Japan was knee-deep in war with China, and with war in

END IN SIGHT

Europe just around the corner the daily route marches through Shanghai's streets would shortly be replaced by detention camps.

My Shanghai stay seemed ready to end, and the way things were the many changes which had occurred since those halcyon days of the early twenties made it comparatively easy to pull out of the place. The Canidrome dog-track was financially back on its feet and the directors were all smiles once more. Our 5.30 p.m. meetings had become popular, as customers were able to get the dogs out of their system by about 9 p.m. then dash off to their favourite night-club. Our lavish breeding establishment, badly bombed at the height of recent hostilities, had been replaced by new premises safely tucked inside the French Concession. New greyhounds were coming forward at a satisfactory rate and quality was high enough to break some of the old track records set by imported dogs.

Then, one night, gangland dropped a reminder in the lap of the management that the time had come to discuss terms. A heavy explosion over at the far side of the Canidrome track took place just before the end of a race and police investigations discovered traces of a home-made bomb. The incident did not cause too much worry at the time, but when a second bomb was tossed on to the track close to the members' section a fortnight later, directors and police went into a huddle. For our night meetings it was customary for all except the track lights to be extinguished while races were being run and during one of these blackouts, again near the end of a race while all eyes were upon the dogs racing to a finish, the third bomb was thrown. It came down from the top section of the main stand, directly behind the official enclosure, but struck a projecting canopy in flight and exploded prematurely, severely wounding the hand of a Frenchwoman in a private box belonging to the French consul-general. Reviewing the line of flight later, I realized that but for the canopy this bomb would have landed plumb in the middle of the stewards' and judges' box—and that was where I invariably stood while races were being run! This night was no exception, so had the bomb reached its target I fancy I would have constituted the bull's-eye. I took that as the omen I needed, quit the Canidrome and sailed from Shanghai a week later.

For the record, I learned before leaving that the bombs were all spade-work for the Green Dragon Society, whose income had been sadly curtailed by Sino-Japanese hostilities. Practical-minded Tu Yueh-sen could see no reason why the Canidrome should not share its prosperity with him, and I understand that after the third bomb he regularly received $50,000 monthly.

Six months after my departure, of course, the balloon went up in Europe, the Japs tightened their control on Shanghai and finally applied their stranglehold on December 7, 1941, almost at the same hour as Pearl Harbour was attacked. When Shanghai suffered from an acute meat shortage in the following year, 1942, my information states that the Japs put the Canidrome's several hundred fine racing dogs into the regimental cooking pots. On hearing this my earnest hope was that those who ate the greyhounds suffered from galloping cramps.

All that remains is to record a few last impressions of a city which has passed behind the Bamboo Curtain and most certainly will never be the same again.

Shanghai was a great business centre, but never a great city. It had few fine buildings, the best of them distributed along the Bund, or riverfront, giving an impression to tourists of solid worth. Why not, since most of the largest banks were among them!

Shanghai was the meeting-place of East and West and there it was proved that all nations could live in harmony if they had a mind to do so. Foreigners led the Chinese, by example, into

END IN SIGHT

adopting things and ways of life which had advantages for them, such as personal cleanliness, domestic hygiene, civic law and order, justice, honest police administration, government by representation. 'The most realistic republic ever known,' one writer once said of Shanghai.

Everything was unconventional in Shanghai and therein, no doubt, lay most of its charm. No one (except perhaps the Christian missionaries, of whom there were legion) ever went to Shanghai with any other thought than to make money. We ran the risks of diseases like smallpox, cholera, syphilis or tuberculosis and we walked at times along streets slippery with the early morning expectorations of the multitude. We coughed to keep alive if we happened to be on the Bund on a sultry afternoon waiting for the southerly breeze when the honey-boats passed upstream.

The outside world accused all of us of possessing 'the Shanghai mind', a term which received prominence soon after the May 30, 1925, shooting of rioters storming Louza district police station. Even J. B. Powell, *Chicago Tribune* correspondent, played up that facet of our existence, but the so-called 'Shanghai mind' was nothing more than the pride of its citizens in their big, warm-hearted city; a most astonishing fact, really, that a cosmopolitan community of some sixty or seventy nationalities could feel so united, such a oneness that it took collective umbrage against anyone questioning their right to have, for example, a few small parks and open spaces reserved for themselves. The Nationalists made much political capital out of this fact. Yet what was wrong with a small foreign community, hemmed in by millions of (let's face it) 'contagious' Chinese, reserving a few small parks and gardens where they might take their families for an outing, weather permitting?

Every big city has its 'green belt', its public parks. To have opened the gates of our parks to all and sundry would instantly have destroyed them, as anyone knows who has seen a public garden in any part of China. In order to keep these parks and gardens unsullied for the use of young children and Western families, notices posted at all gates at one time made unhappy reference to the fact that entrance was forbidden to 'Chinese and Dogs'. Only after these notice-boards had been in use for perhaps a generation, when political agitators were looking around for brickbats for their anti-foreign campaign, did someone remember the obnoxious wording on them. What seemed to be forgotten was the fact that Shanghai started out as an 'enclosure' for the early foreign traders and that Chinese went to live there in increasing numbers because they enjoyed the safety which this enclosure provided, especially when there were Taiping rebels about.

I cannot forget the generally happy relations existing at all times between foreigners and Chinese. Most of the unpleasantness which cropped up between them was caused by tourists, visiting seamen or Red-trained agitators. If Shanghai had a reputation as a 'wicked' city, this could have referred only to its licentiousness, its immorality and, in spite of the presence of so many missionaries, its general indifference to religion. Hypocrisy was not one of its sins, and, on the credit side, it offset its shortcomings with good works such as the Anti-Kidnapping Society, Rickshaw Pullers' Welfare Organization, Anti-Opium Society, Corpse Collecting Society and hundreds of charitable bodies. Foreigners themselves seldom broke the law. On the other hand the Chinese jail in the International Settlement had a more or less permanent population of more than 6,000 with a high proportion of long-term, dangerous criminals.

My years in Shanghai were incredible ones. I saw old China fade away — indeed beat a hasty retreat — before the progressiveness of young, modern China. I saw beautiful young

END IN SIGHT

native girls come out from behind the flat-pressed hairdo, the ancient trousers and satin slippers, and adopt the now world-famous cheon-sam, the permanent wave and the three-inch heels and nylons. I saw the first Chinese couple dancing on a public dance-floor and stayed to watch succeeding thousands of them virtually elbow foreigners off their own dancefloors in less than a dozen years. I heard Chinese musicians rearrange Chinese popular music into Western dance tempo and listened to young Chinese stand and croon into microphones.

I saw, too, open marriages between foreign men and Chinese girls, not merely the clandestine affairs which a generation earlier had produced a crop of Eurasians unwanted by either side, and I stayed long enough to see Chinese cabaret girls dye their hair *red*, with hideous results.

If I should be asked for an outstanding impression I might be tempted to give the palm to that night, Christmas Eve of 1936, when news was received of the release of Generalissimo Chiang Kai-shek who for more than a week had been 'kidnapped' in distant Sian while on a routine military inspection tour. I was wedged in among one of the tightest (in numbers only) crowds of my holiday experience at the Metropole Ballroom. This was the fashion cabaret of the moment for high-class Chinese and it was my invariable custom to go where they went on festive nights. It was always so much more interesting, being among the people creating history and, besides, old Snake-eyes Tu Yueh-sen was always an interesting side-show on holiday nights at the Metropole, one of his favourite haunts. Shanghai, in common with the rest of Nationalist China, was very glum at the prolonged detention of the 'Gissimo. Rumour was not helping the situation and Chiang had already been reported dead at least twice. The Metropole crowd, almost 80 per cent Chinese, was trying hard to make whoopee; but over all hung an air of despondency which in itself was an unusual thing in China, where there is little room for sentiment outside of the family circle.

Suddenly a Chinese was seen pushing his way through the crowd towards the bandstand, waving a paper and obviously excited. He reached the rotunda, tugged at the sleeve of Don José, the Filipino band-leader, whispered something in his ear and showed him the paper in his hand. Don Jose smiled and nodded. Then he signalled his orchestra to stop playing—in the middle of a dance. This, of course, drew attention to the bandstand, which was what he wanted. The Chinese with the paper then spoke into the microphone and his voice choked with emotion. He spoke in Chinese, but I was able to pick up the gist of his message, 'Chiang has been released!' And he waved the telegram bearing the good news.

From here on my indelible impression begins. The several thousand Chinese present rose and cheered themselves hoarse, men and women, old and young, ancients and moderns. Then someone among them began to sing the Chinese national anthem, something I had never heard before. I could scarcely believe my ears. Here was a crowd of Chinese acclaiming a national leader and expressing, as a sort of prayer of thankfulness, its joy and gratitude over the news of his release.

They sang the anthem through twice and then cheered for five minutes. And I could not help thinking of the many past dynasties of China, of the long line of emperors who had ruled her before Chiang. I tried to picture those sovereigns, those impersonal figures of the past, in a similar situation. I wondered if the people of the Celestial Kingdom would have jumped to their feet and sung as this crowd was then doing. I could not imagine it. Then I realized just how much China had changed; how far along the path of nationalism these people had come. And strangely enough, I also thought of a little Cantonese doctor,

END IN SIGHT

shadowed around the world by Peking agents with orders to destroy him for his revolutionary ideas — Dr. Sun Yat-sen, the Lenin of China and the man who started it all.

At that moment another ripple of excitement ran through the Metropole Ballroom. Someone was clearing a path through the dense crowd for a distinguished party, and I presently made out the shaven, bullet-like head of Tu Yueh-sen, mighty underworld boss, complete with retinue of pretty girls and bodyguards. Another thought crossed my mind, not so pleasant this time. This thought told me — 'Here comes the real boss of China!'

Finally, I will lay the blame for the China debacle squarely on the doorstep of Japan. Jealousy of Western domination of Far-Eastern markets and of white influence in China aroused the Japanese to a point which made them determined at any cost to alter that position. Because of Japanese encroachments upon China, General Chiang was unable to put down the Communists and his kidnapping at Sian was carried out by the Young Marshal, Chang Hsueh-liang, as a move to force Chiang to turn aside from Communist suppression and give his undivided attention to resisting Japan. The Young Marshal had a selfish motive, of course. The Japs had stolen Manchuria, his birthright, back in 1931. He apparently overlooked the fact that his father, the Manchurian ruler assassinated by the Japs, had himself taken his country by force when a bandit leader.

The Japs were so determined that Chiang Kai-shek should never rule China in peace and quiet that even after their defeat by the United States and their allies in 1945, and in defiance of orders to the contrary from General Douglas MacArthur, the Allied commander-in-chief, they surrendered themselves *and their arms* to the Communist guerillas in some of the larger theatres of the China war. The Communists thus gained sufficient weapons finally to overthrow Chiang Kai-shek in 1949. The Communists then took over China and Japan had the satisfaction a few years later of seeing long-standing British mills, factories, wharves, shipping, real estate, public utilities, oil installations and all forms of property valued at upwards of k500,000,000 confiscated by the government of Mao Tse-tung, who used Japanese arms and ammunition for the purpose.

As fast as they could get exit permits from the Reds, foreign residents packed up and left. The Reds held on to most of the *taipans* of foreign firms as hostages, bleeding the companies of hundreds of millions of dollars which Peking claimed to be ill-gotten profits made in China over the past century. Even White Russians, who a generation earlier had fled from the Soviet Union, now packed their bags once more and sought sanctuary in other countries.

Shanghai — the old, gay, friendly, rich and colourful city was dead: after 100 years.

There will never be another city like it.

Vale — Shanghai!

About The Author

John Pal, the author of Shanghai Saga, appears to have been one of the pseudonyms used by Alan Palamountain, born in 1903 in Australia. At the age of seventeen, he traveled to England and then to Shanghai to sign up with the Imperial Chinese Customs service, run by foreigners to collect customs duties on behalf of the Chinese government. He later worked as a journalist on the Shanghai Times newspaper, and left the city in 1939 as the threat of Japan was growing.

www.ingramcontent.com/pod-product-compliance
Lightning Source LLC
LaVergne TN
LVHW010313070526
838199LV00065B/5546